Lawmaking in Illinois

Legislative Politics, People and Processes

Second Printing with Afterword

Lawmaking in Illinois

Legislative Politics, People and Processes

Second Printing with Afterword

Jack R. Van Der Slik
and
Kent D. Redfield

Office of Public Affairs Communication
Sangamon State University
Springfield, Illinois
1989

For our heaven-sent children: Franci and Eric, Gary and Randy,
Jenny, Alicia and Renee

Copyright 1986, 1989 by the Office of Public Affairs Communication,
Sangamon State University. All rights reserved.
Published 1986. Reprinted 1989 with Afterword by Jack R. Van Der Slik
Printed in the United States of America

Library of Congress Cataloging in Publication Data

Van Der Slik, Jack R., 1936-
    Lawmaking in Illinois.

    Includes index.
    1. Illinois. General Assembly.   2. Legislation — Illinois.
    I. Redfield, Kent.   II. Title.
JC5771.V36   1986   328.773   86-61343
ISBN 0-938943-01-4

Cover Photo: Sharon K. Carter

Office of Public Affairs Communication
Sangamon State University
Springfield, Illinois 62794-9243

Table of Contents

PREFACE

The Illinois General Assembly is not frequently studied nor widely known to students of politics in Illinois and beyond. Press reports of legislators often highlight their occasional silliness, sloth or frenetic activity near the end of sessions. Our book is intended to describe Illinois lawmaking from a broad perspective. We seek to show that the complex legislative process must be understood in the cultural context of the state and the politics of its regions and its interest groups. Illinois politics is remarkably open, allowing anyone with a point-of-view to gain access to the legislature. Participants are numerous, often loud and sometimes strident. Newcomers are welcome but professionals with the knowledge and patience to work within the system tend to get the most rewards.

We hope that this book will answer questions from many people. It is written first of all for students who want to understand state politics in Illinois. We hope that it stimulates some of them to pursue politics as a career. For the rest, the book encourages active citizenship, avocational political participation and reasonable expectations from state government. Perhaps it will stimulate further research and better understanding of Illinois processes. We hope that professionals in the news media and political science will get a fuller understanding of Illinois politics from our perspectives, but we look forward to their suggestions, differing views and extensions of our ideas.

We intend that this book will help Illinois citizens realize that they have stakes in the politics of the state. Citizens can participate in a variety of political activities that go beyond simply voting. They are welcome to be active in candidate campaigns, local political organizations and interest groups. When they express themselves as letter writers and witnesses at legislative hearings, their views will be taken into account. Our book also makes it clear that those who ignore participation increase the likelihood that they will be ignored by the important players in the policy process. Or as the proverbial Mr. Dooley once said, "Politics ain't beanbag."

We have accumulated a great many debts in the development of this book. Its progenitor was David H. Everson, who chose us and compelled us to do it. People who helped us evaluate ideas and read drafts early and late were Joan Agrella Parker, William L. Day, J. Michael Lennon and Marilyn Huff Immel. Our outside reviewers are special. Gerald L. Gherardini kept us honest from his perspective inside the legislative system. Mike Lawrence, statehouse journalist *par excellence*, helped us to make the story complete. Barbara Brown, one of the best teachers of Illinois politics we know, helped us express our ideas clearly for students. Marilyn Huff Immel, with assistance from Beverley Scobell and Caroline Gherardini, converted our manuscript into a polished book. Despite all of the best intentions of these helpful people, we insisted upon our own interpretations and descriptions. So we absolve them from responsibility for any shortcomings that remain.

We are grateful for the typing skills of Jackie Wright, Cheryl Ecklund and Ann Aldrich. For research assistance we thank Beth Phillips, Tawny R. Meek, Todd Thoman, David Sellman, Porter McNeil, Richard Johnson and Carol Strawn.

For other than professional support, without which this work would not be published, we thank Bonnie Van Der Slik and Jan Redfield.

Although we have drawn upon recent literature about Illinois politics, our debts would not be properly acknowledged if we ignored the people from whom we have learned the nuances of legislative interaction over recent years. We hereby express our appreciation to them for letting us see aspects of the process through their eyes.

Don Adams	Alan J. Greiman	Dorothy Nadasdy
Len Adams	David Griffith	Dawn Clark Netsch
Philip Adams	Fritz Goebig	Richard Newhouse
James Andrews	Phillip Gonet	Ralph Nickell
Ed Armstrong	Anna Mae Goss	Josephine Oblinger
Gregory W. Baise	Linda Hawker	Thomas Ohler
Arthur L. Berman	H. William Hey	Robert E. O'Keefe
Rich Bradley	Maryann Hensey	Janet Otwell
Charles R. Burns	Gene Hoffman	Thomas Pape
Roland Burris	William Holland	Taylor Pensoneau
George Camille	Bruce Johnson	W. Ben Polk
Eugenia Chapman	Stanley Johnston	William Redmond
Robert G. Cronson	Gayle L. Keiser	James Reilly
Michael D. Curran	Linda Kingman	Philip J. Rock
Barbara Flynn Currie	Jenifor Klindt	Sheila Ryan
John Davidson	Herman Knell	Sterling M. Ryder
Jack Davis	Judy Koehler	Steven Sargent
Danny Day	Robert Kustra	Bernie Schoenberg
Garrett Deakin	Marshall Langberg	Charles R. Scolare
Vince Demuzio	Gary J. LaPaille	Terry Scrogum
Kurt DeWeese	John Lattimer	Irv Smith
Kirk Dillard	Paul Lingenfelter	Kelly Smith
Thomas Dodegge	Terry Lutes	Earl W. Struck
Jim Edgar	Cindy McCuen	Calvin Sutker
Daniel Egler	Patricia McKenzie	James Taylor
David Epstein	Frank McNeil	Richard J. Walsh
Don Etchison,	A.T. "Tom" McMaster	Bernard Waren
Mary Frances Fagen	Ronald D. Michaelson	Charles N. Wheeler III
Beverly Fawell	Ken Mitchell	Douglas L. Whitley
James Fletcher	Kenneth M. Mitchell	Paula Wolff
Bill Foster	Bill Miller	James Woodward
Al Green	David R. Miller	Harry "Bus" Yourell.

Lawmaking in Illinois

Legislative Politics, People and Processes

Second Printing with Afterword

Chapter One

The General Assembly: Arena for Conflict

Remember the story about the man whose wife dragged him to the museum to see an exhibit of contemporary art? After some puzzled and bemused minutes, he announced to his wife, "I may not know much about modern art, but I know what I don't like."

Some casual observers of the Illinois General Assembly leave the galleries muttering similar remarks about the legislature. The typical reaction of someone who has made a quick visit to the Capitol in Springfield is that the floor business of the General Assembly is unruly and confusing. As in modern art, classical order and decorum seem to be missing. Actually, a great deal is being accomplished, even if the casual observer cannot follow the process or see the resulting legislation.

For those readers who have not attended a session of the General Assembly, here is a quick sketch of what might be seen on an ordinary day of legislative activity. Ten or 15 minutes after the announced time of beginning, the presiding officer gavels the chamber to order, a visiting clergyman invokes God's presence and blessings upon the business of the day and the members join in a pledge of allegiance. The presiding officer announces a "roll call," but instead of calling off the names, the members press the "present" button on their electronic voting machines, and amber lights show up next to the members' names on the roll call boards at the front of the chamber. From that point, the attractiveness of the proceedings diminishes rapidly. As the clerk begins to read messages, some members begin to walk around, others chat with neighbors or talk on the telephone. A number are eating, drinking or reading newspapers. From time to time the presiding officer will gavel the sound level down to a low roar, but the hubbub of noise gradually picks up again. Hardly anyone on the floor pays any attention even when resolutions are read to honor outstanding people, teams, towns, public officials and other state notables. To the casual observer, it seems hypocritical when the presiding officer calls for the ayes and nays and announces that "the ayes have it," when hardly anybody has cast a considered vote. Even when bills are called and sponsors talk about real legislation, it seems that the attention of most members is elsewhere.

When members vote by roll call, the interest level in the galleries rises. Green, yellow and red lights wink on next to members' names. After several roll calls, a pattern becomes evident: with a few exceptions almost all the lights are green. There seems to be little disagreement, and it is difficult to determine if anything significant is taking place. As the gallery observer looks on, the participants below continue munching snacks, laughing and socializing amid a good deal of traffic on the floor. What is more shocking is that some members seem to be pushing the voting buttons at the desks of absent colleagues. So the casual observer returns home disappointed about representative democracy in action, vaguely uneasy, suspecting that weighty matters are being decided capriciously in the legislative chambers.

There are other reasons why the legislature does not evoke favorable responses from casual observers. Media coverage is often most intense at the end of June when many bills are getting final consideration, days are long and legislators are rushing toward adjournment. Yet, the last week of a legislative session is no more typical of the legislative process than the last week of spring semester is of life on a university campus.

The legislature *is* a confusing, untidy place. It wallows in paperwork. It must accommodate the wishes and needs of hundreds of members and staffers. Much of its business is accomplished face-to-face. There are constant meetings of legislators with staff and lobbyists: scheduled meetings with formal agendas and informal meetings to negotiate immediate problems. Locations and times of meetings are frequently changed. Some expected participants are absent. Chairpersons are late, as are staff reports. Witnesses for committee meetings turn up at the wrong place or the wrong time. Lobbyists loiter in the halls and rotunda, smoking, and cajoling and buttonholing legislators and others.

This apparent disorderliness is compounded by the fact that the House, in the south wing of the Capitol, carries on its proceedings in apparent disregard of the Senate in the north wing. Actually, the two enclaves of Illinois' bicameral legislature are connected by a complicated network of interaction carried on by leaders, committee members and staff. From time to time, one chamber or both will suspend operations so that formal intercameral relations can take place.

THE GENERAL ASSEMBLY: CONGRESS IN MINIATURE?

The most familiar legislature in the U.S. is, of course, Congress. It is often assumed that the General Assembly is a scaled-down replica of it, and there are a great many similarities. For example, many names of committees and titles of officers are the same. Both bodies are bicameral, comprised of a House and Senate. The members of both are called representative or senator. Like its national counterpart, the Illinois House has a speaker, a majority leader and a minority leader. The state Senate is presided over by a president, the elected leader of the majority party, whereas the U.S. Constitution provides that the nation's vice president shall be president of the Senate. Both the national and the state houses have their own standing committees, committee chairpersons and committee staffs, and the senates have fewer members than the houses. The U.S. Senate has 100 members, two from each state. Illinois has 59 senators, each from a single-member district with boundaries that are redrawn each decade after the national census. State Senate terms are usually four years; U.S. senators serve six-year terms, while representatives at both levels have two-year terms. The U.S. House has 435 members, while the Illinois house has only 118. There is less difference, therefore, in size and intimacy between the two state chambers than there is between the two chambers of Congress. In Congress the ratio of representatives to senators is over four to one, but in Illinois it is but two to one. (Illinois cut the size of its House from 177 members to 118 in 1983. Previously, the ratio of representatives to senators was three to one.)

Like Congress, the two chambers of the General Assembly are nearly equal in power, but only a few of the distinctions between the U.S. House and the U.S. Senate are paralleled in Illinois. The state Senate must approve the governor's administrative appointees rather like the U.S. Senate does for presidential appointees. Of course, states don't conduct foreign relations, so the state Senate has no treaty or foreign policy powers. The Illinois House does not originate all revenue bills as does the U.S. House. Common to both institutions, however, is the basic requirement that bills must pass both houses in the same form to become law. The chief executive—president or governor—may veto, and extraordinary House and Senate majorities are necessary, both in Washington and Springfield, to override vetoes. At both levels the Senate is thought of as the "upper" house, not really because it has more power, but, because it is smaller and members usually have more influence, public recognition and status.

Congress and the General Assembly are alike in having a two-year term—called a biennium—to consider legislation. The biennia are numbered. For example, after the 1986 election a new biennium begins in 1987 and continues throughout 1988. In Illinois it is the 85th General Assembly, or the 85th biennium of legislative business since statehood in 1818. At the national level the same period is the 100th Congress since the adoption of the U.S. Constitution.

There are two significant differences between Congress and the General Assembly in how they use their time. The General Assembly's yearly sessions are roughly half as long as those of Congress. After the November election, Congress spends almost the entire next year in session. In an election year it adjourns in early October, sometimes returning to wind up the biennium after the election for the next one. In the General Assembly the chambers begin sessions (actual meetings of the assembled members) in January after the election. The General Assembly is rarely in session until late March or early April. After that members meet Tuesday through Thursday most weeks until mid-May. Then the schedule gets busier until the hectic last two weeks of June and the first week of July. After that there is usually a long break until a month-long session in October to consider vetoes. During the second year of the biennium when fewer bills are allowed, the legislature is rarely in session until April. After that it becomes increasingly busy until the first week of July. Then there is a break until after the election in November, when the legislators meet for a month to consider vetoes. The actual end of the legislative biennium is the morning of the day the newly elected (but mostly re-elected) members convene a new General Assembly and begin a new biennium.

The Illinois House and Senate conduct a much greater proportion of their respective activity "on the floor" than does Congress. The floor debates in the state legislature may be conducted before an inattentive membership, but congressional debates are conducted in nearly empty chambers. Appearances are misleading in both cases. Congress does most of its lawmaking in committee, while floor proceedings are usually routine. In the General Assembly, committees are far less important in shaping legislation; the real deciding happens on the floor where most of the work of the General Assembly takes place.

There are more differences. The General Assembly handles more bills, its processes are faster and its legislation more specific. It has less staff than Congress, more members have second jobs and salaries and benefits are smaller. Finally, the families of state legislators do not usually live in the state capital. All these differences, and others which will be noted later, affect the way the General Assembly functions.

LAWMAKING: AN UNFINISHED BUSINESS

Americans must love laws, they have so many of them. Every odd-numbered year, under the sponsorship of the Illinois State Bar Association, a new edition of the *Illinois Revised Statutes* is published. It contains all the laws of the state codified into 148 chapters, printed on more than 7000 pages, in four heavy, maroon volumes. The index comprises another volume of 1800 pages of entries from "Abandoned lands" to "Zoos." By the time the new edition is published, it already has a supplement because the General Assembly has passed new laws and rescinded some of the old ones. The state's legal framework is continually shifting. This flux can be irritating, but it is symptomatic of the dynamic character of a democratic society with representative government.

The importance of state laws to our daily life is immeasurable. Most Americans are unaware that the bulk of their ordinary relationships, in matters both "private" and "public," are framed by state laws, and that state laws are much more comprehensive than federal laws. When we drive our cars, buy and sell property, operate businesses, educate our children, marry and divorce, vote, arm ourselves or ask for police protection, we do so under state law. All of our local governments are organized and empowered within the constraints of the state. Consequently, as our values, technology, demographic and social forces change, so must our laws. These forces make the legislature a place for action.

GOOD LEGISLATORS OR GOOD REPRESENTATIVES: A CONTINUING DILEMMA

Laws are made by majorities of members, but majorities are combinations of individual lawmakers. These individual lawmakers are subjected to an amazing variety of external pressures. All must regularly face the same question: should I be a *legislator* or should I be a *representative?* When these roles clash, as they frequently do, the lawmaker has to decide which to advance at the expense of the other.

The member as *representative* is the advocate, the bill sponsor, the delegate who arrives at the legislature to serve as an ambassador from a constituency. Representatives are special pleaders in behalf of their constituents. They take care of the folks back home, make sure that the district "gets its share" or, if possible, gets more than its share. That share may be material—school aid, highways and mass transit support—or symbolic, such as getting the governor to come to the district to open the local chili festival. The rhetoric of exchange between the representative and constituents insists that the member not permit "those people in Springfield" to overlook "our people" back home.

An important part of this effort is attention to constituents' problems. Members call this casework. Typically, the representative is a broker, a mediator between a constituent and an agency of the state. The range of mediations is enormous. The constituent may be waiting for a public aid check, a set of license plates, incorporation papers for a small business, an income tax rebate, a gun owner's permit or countless other "minor" state services. These may seem inconsequential in the abstract, but they are not to the constituent. "The State" is impersonal and powerful, and the constituent may not know where to begin. So it is up to the representative—the constituent's agent—to deal with the state. Dealing successfully creates good will, which often translates into a campaign contribution, or at least a vote on election day. Even when constituents do not get all they want, government seems more responsive because of the representative's intervention.

These expectations define the legislature as a representative assembly, a forum for local champions to articulate the special needs of their districts. The resulting legislative debates reflect the diversity of specific interests. Individual lawmakers must convince the majority that solving specific, often local, problems is in the public interest. Frequently, the governor is cast in the role of advocate for and defender of the public interest, so there is rivalry among representatives to obtain clout with the governor.

"Politics" has particular meaning in the representative assembly. Each member, striving for a fair share or more, must bargain and negotiate with the representatives from other districts. A common bargaining technique is called "logrolling": "I'll vote for your bill if you vote for mine." By extension, the representative does nothing without accumulating obligations and credits which can later be exchanged for constituency benefits. Of course, the tactics of compromise, vote trading and negotiation can be part of a larger strategy of forming political blocs and building party loyalty.

The member as *legislator* considers his or her task to be that of making the best possible laws for the entire state. As one member of a larger body, the legislator takes part in the division of labor. That may entail developing and using expertise, as well as providing leadership in committee, task force or party. On a particular issue, some members will take the lead, while the others defer to those with greater expertise in that area. In contrast to representative as advocate, the legislator as colleague shares in the responsibility for policies that are intended to achieve the greater good on statewide issues and problems.

The legislator, more than the representative, perceives the General Assembly as a legislative body, institutionalized to process bills into laws. This body should be organized and staffed to take greatest advantage of specialization of effort, and attempts to resolve and meld differences into consensus. The individual legislator does not approach a particular policy area—mental health, election laws, highway safety—with the view of getting something for the district. The objective is comprehensive policy in the public interest. Proposals are weighed and evaluated without regard to which person, party, block, region or interest originated them. The legislative process—how a bill becomes a law—is not seen as a set of hurdles to be leaped; rather, it is a screening process for sorting out policy solutions of various degrees of effectiveness. The emphasis is on determining the best policy, not the most personally advantageous.

To be an expert legislator, one whose judgment is respected and followed by others, is time-consuming and requires resources that might otherwise be used to win reelection. The legislator has to become immersed in a subject matter, learning its vocabulary, the biases of professional practitioners and the range of problems throughout the state that are tied to the subject matter. So immersed, the legislator may fail to represent Farmer Jones or Business Executive Davis when they call for a favor. Alternatively, the *representative*, faithfully available to his or her constituents, may never obtain recognition for special policy expertise.

The claims for *legislator* and the demands for *representative* are not always contradictory. The concerns of Farmer Jones and Business Executive Davis are not necessarily unique. The casework of the *representative* may lead to the creation of important legislation. Conversely, the policy expertise of the *legislator* may generate political capital to exchange for constituency advantages.

CLAIMING CREDIT/AVOIDING BLAME

One Illinois lawmaker, in an interview, began by saying, "Of course, you know we're all egomaniacs or we wouldn't be around here." That is one way to make the point that lawmakers are public people. They work, to a great extent, in the open. They are accountable both to their constituents and the citizens of the state at large. Much of their interaction is with other public figures—colleagues, bureaucrats—all of whom also desire to leave favorable impressions about themselves with other people, and the various intermediaries who take part in communications processes: reporters, lobbyists, staff and opinion leaders. Lawmakers judge each other, compare themselves, and often, pass these comparisons around. "Wilcox had all the answers on the environmental protection bill." "Morton really made the governor's staff look stupid on the highway appropriation amendment." As *legislators*, members disagree about what is wise policy. As *representatives*, members compete for constituency advantage. In both roles they wish to gain credit for accomplishments; for the same reason, they want to avoid blame for efforts that fail.

Often, it may seem that legislators are hypocritical or vain, or both. But much of their posturing is imposed upon them by the public, democratic political arena in which they serve. To be perceived as an "expert" on some matter, such as nuclear waste disposal or soil conservation, requires that one speak up about those bills, go to hearings, ask questions, dispute with witnesses, deal harshly with inefficient bureaucrats, obtain attention from reporters, speak on the floor and generally take an active role in the various stages of the legislative process when nuclear waste disposal or conservation bills are being considered. Sometimes it is difficult to differentiate between hard, earnest effort and grandstanding.

Reputation is very important in politics, to say the least. Claiming credit and avoiding blame is an often subtle art that legislators and other political participants refine to their advantage, however crass some of its manifestations may seem. Like other art forms, some can do it well and others can't. A favorable reputation is like a painter's sense of perspective—essential for the task at hand. For lawmakers this task is influencing other people—particularly those who make public policy. The media, constituents, lobbyists, bureaucrats, as well as the governor and party leaders, all must be influenced. Lawmakers are endlessly seeking to maximize the credit they can take and minimize the blame they have to bear, not simply to satisfy the demands of ego, but to add luster to their all-important reputations and improve chances for reelection.

REFORM OR CHANGE

The word "reform" means, literally, "to form anew," or "to form again." Much of what government does is accomplished by forming again the structures of government responsible for delivering services or making policy decisions. A legislature in which the task of considering bills is divided equitably among many—say 30—standing committees will function in a more decentralized fashion than one in which the bills are handled by only ten committees. For a legislature to go from ten to 30 or from 30 to ten committees is a reform in the literal sense.

But in politics reform is usually understood to have another meaning. "To reform" is to make something better; to correct faults or flaws. In fact, in the parlance of some political participants, reform is an attempt to eliminate corruption and bias from politics.

It is important to realize that the particular structure of government usually does skew its processes. Consider the implications of the structure in two hypothetical houses, one comprised of 150 members in ten committees, and another with the same number, but 30 committees:

House With 150 Members

10 committees of 15 members	*30 committees of 5 members*
1. Broader policy jurisdiction and discretion.	1. Narrower policy jurisdiction and discretion.
2. Harder to form a committee consensus.	2. Easier to form a committee consensus.
3. Committee consensus more typical of whole house.	3. Committee consensus less typical of whole house.
4. Less time to hear diverse opinions from many witnesses.	4. More time to hear diverse opinions from many witnesses.
5. Chairperson influence in committee less, but greater on the floor.	5. Chairperson influence in committee greater, but less on the floor.
6. Committee recommendations likelier to be enacted on the floor.	6. Committee recommendations likelier to be rejected or amended on the floor.

The way the committees of a house are structured will affect the way the legislative process works. If one wants legislation substantially shaped and refined by committee and then ratified on the floor, then committees should be relatively large and heterogeneous with processes intended to achieve a consensus that will be satisfactory to lawmakers not on the committee. For this outcome, the "10 committee system" is better. But if one prefers that bills be amended and decided on the floor rather than in committee, the 30 committee structure is superior to the 10 committee structure. Arguments can be made for either mode of organization. The 10 committee structure will tend to make committee deliberations more important for shaping legislation, therefore it favors the *legislative* mode of lawmaking. The 30 committee structure necessitates small committees with fewer votes and therefore less impact on the floor. This structure encourages members to pursue the *representative* mode.

Because structure does bias political processes, certain interests in society will find, from time to time, that what they want is hard to get under the existing rules and organization. These interests may seek, therefore, to change the rules or the organization. From their perspective these changes are reforms to eliminate flaws and remove unfairness. Perceived flaws, of course, depend upon the eye of the beholder.

Here is a simplified example relevant to Illinois politics. Until 1983 the rules of the General Assembly required a three-fifths majority in both houses to ratify proposed amendments to the U.S. Constitution. This rule was established in consistency with the three-fifths requirement to propose amendments to the Illinois Constitution. The "fairness" of requiring an extraordinary majority for passage of state amendments has not been seriously questioned, but the fairness of the three-fifths requirement on ratification of U.S. constitutional amendments has been bitterly argued, especially by proponents of the Equal Rights Amendment. ERA got majority support in both the House and Senate and once obtained three-fifths in the House, but failed to get the extraordinary majorities needed for passage in both chambers during the same biennium. ERA supporters wanted the Illinois legislature to reform what they considered to be an unfair rule. After ERA died at the national level (partly because of its failure in Illinois), the Illinois House changed its requirement to a constitutional majority—60 votes (one more than half the membership)—to ratify amendments to the U.S. Constitution. The Illinois Senate continues to require three-fifths, or 36 votes. People tend to judge the fairness of a particular reform according to how its consequences fit their policy preferences.

One of the chief purposes of this book is to analyze the implications of structure and organization in the General Assembly. When useful, we will consider alternate structures. In some instances we will argue for certain structures or organizations, thus presenting our own perspectives on reform.

A GLANCE BACK AND A LOOK AHEAD

The best way to understand the General Assembly is as an arena for the development and resolution of conflict. What is not much appreciated is the success lawmakers have with the *resolving* part. More often than not, the media are drawn to report on the body's more dramatic and obvious *conflict*. The legislature, in the eyes of many, is a carnival of bickering and showboating. And those who cannot get their way are especially prone to denigrate it and demand that it be reformed to suit them. But the careful observer will consider who will benefit from such reform.

In the following chapters, we will describe how the people in the legislature and the processes for lawmaking in Illinois do resolve conflict. But before that we need to sketch the diversity of interests in Illinois, and how it affects the state's political culture and party composition. To appreciate the clash of *representing* and *legislating* in the General Assembly, we need to consider the goals of these efforts. Chapter Two describes some of the most significant characteristics of Illinois and explores differing beliefs about what issues government should address. The perspectives of the two major parties will be prominent in this discussion. Chapter Three describes how these differing partisan beliefs are deliberately organized into political programs through the legislative districting process. Chapter Four explains how the nominating and electing process works in the various districts across the state.

In Chapter Five the people of the legislature are examined. The most important of these are the lawmakers, mostly men, mostly white, mostly well-educated and mostly middle-aged. But women, blacks and senior citizens are also lawmakers. The staffs are described in Chapter Six, people who are hired for their competence and knowledge. Chapter Seven examines the legislative process. How does a bill become law? The answer depends upon the nature and importance of the bill. The emphasis of this chapter is on the processes inside the legislature. Chapter Eight describes the governor and his leadership role in the legislature. The governor can, if he chooses, set the agenda for legislative policymaking, as well as manage the budget so as to influence lawmakers. Other statewide elected leaders can occasionally rival the governor in policymaking, but this is rare. Chapter Nine explains the variety of external factors and forces which influence the lawmakers, with special emphasis on lobbyists and interest groups.

Chapter Ten seeks to summarize the results of the legislative process. In what accomplishments do lawmakers take the greatest pride? How do they vote? How do some of Illinois' policies compare to those in other states? How has the legislature taken care of itself?

Our primary purpose is to describe and analyze, although there will be some judicious criticism and praise. While trying to breakdown some simplistic stereotypes, we will leave evaluation to our readers. One old joke at the expense of legislatures precedes the days of the federal Food and Drug Administration. It goes like this: "There is a similarity between laws and sausages. If you like sausages, don't ever watch them being made. And the same goes for laws." The General Assembly may appear to be unruly and confusing, but a careful examination of its processes reveals a well-organized, representative and generally effective body. In sum, we seek to make Illinois people, politics and processes more understandable so that citizens can judge the legislature's work more competently than the man who, in his ignorance of modern art, knew what he did not like and dismissed it without careful consideration.

Chapter Two

The Political Context of Lawmaking: Pluralism and Competitiveness

Several colorful figures in Illinois politics spent part of their careers in the General Assembly. Paul Powell, who died while serving as secretary of state leaving a hoard of cash in a shoe box, spent 30 years in the Illinois House. Chicago Mayor Richard J. Daley served in both the House and the Senate; his son, Richard M., served in the Senate too. Other legislative veterans include Mayor Harold Washington, Adlai Stevenson III, Secretary of State Jim Edgar, Lieutenant Governor George Ryan, and U.S. senators Alan Dixon and Paul Simon. Their stories, and those of many others, are stories of conflict: who will prevail in policy decisions, who will hold key offices, where the boundaries of legislative districts will be, when public interests will prevail over private interests and whether benefits will go to Chicago, its suburbs, rural interests, poor people or others. Some citizens judge these decisions with a great moral sense of right and wrong. Others think of them as the normal business of politics. Some people feel threatened because the decisions cause changes in the status quo. To understand the complexities of legislative politics in Illinois, one must have an understanding of its people, their culture and what they expect of government.

ILLINOIS AS A MICROCOSM

If Illinois were to declare its independence as a nation, it would rank with some of the major countries of the world. In area it is larger than Austria and Switzerland put together. It is roughly comparable to Australia in population, productivity and social diversity. It has more students in colleges and universities than Mexico and more motor vehicles than Argentina and Venezuela combined. Illinois is a big, complex and diverse state. Its riches are evident in the heavy, dark soil that mantles the northern three-fourths of its surface, as well as in the residential "Gold Coast" north of Chicago's "Magnificent Mile." There is also deep and stubborn poverty in parts of Chicago, East St. Louis and some of the small towns downstate.

When it comes to governments, Illinois is Number One. No state in the nation has as many governmental units as Illinois. Within its 102 counties, Illinois has approximately 1,300 cities and villages, 1,400 townships, 1,000 school districts and over 2,500 "special districts." This last category includes single-purpose units of government which administer fire protection, libraries, flood control, soil conservation, recreation and parks, mosquito abatement and several other functions. All these governmental units have elected or appointed councils and executives, and each official plays some sort of role in the political and governmental processes of the state.

When Illinois is compared to the United States there are many parallels. The median age of the population, the median education, the birth rate, the death rate and the ratio of employed to the Illinois population are nearly the same as in the nation as a whole. There are some differences, too. Compared to the nation at large, Illinois has a higher average income, union membership and crime rate, more Roman Catholics and nonwhites. Literacy is higher in Illinois than the nation. On the whole, however, these differences are not great.

A line drawn across Illinois from Terre Haute, Indiana, to Keokuk, Iowa, would designate a familiar cultural demarcation. The 1880 census showed that most settlers south of the line were from Virginia, Tennessee or Kentucky. The northern and urban Illinoisans spring from Yankees and the waves of immigrants from Ireland, Scandinavia, Germany, Poland, Italy and eastern Europe. So the accents are different north and south, and to some extent, so are the politics and cultural perspectives. Illinois is a microcosm of the United States—a miniature of the nation's diversity.

The state's peculiar demographic pattern affects its economy and politics. The sparsely populated counties in parts of the southern end of the state stand in stark contrast to Chicago with its population of nearly three million. But "Chicagoland," as its media people call it, is more than the city. The rest of Cook County contains an additional 2.3 million who live in a hundred towns and villages. These too are diverse—the Jewish enclave of Skokie, the black suburban town of Robbins, the people of old wealth in Barrington Hills and new wealth in Schaumberg. Cook County is bounded by Lake Michigan and five counties—Lake, McHenry, Kane, DuPage and Will, the "collar" counties—which are culturally, socially and politically tied into Illinois' greatest metropolitan center. Another 1.8 million people live there.

The remaining 4.3 million people of "downstate" are more broadly distributed. There are nine other metropolitan areas in the state: Rockford, in the north central part of the state; Rock Island-Moline in the northwest; Kankakee, just south of Chicago; a circle of cities in the central part of the state: Champaign-Urbana, Bloomington-Normal, Peoria, Springfield, and Decatur; and Alton-East St. Louis, on the southwest edge of the state. But a great many Illinoisans live in the hinterland, 20 miles or more distant from a city of 25,000 or more in population. In fact, half of Illinois' counties—51 of 102—have populations of fewer than 25,000 people.

POLITICAL CULTURE

Another way to characterize Illinoisans is by their political culture. Daniel Elazar developed a set of categories to differentiate what he called the individualistic, moralistic and traditionalistic political cultures. His categories were substantively affected by his personal exposure to Illinois as a student at the University of Chicago and a researcher at the University of Illinois (see Elazar, 1972; Elazar and Zikmund, 1975).

Political culture refers to the beliefs, values and habits of mind by which the people of an area, community or state perceive and understand the world they live in, with particular reference to politics and government. While the details of these patterns change, their main contours are passed on from one generation to the next. They are imbedded in the cultural institutions of the community—the family, churches, schools, news media, work places and government units. The political culture shapes the meaning and emotions that people associate with the symbols of governmental authority—the flag, the policeman, the voting booth and political institutions. It determines how political candidates appeal for power, and how officials apply the authority of their offices.

Elazar explains American political culture as a synthesis of three distinct types which were present in the colonies and founding states. *Individualistic* political culture is very pragmatic. It takes matters as they are and moves toward personal gain. The individualist invests time and money in order to turn a future profit. Profit should be understood broadly—what gratifies me, what I want. A helpful stereotype is the rugged frontier individualist. "I can take care of myself. I take care of my own. I do what's necessary to get the job done." That could include breaking the rules, if nobody is looking. "But I'm a man of my word, and a deal is a deal. My reputation is important. Personal relationships are important. I see myself when I see my product, ideas or services. You help me and I'll help you—or the opposite." Personal connections are important and should be cultivated. Ethics develop on the basis of "Do unto others as they do unto you."

Moralistic political culture places high value on virtue, especially virtue in and for the community. "Community" may be conceived at various levels—the ethnic group, town, metropolitan area, state, nation or even "community of nations": humankind. Moralists have a broader view than individualists about what is a "public" issue. Individualists see conflict and competition as "private business" but moralists often argue that they are "public business." So the moralists tend to judge matters of right and wrong with a view of the community good. They attach importance to abstract matters such as community reputation, free speech and equal opportunity. They share a desire to reform government and politics. "I am a citizen of this place. I am affected by and care about its reputation, free speech and humane concern about its people. I feel a responsibility to continually reform government to be more just and compassionate." The extinction of a bird, animal or flower, for example, is perceived as a loss to the community. The moralists are the defenders of natural shoreline, the prairie or endangered species. Their ethic is built upon the notion of "looking above individuals' material interest." Their appeals are highminded. And they behave judgmentally, whether condemning from moral outrage or righteously praising. They do not compromise easily. "How can I compromise? This is a matter of right and wrong."

In the *traditionalistic* political culture people accept things as they are because that is how they have been. They accept, respect and even defend the inherited hierarchy of society, distribution of wealth and power, and set of rules. The community is proud of its leading families. "I like doing business with Banker Jones. His daddy helped my grandad keep the farm during the Depression." Traditionalists are not necessarily hostile to technological change. They may welcome it. But they are suspicious of outsiders with different ideas of what is good, right and proper. Newcomers who seek to intrude upon the prerogatives of community elite or contest with its decision makers are rejected. Ties in the traditional culture are based on associations of family (clan), lodge, alumni and social caste. Rewards are distributed more by inherited characteristics than achieved ones. Traditionalists tend to be tied to the land—the homestead, estate, ranch or farm. Although scions of the elite may go off to college, or on to business enterprises, they keep in touch with the activities of clan and community, even resuming full involvement later in life. The proper response to tradition is deference. Ethics are built upon "Thou shalt honor thy father and thy mother, and what they honored."

The origins and spread of the three cultural streams are easier to explain by proceeding north to south with the original states. The moralistic stream originated with the Puritans in the Commonwealth of Massachusetts, and dominated New England in the 17th, 18th and 19th centuries. Then it migrated westward across the northern tier of states in the old Northwest Territory. But it was reinforced by Scandinavians and Northern Europeans with religious roots in groups and sects that emphasized the integration of moral and community values. Beginning with Calvinists of Presbyterian, Congregational and Reformed stripe, it was supplemented by Scandinavian Lutherans, Quakers, Mormons, Jews and Scotch-Irish Protestants.

The individualistic stream emerged from the middle Atlantic states of New York, New Jersey, Pennsylvania, Delaware and Maryland. They, and later generations like them, came to America to "get ahead." Yeoman farmers, merchants and tradesmen, they sought individual opportunity. These states were more pluralistic in religion. Personal liberty was important so there was emphasis on religious free exercise and tolerance;

religious morality was a private affair. They worshipped in churches that did not emphasize collective behavior; rather, personal morality and the performance of rites. They were Episcopalians, continental Lutherans, Catholics, and Methodists who would tolerate one another's preferences in order to get on with family life, business and the accumulation of wealth. These were the folks in the forefront of the westward movement, bold and self-reliant individuals who carved out new settlements and rushed for land, gold or silver. Later additions were from southern and eastern Europe.

The traditionalistic culture was nurtured on the eastern seaboard in the plantation economy and lifestyle made possible by slave labor. Its society had well-delineated layers, with the landed and commercial gentry on the top. A compatible French version settled in the south along the Mississippi. This cultural stream socialized people to "know their place," and all but a few members were taught to accept decisions, not take part in making them. This stream moved west across the southern tier of states, and was added to later by Hispanics from Spain, Mexico and the Caribbean Islands.

The streams of course, have flowed and mixed together over time. Various sections of the country were changed by later waves of immigrants. The blue laws of English Puritans fell to the more individualistic values of the Irish Catholics in Boston during this century. Orange County, California got its moralistic, right-wing politics from transplanted Yankees and midwesterners. A measure of traditionalism in Hawaii is a unique combination of native heritage, Asian migration and the defense of advantage by the heirs of early individualists.

POLITICAL CULTURE IN ILLINOIS

Illinois inherited a unique mix of the three cultural streams that Elazar identified. This is not surprising when one realizes that the state reaches nearly 400 miles from the Wisconsin border to the confluence of the Ohio and Mississippi Rivers on the south. The traditionalistic stream moved into southern Illinois from Virginia, Tennessee and Kentucky. Early in Illinois' statehood this political culture dominated the state, and most of the people lived south of Springfield and along the rivers. The biggest issue at and after statehood in 1818 was slavery (Kenney, 1974, Chaps. 1-3). Later streams of southern, largely black, migrants moved to Chicago, East St. Louis and other urban centers. The Hispanics later added to that stream, especially in Chicago.

The moralistic stream dominated the northern third of the state for most of the 19th century. Some of its adherents wanted to secede from the state in the 1840s to become part of Wisconsin. They were abolitionists and Republicans at mid-century. But they were outnumbered in Chicago as the century turned, and Irish Catholics and European immigrants became a majority. Moralists dominated in the northern plains, particularly Rockford and the northeast, but were a minority elsewhere.

The individualistic stream has been prominent in Illinois through most of its history and has shaped its state, county and local governments. During the western movement in the nineteenth century, it came to dominate the central part of the state. Middle Atlantic natives also came to Chicago after the opening of the Erie Canal. And Chicago attracted individualists from all over Europe during the last of the 19th and early 20th centuries. Chicago has been a marketplace, a manufacturing center, a transportation hub, a financial bastion, a communication nucleus; indeed, until recently the nation's second city. Chicago is a polyglot of people organized not to determine the "community good," but to "make it" via enterprise.

LINKING THE CULTURAL STREAMS TO POLITICS

Figure 2:1 summarizes and differentiates how subscribers to the three main cultures see the public interest, government's tasks, the public bureaucracy and political parties. The points mentioned are, of course, oversimplified, for emphasis. The relevance of the types for politics in Illinois will increase as Illinois political patterns are revealed.

Individualistic

Self-interest is the primary concern. Emphasis is on the marketplace and private enterprise. The public interest lies in preserving an open marketplace. Government should invest in collective goods—waterways, roads, clean air and water, and people, their education and skills for productivity, so that the private enterprise system will make everyone better off. The test of merit in people, ideas and products is the marketplace. If it works and if it sells, it must be good.

Politics is just another form of business. It is pursued best by professionals. For the person not in politics, it is mostly a spectator sport. But when one has self-interests which can be served by government, one must be ready and willing to do business with politicians. Individuals invest as much time, effort and money into politics as they want to get out of it.

Government should regulate enterprise and people, protect private wealth and referee private conflicts. But its role in these conflicts should be limited. In most matters private enterprise is self-regulating. Views vary a great deal about what goods and services government should provide and whether or not these might be more profitably and properly produced by private interests. Government should be opportunistic, like private enterprise, in some matters. For example, it can risk its capital

Perspectives	Individualistic	Moralistic	Traditionalistic
View of the Public Interest	Self interest is primary. It is important to protect the market place and encourage private enterprise. Test of merit: Does it sell? Does it work?	The community good is primary. Seeking selfish advantage is wrong. Test of merit: Does it make the community a better place?	The protection of traditional privileges and responsibilities is primary. Social stability is good. Test of merit: Do the elders or elite approve?
View of Politics	Politics is like business. The process emphasizes jobs, profits and working at politics as a career. People who need political help should be willing to pay.	Politics is a civil duty. The political process emphasizes citizen participation and amateurs in office and party affairs. Politics is a means to right the wrongs of society.	One's view of politics depends upon one's status: if low, citizen duty is subservience; if high, citizen duty is to defend tradition and protect the subservient. Politics should be issueless.
Tasks of Government	Government protects a fair marketplace and facilitates initiative. Government minimizes expenditures for social welfare.	Government intervenes to do good. Emphasis is on community advancement. Government protects the weak.	Government is the agency of the elite to preserve traditional values.
Government Initiative	Government is opportunistic and business-like. Government ventures in lotteries and enterprise zones should produce profit. Officials are open to new ideas from insiders.	Government takes initiative. Novel government ventures should help people to better themselves, even if that is costly to the community. Officials are open to new ideas from anybody.	Government is custodial and makes changes incrementally. Officials evaluate new ideas according to the community status of those who propose them. Proposals from newcomers are suspect.
View of Bureaucracy	Appreciates and encourages efficiency, but patronage and favors often take precedence. Bureaucracy submits to politics.	Appreciates expertise, merit selection and bureaucratic standards. Bureaucracy should be humane and bureaucrats may propose policy ideas.	Appreciates a bureaucracy that defers to elite and tradition. Bureaucratic standards do more harm than good.
View of Parties	Party organizations should be strong. Parties contest elections to control public offices and reward faithful workers.	Parties should be programmatic and principled. Internal party operations should be democratic and open for newcomers and insurgents.	Party organizations are personal and informal. They should preserve consensus and recruit officeholders that the elite can trust.

Figure 2:1   American Subcultures

and resources to organize a World's Fair, run a lottery, conduct urban renewal or establish industrial parks and enterprise zones, all of which may pay off in the long run. Expenditures for social services to the poor like welfare, however, are viewed as dubious investments, unlikely to produce much return.

The government's bureaucracy ought to perform efficiently, cost-effectively and in a "business-like" manner. But it should be responsive to particularistic needs too. Businessmen provide favors for their friends; so should the bureaucracy. So it is both appropriate and desirable that the government provide patronage and favors to its supporters. Merit selection of personnel and ideas ought not be overlooked, but the merit principle need not be rigidly followed.

Political parties are organized to win offices and control government. They should be as strong and well-structured as any successful business if they are to carry out their function. Organization members work for benefits—pay, favors and the fun of being part of the action. Faithful service is a kind of investment in the future, and the payoffs should be dependable and continuing. Newcomers may be dabblers or undependable and, therefore, not to be quickly trusted. So working one's way up the greased pole of success is likely to take time. One fits his or her ideas to those of organization leaders rather than the other way around. Compromise is commonplace and virtuous. People who resign on principle are bullheaded; they are called "quitters" and "losers."

Moralistic

Primary emphasis should be upon community good; that is, the well-being of many, even most, individuals. It is wrong—an offense against the community—if there is a well-off elite while the community suffers. Virtues in such a circumstance are integrity, selflessness and sacrifice for others. It is important to improve the lot of the dependent and poor. In fact, it is a community responsibility, and the dependent are entitled to assistance because of their membership, or partnership, with the rest of the people.

Politics in the moralistic society is a matter of citizen duty. The citizen ought to be as active as possible. One affirms his or her good intention toward the community by taking part, and one appreciates neighbors for doing the same. There is a steady reaffirmation about what is the public good, and a pricking of the conscience to continue the pursuit of that good. Citizens pursue principles through politics—civic participation. Politics is a noble means for righting the wrongs that may occur in the community. Of course, all citizens have their special interests, careers and problems, but all should set time and energy aside for citizen duties in politics.

It is the task of government to intervene in private affairs to do good, and protect citizens from harm. Community resources should be developed and made accessible to all. Government assumes a regulatory role and enforces community standards against sleazy enterprises. Moreover, government is expected to take the initiative and right obvious wrongs that endanger the commonwealth. Government is progressive, always looking for new solutions to old problems, not just new technology, but new ways to distribute burdens and share benefits. This progressivism welcomes new participants. It encourages and supports newcomers who want to take part in public debate. Their ideas are important, not their seniority.

The governmental bureaucracy has high standing in the community. It should be efficient and expert, and those qualities mean its administrators should be able to bring insights from technology and management to problem solving. Bureaucracy should be well organized. People are appointed strictly according to merit and promoted for ability. There is nothing inherently bad about a bureaucracy; indeed, it provides public service with civility and civic pride. It ought not demean either those at its low echelons or the clients that it serves.

Political parties are organizations, mostly made up of volunteers, to pursue ideas and programs, to stand for principles and issues. Participants, then, may be ideologues. Party meetings are issue oriented. There is constant concern about the ways to transform ideas and principles into policies for solving problems. It is very important that party organizations be forums for participation, and when conflicts arise, resolution is by majority rule. So the party is a community institution, a means by which people learn community participation and civic duty. Because loyalty is to ideas and principles, rather than to leaders and the organization, a disaffected person or group should be able to form a new party. To resign or revolt on the basis of principle is an honorable form of political behavior.

Traditionalistic

The public interest of this culture is to protect and defend the existing social order. Its people continually refurbish their rationale for why the people at the top are entitled to have their exalted positions, why those at the bottom are properly there and similarly for those in between. The community emphasis is upon stability. The test of ideas and merit are tradition and what the elders and betters think of them.

One's view of politics is greatly dependent upon one's status. For those with low standing, citizen duty is to accept one's place and be subservient. Members of the elite reward the subservient with benevolent protection against physical harm, economic disaster or exploitation by outsiders. One has work, a place to live and security, but as far as public issues are concerned, persons of low status should be passive, not active. For people of high standing to assume responsibility for leadership is a public duty. The main lines of responsibility are to honor tradition, protect the subservient and grant patronage to the loyal. The tasks of government are simple. Government is one of the agencies of the elite to defend and preserve traditional values and the division of labor and benefits.

Government is not thought of as an initiator. It is custodial. It may well be the agency for taking care of dependent people, but the objective is not to eliminate their dependence. Rather, government minimally meets their needs while keeping them in continuing dependence. Government is difficult for outsiders or newcomers to penetrate. Demands from such people that government agencies "do something" about a particular problem are often met with indifference or annoyance.

Bureaucracy may be efficient and specialized at its lowest, operational levels, but its major administrators defer on policy judgments to the elite, whether or not the elite members hold public office. Apparent and real decision-makers are not necessarily the same. A school superintendent, for example, does not look up the statutes or the board minutes to discover the limits of his or her authority. Instead the superintendent defers tough policy questions to the community fathers. Emphasis is on common law, tradition and good judgment, rather than professional standards, state regulations or civil service rules. When administrative problems arise, the civil servant is well advised to consider the status of the people involved.

Political parties are informal in all their aspects—rules, membership, who will be in charge, discretion over candidates and issues and the like. Party organizations are agencies for preserving the consensus about the social order. The elite controls the recruitment of trustworthy people for offices and jobs which elite members do not themselves wish to hold. Elections are held to ratify those already anointed for office. Contests are usually avoided and citizen participation, especially by newcomers, may be discouraged.

ILLINOIS POLITICS AS CULTURAL CLASH

Most political observers consider Illinois to be dominated by the individualistic political culture. But all three cultures are present in the state, and politics occurs everywhere: in the statehouses, in the county courthouses, in the precinct and ward offices. Often participants at the state level have gained their orientations at the lower levels, so there is a real mixture of perspectives. This mixture is represented in the state legislature, where clashing expectations of government, the executive, the bureaucracies, the civil service, the parties and the legislature itself are expressed by members.

The most obvious example of individualistic political culture is the regular Democratic party of Cook County. Its ward committeemen are professionals in politics. Its control over the city, much of county government and parts of the state administration and legislature is largely an exercise in enterprise. Positions in governmental bureaucracy and elective office constitute a ladder of upward mobility for people who serve with loyalty and faithfulness. When there are factional fights such as between the "old guard" of Edward Vrdolyak, the Cook County Democratic party chairman, and the new administration of Chicago Mayor Harold Washington, each group takes jobs and patronage from the other wherever possible. These fights have policy and ideological aspects, but they are primarily factional and ethnic struggles within the political section of the marketplace.

An excellent example of moralistic culture is former Rockford Republican Congressman, John B. Anderson. Always highly issue oriented, Anderson over time changed his views on specific issues, but the essence of politics for him was always the issues and the arguments for and against them. His presidential campaign in 1980 was primarily a method for contesting the issue positions of Ronald Reagan and the conservative wing of the Republican party. When Anderson lost the battle for the Republican presidential nomination, he left the Republican party to contest both Reagan and Carter on the issues as an independent, despite his hopeless prospect for victory. Another Illinois example of the moralistic tradition is Jesse Jackson, the black spokesman for Operation PUSH (People United to Save Humanity). His style is not to do business with the Chicago regular Democrats, but to make moral appeals and call upon government to right wrongs. He urges political participation in the black community and seeks programmatic change in government policies. His candidacy for president in 1984 was not based on the expectation of winning, but was an effort to introduce questions concerning justice for minorities into the presidential campaign.

Traditionalistic leaders are less conspicuous in Illinois politics. Indeed, such leaders might hurt themselves by being noticeable. This culture lends itself, nonetheless, to the operation of stable communities, where shifts in population and economy can be prevented or controlled. Traditionalistic lawmakers tend to come from small, homogeneous communities. Often they are veterans of politics at the town or county levels of government. From time to time particular lawmakers who represent the traditionalistic values of their towns and heritage come into the public eye. One of their frequent goals is to obtain patronage jobs for the people of their districts. At the same time, they resist the intrusion of the state and its policies into local and community affairs. One example is Representative Dwight Friedrich who served in the Senate from 1952-1964. He was defeated in a close race after reapportionment in 1964, but he was elected to the constitutional convention in 1970. Since then he has been reelected continuously to the House, most recently in 1984. He lives in the county where he was born, and is a central figure in the financial institutions of his hometown. During the constitutional convention he spoke for an addition to a statement on the Fundamental Principles of the Constitution. To explain the blessings of liberty he moved to add: "These blessings cannot endure unless the people recognize their corresponding individual obligations and responsibilities." His argument was that he learned this principle in his youth from his father, and that the constitution should be a way of passing it on to school children in the years ahead (Sixth Illinois Constitutional Convention, 1972, Vol. 3, p. 1399). That sentence stands today in Article 23 of the constitution's Bill of Rights.

THE CONSEQUENCES OF DIVERSITY AND CULTURAL CLASH

One of the highly prized traits of American government is its constitutional protection of the rights of people. One of those rights is to organize and petition government for "redress of grievances." People can call on government to "do something" or "stop doing something" about issues of their concern.

People do organize, especially to protect their economic interests, their homes, their children and to further their various causes. They set up groups like local parent-teacher associations, the Illinois Pork Producers Association, Illinois Collaboration on Youth. These groups, and hundreds like them, articulate and advance the interests of their members, and hire lobbyists to present those ideas to various agencies of government. (Those processes will be discussed in Chapter Nine.) Thus the actions of political authorities are under the watchful attention of many specialized operatives from organized interests. These individuals are often in competition with one another. Lobbyist A feels his success is in doubt because executive director B is getting her way with the governor or a legislative committee. So the plurality of interests, the diversity of the Illinois economy, the unequal distribution of people across the state, the disparate economic health of different industries and the varied expectations of individual citizens engender the conflict and competition that is expressed in Illinois politics.

An enduring characteristic of Illinois politics is the competitive balance of the two major political parties. Although each party has had its popular heroes whose reelection was considered "safe," the state as a whole can be won by either party, although some areas are securely controlled by one or the other party. Moreover, the cohesiveness of the two parties is subject to tensions of both a regional and ideological nature.

The Statewide Balance of Partisans

There are many ways to point out the partisan balance in Illinois, but one that is striking is its representation in the United States Congress. First consider the Senate. Since 1940, with two brief interruptions, Illinois has had one Democratic senator and one Republican senator. In 1949 Democratic Senator Paul Douglas joined Democratic Senator Scott Lucas in the Senate. But in 1950 Republican Everett Dirksen beat Lucas, and for 16 years Douglas and Dirksen served together. Charles Percy defeated Douglas in 1966. After Dirksen's death in 1969, Ralph Tyler Smith, a Republican, was appointed but in 1970 that seat was recaptured by the Democrats in the person of Adlai E. Stevenson III. After Stevenson's retirement the Democrats retained the position with a victory by Alan J. Dixon. The two party balance continued with Dixon and Percy until Democrat Paul Simon defeated Percy in 1984.

The partisan balance in the U.S. House has been similar. A recently published study reports the following:

> Viewed statewide, the outcome of Illinois congressional elections is quite evenly divided in partisan terms. Party control of the Illinois delegation to the U.S. House over the past five elections has ranged from a Republican advantage of 14-10 to a Democratic advantage of 13-11. Of the more than 19 million total votes cast for Illinois congressional candidates in all elections from 1972-1980, only slightly more than 20,000 votes separate the two parties (Everson and Parker, 1982, pp. 57-58).

After redistricting, the 1982 congressional election produced a party balance of 12 Democrats and 10 Republicans, but in 1984 Dan Crane lost to Terry Bruce and the balance moved to 13 Democrats and nine Republicans.

In the governor's office there have been repeated partisan turnovers. In 1940 the Republicans captured the governorship from the Democrats with Dwight Green, who served two terms. Adlai E. Stevenson II became the Democratic governor, winning in 1948. When Stevenson ran for president, William G. Stratton, Republican, won the office and was reelected for a second term. Democrat Otto Kerner won two terms, resigning near the end of the second term to accept appointment as a federal appeals judge. His successor, Samuel Shapiro, a Democrat, was defeated by Republican Richard B. Ogilvie. One term later, in 1972, Democratic candidate Dan Walker defeated Ogilvie. In 1976, in an election to a two-year term (specially set in the transition schedule of the 1970 Constitution to uncouple the governor's election from the presidential election), Republican James R. Thompson defeated Democrat Michael J. Howlett who had defeated Walker in the primary. Thompson won reelection in 1978. Then the 1982 contest between Adlai E. Stevenson III and

Thompson was the closest in the state's history, and was not resolved in Thompson's favor until the state Supreme Court decided that a recount was not necessary. Thompson won by 5074 votes out of more than 3.6 million cast.

Without detailing the history of the other constitutional offices, it is accurate to say that the other statewide elected positions have also alternated between the two parties. In 1985, Republicans held the offices of lieutenant governor and secretary of state and Democrats served as attorney general, treasurer and comptroller. Both chambers of the General Assembly are usually closely balanced. The 84th General Assembly, which convened in 1985, had 31 Democrats and 28 Republicans in the Senate; 51 Republicans and 67 Democrats in the House. The Illinois Supreme Court, in 1985, consisted of four Democrats and three Republicans.

Uneven Distribution of Partisans

Despite a near balance between Democratic and Republican voters statewide, partisans are not evenly distributed across the state. Moreover, the unevenness is quite firmly fixed. Electoral districts in Chicago are solidly Democratic, while outside of Chicago, in the rest of Cook County, most electoral districts are predominantly Republican. Republicans also dominate in the "collar" counties that surround Cook: Lake, McHenry, Kane, DuPage and Will. The population is more sparsely dispersed over the remaining 96 counties. The rural counties of central and northern Illinois favor the Republicans. The central and northern counties with major cities, like Winnebago (Rockford), Peoria, Champaign and Sangamon (Springfield) are quite competitive. Only three counties with substantial population—Madison, St. Clair and Rock Island ("Quad Cities")—regularly return significant Democrat pluralities, but most of the counties south of Interstate 70 tend to favor Democrats.

The distribution of partisans links the parties to particular interests that turn to government for relief from a variety of problems. The most conspicuous "bloc" in Illinois politics is the Chicago "regular" Democrats, individualistic politicians who represent the concerns of the ethnics, working class and poor from the city. Despite their enduring dominance over the city administration, their power is diminished by racial and ethnic tensions. White ethnic voters, generally better off economically than blacks and Hispanics, may be vulnerable to pressures for realignment into the Republican party.

Many of the social and fiscal interests of the Chicago Democractic politicians are determined by state law and state fiscal resources. Chicago interests often clash most sharply with those just outside the city, in the "balkanized" surrounding suburbs. Suburban Republicans, many just as individualistic as their Chicago counterparts, often favor what the city Democrats oppose, and reject what the city Democrats seek. These Republicans represent middle and upper economic strata from business and the professions, who resist having to pay for economic and social programs to benefit the urban needy. Sometimes moralistically liberal on civil rights and equal opportunity questions, they are also zealous to defend their property rights, schools and local community homogeneity.

Downstate Republicans are more heterogeneous, some representing small town values, others the highly technological agricultural industry. Some feel only nominal loyalty to their political party; they are moralists about issues who will do what is "right" about abortion, no-fault divorce, women's rights, election laws or the like. But they are not necessarily in agreement with one another about what is appropriate policy on such moral questions. Others are partisans who protect the prerogatives of the courthouse regulars as loyally as their Chicago Democrat counterparts.

Democrats come in several varieties. Those from Madison and St. Clair counties usually cooperate with Chicago Democrats. On the other hand, some of the "independent" Democrats from the greater Chicago metropolitan area are more liberal and moralistic on civil liberties and social issues, seek "good government" reforms and question the principle of partisan loyalty. Southern Illinois Democrats are advocates for the rural poor, but are defenders of traditional morals, small town virtues and rural political organization.

The intense competition between Democrats and Republicans usually helps each party achieve an appearance of unity at election time. But between elections a good deal of diversity within each party can be seen in the legislature. Suburban Republicans are in conflict with Republicans from downstate Illinois. Suburban Democrats are suspicious of the Chicago regulars, as are insurgent black Democrats from the city who have, in recent years, defeated the regulars in a few districts. The moralists in both parties decry the "business-as-usual" politics of bargaining and compromise practiced by the individualistic professionals of both parties.

This pluralistic political activity is frequently loud and vituperative. Appeals for loyalty and expressions of hostility are the means by which leaders—the governor, the legislative leaders, the mayor of Chicago and interest group spokespersons—try to mobilize supporters and suggest that otherwise disinterested groups have stakes in the contest at hand. Sometimes these battles come to an impasse. Often, however, when the noise level reaches a plateau, the competing leaders come together and hammer out a compromise to the conflict that yields something satisfying to all the contestants. A notable example is the 1983 tax increase package (Parker, 1984).

Because the individualistic culture dominates Illinois, there is a market atmosphere to its politics. Trades, compromises and making deals provokes critical, sometimes cynical, responses from two categories of Illinois citizens. First are the people with many needs, who feel unable to influence the politicians—the poor, the minorities, the old and the alienated. Many have their roots in the traditionalistic culture, but they no longer believe that powerful leaders care about them. They feel fearful and unprotected. The other group consists of people who want politics to focus on issues and principles. They despise compromising and trading this for that. For them issues are built upon ideals, and each should be settled on the basis of analysis and merit.

If the pragmatic politics of Illinois does not please all the people all of the time, it satisfies many of them much of the time. There are occasion major policy changes, such as the educational reforms of 1985. But most of its issues are resolved little by little through barter and exchange, rather than by reform or comprehensive programs. Because of this incrementalism, the ordinary citizen sometimes does not detect very substantial consequences when the governorship or the legislature turns over from one party to the other. But for insiders such turnovers are very important. Their positions, their influence and their advantages change. In sum, the policy shifts are gradual, but the very competitive nature of Illinois politics provokes the politicians to respond to pressure from the people.

Chapter Three
The Representational Context
of Lawmaking:
Districts and Districting

In business, politics, sports and every other social process, the "rules of the game" set the context of interaction. Legislative politics in Illinois is shaped by the mechanics of the representational system. Apportionment rules and district lines can greatly affect who will win legislative elections and whether or not incumbent legislators will be reelected. For politicians these issues are both highly partisan and personal. So if the idea of representation at first seems only philosophical, keep in mind that it is of immense practical importance to the lives and careers of politicians who seek and hold public offices. The political history of representation in Illinois is especially complex and colorful. Conflicts about it have occasioned some of the most bitter battles between Republicans and Democrats that the state has ever seen. In this chapter we will describe the major conflicts that have produced the present representational setting.

There are numerous ways for an electorate to choose the representatives in its lawmaking body. For example, they could be chosen *at large*. An at-large election would permit all voters to cast ballots for as many candidates as there are positions to be filled. This is the practice in some medium-sized cities, small towns, counties and for some governing boards of education and other special districts. Commonly, however, such bodies are relatively small. The number of persons elected is usually ten or fewer. American legislative tradition inherited much from our English forebearers. Two specific legacies from that heritage are: (1) the size of the legislature should be relatively large, and (2) representation is in behalf of people in a district, an area of land with specific boundaries. Therefore, while at-large elections are feasible for smaller governing bodies, they are not suitable for the election of members to a state legislature.

Compared to other states, the Illinois General Assembly is fairly large. The House has 118 members and the Senate 59. A legislature of that size is likely to be diverse in membership, thus bringing a variety of viewpoints to the lawmaking process. Compared to the other states, the Illinois House ranks 18th in size. Most of the bigger ones are in states east of Illinois. Only two states, Minnesota and New York, have larger Senates than Illinois. Of course, the House was only recently (1981) reduced in size from 177. Previously, it was the fourth largest House in the country. These ranks are not unreasonable given that Illinois, with its 11.4 million people, is the fifth most populous state in the nation.

The practice of representing people by districts is feudal in origin. People belonged to the land—the estates, shires and other subdivisions. That tradition was brought to the American colonies and passed on to the states. Legislative district lines in Illinois, as in other states, usually followed city, county and township lines. Over time, of course, populations change and concentrations of people shift. Demographic alterations—migration of people from the farms to the cities, from the cities to the suburbs—created political pressure to change the boundaries of legislative districts. Illinois was not unique in these population changes, but its redistricting problems helped to bring about the "reapportionment revolution" of the 1960s.

THE POLITICS OF LEGISLATIVE REDISTRICTING

Legislative districts were established in Illinois in 1818 when statehood was achieved. Half a century later, when the 1870 Constitution was written, the number of districts was fixed at 51, each to have a senator and three representatives. The representatives were to be elected by cumulative voting. (In Illinois until 1982 a unique system of cumulative voting allowed the voter to cast three votes in a variety of ways: one vote for each of three candidates; two votes for one candidate and one for another; one-and-a-half votes for each of two candidates; three votes for one candidate.) Districts were to be roughly equal according to population, with regular redistricting after each decennial census.

Within four decades the population growth in Cook County led to a redistricting stalemate. In 1882 nearly 20 percent of the population was in Cook County, and it had 10 of the state's 51 districts. Nine were in Chicago and one in suburban Cook. In 1893 Cook County had 31 percent of the residents and 15 districts, 14 in the city and one for the rest of county. In 1901 Cook's population was 38 percent of the population and it was accorded 19 districts, 18 of which were in the city. From then on, however, the legislature failed to redistrict itself. By 1931 more than half of the state's population was in Cook County, but its share of legislative districts remained 19 of 51. The majority of members from downstate were unwilling to give up their legislative control to a Cook County majority. The General Assembly also refused to redraw congressional districts. Despite many attempts between 1922 and 1952—there were at least 20 resolutions to change the constitution—the downstate majority stood firmly against such change.

Illinoisans took the failure to redistrict the congressional seats to federal court. In *Colegrove v. Green* (1946) it was argued that with district populations varying from only 112,000 to more than 900,000, citizens were not accorded the equal protection guaranteed under the U.S. Constitution. However, in a 4-3 decision in 1946, the U.S. Supreme Court said the remedy for such evils was in the political processes. "Courts ought not enter this political thicket." This meant any solution to inequitable representation in Illinois would have to be solved through the state's own political processes.

The Bipartisan Compromise: 1954-55

By the mid-1950s not only was the Chicago regular Democratic organization disadvantaged by the existing districts, the situation was even worse in the Republican dominated outer Cook and the collar counties. Because most of the voters for both parties were located in the northern metropolitan area, both state political party platforms called for redistricting, and Republican Governor William G. Stratton worked hard for it. In 1955 the constitution was amended to substantially change both legislative chambers and to disconnect the Senate districting from population. A new balance would allow downstate to control the Senate and Cook County to control the House. The Senate was to have 58 members: 34 would be permanently reserved to 101 counties, and 24 assigned to Cook, of which 18 would go to the city and six to suburban Cook. The House was enlarged to 59 three-member districts. Thirty districts would go to Cook County, with 23 assigned to the city. The remaining 29 would be divided downstate. These political subdivisions and county lines were to be used for district boundaries and after each census, seats were to be redistricted according to population. If the legislature failed to accomplish this, a commission would; if the commission failed, candidates for the House would have to run at-large. Proponents of this arrangement believed that an at-large election would so terrify legislators that they would agree on House redistricting with due regard to population changes. Meanwhile, downstate interests would be protected from that danger noted by southern Illinois leader, Paul Powell: "The Cook County boys practice a different brand of politics than we do downstate" (Olson, 1954, p. 345). That protection would be provided by a constitutionally permanent downstate majority in the Senate.

In 1955 the General Assembly did redraw the districts for both House and Senate. Without reviewing all of the details, it is important to note how the districting was conducted. First, the House and Senate each agreed to take care of its own districting. The House would not disturb the Senate's districts if the Senate would accept the House decisions on its districts. Second, work groups divided the responsibility for drawing districts in specific areas: Chicago Democrats drew city districts, suburban Republicans took care of Cook County outside the city and downstaters handled the rest. Third, great effort was made to preserve districts for sitting members who wanted to run for reelection after redistricting.

The redistricting solution for Illinois was highly pragmatic, and was dominated by the party leaders in the legislature, in the local party organizations, especially Chicago, and by the governor. House districts were made more equal in population—but nothing close to current standards. They ranged from 120,000 to 206,000. In the Senate, where districts were to be by area and not by population, and were drawn to be enduring (not subject to future decennial redistricting), populations varied from 54,000 to 384,000. No substantial change in partisan balance was attempted. After the number of seats for specific regions and the hegemony of party leaders in each area were established, the prime political consideration was to draw relatively safe districts for incumbent legislators. Finally, district boundaries respected the lines separating Chicago, suburban Cook County and downstate counties.

The Redistricting Revolution

By 1963, the first biennial session after new census data were available, several legal and political changes had occurred that promised to make districting more complicated. Unequal populations in legislative districts and congressional constituencies was a big political issue nationwide. Although urban populations had long been underrepresented, the 1960 census results showed unprecedented inequalities in the suburbs of large and medium-sized cities. The inequities were common across the United States, not just in metropolitan areas the size of Chicago.

On March 26, 1962, in the case of *Baker v. Carr*, the Supreme Court decided that it would enter the political thicket that it had avoided ever since the Illinois case of *Colegrove v. Green*. Charles W. Baker, a resident of Nashville, Tennessee, objected to the fact that the legislative district where he resided was many times larger in population than that of the smallest state legislative district in Tennessee. Although the Tennessee state constitution had a population principle in its apportionment provisions, no redistricting had taken place since 1901. Baker could not get relief from the legislature. The state courts dismissed his case. So, via the federal courts, the matter came to the U.S. Supreme Court. Baker won. Despite a great many ambiguities in the court's written decision, it was understood across the land that legislatures were under federal pressure to provide "equal protection of the laws" as guaranteed by the 14th Amendment to the U.S. Constitution (*Baker v. Carr*, 1962).

A political factor making redistricting complicated in Illinois was the partisan balance. Whereas Republican dominance of the governorship and the legislature had been secure in the mid-1950s, the situation had changed since then. The national surge in support for Democrats in 1958 brought a 91-86 Democratic majority to the Illinois House in the same election. In 1960 Democrat Otto Kerner was elected governor, and although there were 89 Republicans to 88 Democrats in the House, Democrat Paul Powell was reelected speaker with help from three House Republicans. Republicans held a 31-27 majority in the Senate. By 1963 Republican control was firm in the Senate, with a 35-23 margin, but close in the House, with a 90-87 balance. One more thing: Richard J. Daley won reelection to his third term as mayor of Chicago in April 1963 and was at the height of his power in the regular Democratic organization.

The result was a highly partisan battle. The House Republican leadership sponsored a redistricting bill that was passed along strict party lines in the House and Senate. After the legislature adjourned, Governor Kerner vetoed the bill, leaving the state without a redistricting act. Thus, according to the constitution, the governor was empowered to appoint a bipartisan commission to draw up districts.

According to the constitution, as amended in 1955, the two major parties would each nominate 10 members for the bipartisan commission. The governor would appoint five from each list, and this body would create districts according to the provisions of the constitution. The commission was appointed. Interestingly, Governor Kerner named two Democrats and two Republicans from Chicago, one from each party from suburban Cook County and two from each party for the rest of the state. The commission had four months to make a decision.

The commission considered a variety of options. The enduring disagreement was whether or not Chicago would be reduced to 21 districts, in line with its portion of the state population. When the time for negotiations expired, the two sides were still deadlocked. All other remedies having been exhausted, the constitution required an at-large election for the House during 1964.

The Yard-long Ballot

Governor Kerner called the General Assembly into special session to establish procedures for the nomination and election of House candidates. A bill was enacted to let party conventions each nominate 118 candidates. Then each party slate would be voted on by all the voters of the state, each voter allowed to cast votes for as many as 177 candidates; in this election, no cumulative voting was allowed. Election officials used an orange ballot with 236 names—the "bedsheet ballot"—that was a yard long (actually 33 inches).

Each party convention fulfilled its nominating task during June 1964. Slates for both parties included most of the incumbents who wanted renomination, some former legislators and a sprinkling of "name" candidates. The Republicans' most prominent name candidate was Earl D.

Eisenhower, brother of the former president. The Democrats had Adlai Stevenson III, son of the former governor and presidential candidate.

During the election campaign the stakes for the contest went up. In a succession of cases concerning apportionment and districting, the U.S. Supreme Court established the one person, one vote principle. Districts within a political jurisdiction, such as a state, were to be as equal in population as feasible. That would be true for congressional districts and legislative districts. Moreover, despite state constitutional arrangements which disconnected districting from population in state senates, the U.S. Supreme Court would require the population principle to apply here also. Illinoisans were put on notice that the General Assembly elected in 1964 would have to draw new districts for both the House and Senate of the General Assembly and the congressional delegation.

In November 1964, the nation elected Democrat Lyndon Johnson in a landslide victory over Republican Barry Goldwater. In Illinois, Otto Kerner was reelected governor over Charles Percy. Republicans kept control of the Senate with a 33-25 majority; but in the at-large election for the House most voters marked the party circle at the top. The Democrats, therefore, won a 118-59 majority. All 118 Democrats got more votes than the Republican ticket leader, Eisenhower. In the peculiar dynamics of that election the Republicans who got the most votes were the ones who got endorsements from the Field newspapers of Chicago, the *Sun-Times* and *Daily News* (Andrews, 1966, pp. 255-257).

Courts and Commissions

With the Democrats in control of the governorship and the House, and Republicans dominating the Senate, the 1965 General Assembly deadlocked on the three districting tasks: Congress, Senate and House. Because of earlier appeals to the state and federal courts concerning congressional districts and the state Senate, those two remaps were accomplished by unusual cooperation between state and federal judges. A panel of judges produced a congressional map by combining proposals from the Democrats for Cook County and the Republicans for downstate, which gave safe districts to nearly all the incumbents. The result was a plan likely to elect nine Democrats in Chicago and three in southern Illinois as well as three Republicans from suburban Cook and nine in north and central downstate.

The Senate districts were created by a similar panel of federal and state judges, and (like those of the House) were supposed to be relatively equal in population. There were 21 districts in Chicago, nine in suburban Cook County and 28 for the rest of the state. As a whole, the map was expected to favor Republicans. By judicial order all the new Senate districts would have elections in 1966 and 1970, allowing redistricting again after that. The previous requirement was for Senate elections every two years, in half the districts, with members elected to four-year terms.

As for the House districts, the legislature remained under the constitutional provision that if the General Assembly could not establish a districting plan—and it did not—the governor would appoint a commission to do the job. If the commission failed, another at-large election would take place. Despite pessimism and repeated deadlocks, the 1965 commission kept negotiations going to a successful conclusion. The discussions were helped by the fact that the court had already drawn 30 new Senate districts for Cook County. With reluctance, Democrats agreed to 30 House districts using the same lines: 21 in Chicago and nine in suburban Cook. The 29 downstate House districts were last to be agreed on, and their boundaries were somewhat different from that of the 28 Senate districts. Only one of the 10 commissioners, a southern Illinois Democrat from Shawneetown, was in disagreement. He called the settlement a "sellout of the Democratic Party in southern Illinois" (McDowell, 1967, p. 81).

The result was an apportionment which experts in both parties agreed would result in a very close balance of Democrats and Republicans in the House—either party could win control in a favorable year. Both in Chicago and suburban Cook, House and Senate members had the same constituencies, which would help party leaders maintain control of nominations and primary contests. Downstate, however, House and Senate districts differed, making opportunities for office more individualistic. Except in counties with populations entitling them to more than one House or Senate district, boundaries coincided with county lines.

A factor that probably facilitated the drawing of House districts was the very peculiar membership of the House following the 1964 at-large election. It was well understood among Democrats that despite having 118 incumbents, a district arrangement could elect roughly 85 to 95 Democrats. Moreover, the incumbents of both parties were disproportionately from metropolitan Chicago. So the surplus of incumbents residing upstate and the paucity of them living downstate meant that the mapmakers were under fewer constraints and less pressure from incumbents than in typical districting situations. Upstate contests between incumbents were inevitable, and downstate ones could be avoided.

Redistricting for the 1970s

All that politically painful work on redistricting stayed in place only until the results of the next decennial headcount became available in 1971. By that time it was clear that the U.S. Supreme Court would accept no substantial variations from population equality in the districts of either the House or Senate. In addition, Illinois now had a new constitution which reestablished legislative districts with one senator and three representatives. There would be 59, thereby adding one additional member to the Senate, and keeping three-member House districts elected by cumulative voting. Districting would remain the responsibility of the General Assembly.

Two other considerations are noteworthy. First, the constitution was silent concerning regard for existing political boundaries in districting. The district redrawing would not necessarily begin by apportioning seats to Chicago, suburban Cook, and the remaining 101 counties. The simple requirement of the 1970 Illinois Constitution was that "Legislative Districts shall be compact, contiguous and substantially equal in population" (Art. 4, Sec. 3a). By that time it was clear that the U.S. Supreme Court would enforce the "equal in population" ruling rather strictly. "Contiguous" means all connected together. A district cannot consist of, for example, a county, plus a township outside—but not touching—the county. "Compact" means not having widely separated parts connected by narrow corridors of land.

The second consideration is that the machinery for redistricting was designed to prevent partisan deadlock. If the legislature failed to redistrict by June 30 in the year following the census, the legislative leaders would be required to appoint a Legislative Redistricting Commission—consisting of eight members, expected to be four Republicans and four Democrats. If they failed to adopt a plan, a ninth member—a tie breaker—would be chosen by lot from two additional partisans. Each party would have an even chance to get the advantage.

The dynamic character of Illinois' demography must be kept in mind to understand the politics of redistricting. From 1901 to 1955 population grew most in and around Chicago, but districts were frozen to the advantage of downstate. After 1955, the House was supposed to reflect population change, not only in Chicago, but also in the suburbs. Actually, however, the population of Chicago ceased to grow. But migration in and out of the city made its voting population increasingly Democratic. The Democrats kept their numerical strength in the legislature by capturing previously Republican districts in the city. Population growth continued in the rest of Cook County, and these districts were predominantly Republican. Increasingly too, populations in the collar counties grew and districts there were won mostly by Republicans.

If after the 1970 census, districting had been done according to previous subdivisions, population required the following:

Chicago—17 and a fraction, down from 21
Suburban Cook—11 and a fraction, up from 9
Downstate—30 and a fraction, up from 29

The Chicago Democrats, however, tried to get a plan that established some districts, mostly in Chicago, which overlapped into suburban Cook County. Their goal was to retain control of 21 districts. The Republican speaker, W. Robert Blair, was a Will County representative first elected on the yard long ballot of 1964. He negotiated an agreement with the Democrats which passed the House. It nearly satisfied the Chicago Democrats' objectives while Speaker Blair got to draw downstate boundaries to the Republicans' advantage. In the Senate, Cook County Republicans were outraged and they prevented the bill from passing. When the deadline passed without a redistricting law, the Legislative Redistricting Commission had to be appointed.

Each of the four legislative leaders was allowed to appoint two members. Three leaders—Blair, Cecil Partee, Chicago Democratic Senate leader, and Clyde Choate, downstate Democratic House leader—appointed themselves and a loyal staff member to the commission. The Senate Republican leader appointed a Senate assistant leader, Terrel Clarke from suburban Cook, and former Republican Governor William G. Stratton, who had broken the locks on suburban representation in 1955. The commission decided by a 6-2 vote, over the angry opposition of Clarke and Stratton, on a map very similar to the earlier Blair map, containing districts which overlapped the city boundaries. It placed 11 districts entirely in the city, and nine others on the city's outer rim that extended sufficiently into the suburbs to garner the needed population, but not so much that Democrat control would be in doubt. Suburban Cook contained only eight districts completely, and two more extended beyond Cook into neighboring counties. Downstate got the remaining 29. Opinions on the new map differed. It contained 28 safe districts for each party, and three leaning Republican. Chicago regular Democrats had preserved control of 20 districts, unwarranted by the city's population, by establishing districts that extended beyond the city's boundaries into the suburbs.

Despite a court challenge of the map's constitutionality, it was judged to meet current standards. By later enactment, the map remained in place until 1982.

Cutback and Single-member Districts

The most recent redistricting was marked by unique circumstances. In 1980 Illinois voters adopted a constitutional amendment, often referred to as the "cutback amendment," by a popular vote of 68.7 percent of those voting on the proposition. That ended an era. No longer would Illinois have 59 districts, each electing a senator and three representatives. No longer would the three representatives be chosen by cumulative voting (Everson and Parker, 1982). Cutback reduced the House membership by one-third, and required representatives to be elected from single-member districts. Thus the new district plan would again have 59 Senate districts, and each of those would be divided into two House districts, for a total of 118. An obvious consequence was that many House incumbents would not get safe districts, particularly those who were from the minority party in the old three-member districts. Republicans would be eliminated from Chicago districts and Democrats would be decimated in Cook and the collar counties. In the remaining 96 counties, both parties would retain their approximate pre-cutback strength. Although Senate incumbents might be allowed to keep most of their old districts, doubtless some of the displaced House members would compete for them as well.

The population shifts of the 1970s only exaggerated previous patterns. Chicago's population became smaller, more black and more Hispanic. Population growth was mostly in the Cook and collar county suburbs. The remaining 96 counties grew at a rate slightly above that for the state as a whole. If the old political boundaries of Chicago, suburban Cook and downstate had been maintained, Chicago's population would get 15.5 Senate districts and 31 House districts, suburban Cook would get 12 and 24, and Downstate would get 31.5 and 63.

The political setting for drawing districts was somewhat balanced, but favored the Republicans. They controlled the House 91 to 86, while Democrats had a 30-29 edge in the Senate. The governor, James R. Thompson, was a Republican. Neither party could win alone but if Republicans could win in the legislature, they would not fear the governor's veto. For Democrats to win would require Republican help in the legislature and from the Republican governor.

The political strategies of turf protection were described by Charles N. Wheeler like this:

> Republicans adopted a fairly simple game plan: draw as many strong black districts in Chicago as possible, throw in a Hispanic district or two—all at the expense of white ethnic machine Democrats, of course—and hope for enough crossover votes from independent-minded black Democrats to send to Thompson's desk a redistricting plan that would guarantee Republican ascendancy elsewhere. Republicans also planned to draw "dream" districts for a few downstate Democrats, on the "if you can't beat them, co-opt them" theory.

> Democrats drew up their own map.

> Not surprisingly, it was drawn to preserve Chicago's 20 districts by overlapping half of them into the suburbs.

> Elsewhere, the plan sought to save Democratic incumbents and carve out safe Democratic districts wherever possible . . . . [T]he Senate Democrats' map also pitted GOP incumbents in several districts. Besides the predictable Republican criticism, the Democratic plan also

came under fire from independent blacks, who charged it would dilute black political strength (1982, pp. 73-74).

In the legislature each party coaxed some dissidents from the other party to its side, but frustration prevailed. The June 30 deadline came before the legislature could pound out a compromise. That triggered the formation of the Legislative Redistricting Commission by appointment from the Republican and Democratic leaders of the House and Senate, and negated the Republicans' gubernatorial veto advantage.

The constitution required the commission, four Republicans and four Democrats, to do its job by August 10. Failure would mean random selection of a tie breaker. Despite some early signs of cooperativeness, the four Democrats and four Republicans could not get together on a plan. The greatest conflict concerned the districts that overlapped from Chicago into suburban Cook. The Senate Republican on the commission, James "Pate" Philip, was from suburban DuPage County and was an aspirant for Senate president if Republicans could regain control. The pushing and hauling between the preferences of suburban Republicans and Chicago Democrats resulted in stalemate.

As required by the constitution, the Supreme Court nominated a member of each party for the role of tie breakers. Former Governor Richard Ogilvie was named for the Republicans and former Governor Samuel Shapiro for the Democrats. Shapiro's name was drawn from Lincoln's hat by Secretary of State Jim Edgar. Negotiations thereafter were essentially among the Democratic majority about which incumbents would be protected. Wheeler describes the product of the Democrats' efforts:

> Although losing some 364,000 residents from 1970 to 1980, the city stands to yield control of only one Senate district, thanks to the map's overlapping of 10 districts into suburban territory. Each of the hybrid districts has enough city precincts to be rated firmly Democratic, and along with 9 other districts wholly in the city, should elect city-oriented Democrats in the future. . . .
>
> The key to the city's anticipated hegemony among House Democrats, of course, is the map's creation of 21 city and 16 hybrid, city-suburban House districts, all of which are expected to elect city-oriented Democrats. If that occurs, Chicago Democrats will lose less than 10 percent—just 4 of 41—of their current House seats, despite the one-third reduction in House size (1982, p. 70).

The Legislative Redistricting Commission ratified the map, five Democrats against four Republicans. Challenged subsequently in a federal court, some adjustments were negotiated on behalf of black and Hispanic interests in Chicago and some Republican incumbents. But the strategic objectives of the Chicago leaders of the Democrats were approved by a majority court decision (two Democratic judges against one Republican).

In passing, it should be mentioned how complete the Democratic victories were in the districting process after the 1980 census. The General Assembly also deadlocked over rival party plans for congressional districts. This issue also was handed over to a three-judge, federal court panel. The existing 24 districts, held in 1980 by 14 Republicans and 10 Democrats, were reduced to 22 seats because of Illinois' relatively small population growth. The federal panel approved a plan largely reflecting the map proposed by the legislative leader of the House Democrats, Michael Madigan. City districts were extended into the suburbs, and downstate districts were made secure for two incumbent Democrats, and less safe for a couple of incumbent Republicans. Suburban Republican incumbents were crowded together. Although the outlook was possible for a 12 Republican to 10 Democrat lineup after the election, in the 1982 election a Democratic surge actually brought a 12-10 edge for Democrats.

INTERPRETING ILLINOIS REDISTRICTING POLITICS

This brief history of redistricting the Illinois General Assembly reveals a good deal about the partisan context of all the state's politics. Consider these generalizations:

(1) Enduring party and factional advantages can be won or lost in the redistricting process.
(2) The more cohesive a party or faction, the better its chance of obtaining favorable results in negotiations over legislative boundaries.
(3) External forces can affect the outcomes and consequences. Federal court decisions have been especially important.
(4) Incumbent legislators constitute an in-group, which both parties try to protect if possible.
(5) The election after redistricting attracts new candidates for the legislature.

Each of these points deserves some elaboration.

Party and Factional Advantage

Although individuals move and some voters change from Republican to Democratic and vice versa, the political characteristics of residential areas change slowly. Whether one focuses on the Polish, Irish or German wards of Chicago, or the WASP New Trier Township and DuPage County, the biases of various areas do endure. What this means is that districts in Cook County and downstate can be drawn to provide an enduring political advantage. The principles for doing this are simple. Each party has areas of concentrated voter strength. One side tries to concentrate the opposition's voters into as few districts as possible. Let them win on their own turf by wide margins, but prevent them from winning in neighboring districts. If conceding one district to the opposition will yield two or more districts for the home team, try to draw the districts to get such advantages.

To the Cohesive Go the Spoils

The stronger the unity in a party or part of a party, the better it can negotiate for advantages. For one thing, organization brings information. Whether at the precinct, ward, township, county or state level, the organized party unit knows which citizens vote, and which party they usually support. That helps when it is time to draw lines and bargain for advantages. From 1955 to 1982 the Chicago regular Democrats have been the biggest and best organized faction in Illinois. Republicans in suburban Cook and the collar counties have never acknowledged one leader. Downstate legislators have won party positions in the legislature from time to time for both parties, but none has had an enduring party base to work from. So, when it has served the Chicago Democrats to do so, they have given away downstate strength to preserve or extend their control in and around the city. Individual Republican leaders have differed in their concern about suburban Cook and the collar counties. In 1971 Chicago Democrats capitalized very importantly on the split between Blair and downstate Republicans versus the suburban Cook Republicans. That opened the way to overlapping districts and a renewed opportunity for majority control by Democratic legislators in both houses.

External Forces Shape Outcomes

In 1955, downstaters accepted a compromise that gave more House seats to the suburban Republicans and city Democrats at the expense of downstate in exchange for a permanent arrangement fixing Senate districts by area instead of population. But in 1964 the U.S. Supreme Court interpreted the U.S. Constitution to mean one person, one vote would apply to both houses in the states regardless of previous state political agreements.

The 1964 at-large election turned into a big Democratic advantage, not because of the special merit of its 118 candidates, but because the at-large election coincided with a smashing presidential victory by Democrat Lyndon Johnson over Republican Barry Goldwater. In 1980 the Democrats skillfully staved off the Republican advantage of having control of the governorship and got a deadlock in the legislature. Then they won the tie breaker on the luck of the draw. Having gained the advantage, they passed an advantageous districting plan and, an election later, won a majority in both legislative chambers.

Legislators as an In-Group

After two or more terms in the legislature, a member is considered to be a veteran. This is an honorable status. Ordinarily—there are exceptions—veterans like and respect one another, even "across the aisle." (Republicans and Democrats sit on opposite sides of the middle aisle of the House and Senate.) When redistricting takes place the major battles pit the parties against each other. What quota of seats will Republicans/Democrats get? Apart from that, when particular boundaries are drawn, districts are usually drawn to be safe for veterans of both parties. On the other hand, if a veteran is planning to retire, that old district may be carved up to the advantage of neighboring veterans. Usually very few districts are drawn to be closely competitive between the two parties. The few that are often have no incumbent, or the incumbent is only a freshman.

Redistricting and New Blood

Inevitably, new districts mean new boundaries, confronting incumbents with new constituents. Sometimes the incumbent knows the new district will be tougher to run in than the old. Some Republicans in and close to Chicago had to run for their political lives in 1972 and 1982 because of the district changes; that was also true for some downstate Democrats. More than the usual number of legislators retire at redistricting time, and the untested electoral situation stimulates a larger than usual crop of new legislative candidates. This means that more freshmen are elected following redistricting—all other things remaining equal—than in typical years.

CONCLUDING OBSERVATIONS

A champion salesman was asked, "What is the secret of your success?" His answer was not a credit-claiming one: "I've got a great territory." Many legislators understand that their electoral success depends in large measure upon their "territory"—their district or constituency. Keeping control of the district is beyond their power. That is why redistricting is such a threatening process. Party leaders, and previous loyalty and friendship help, but members have the lurking fear that they will be caught in the collision of larger forces. After redistricting, members consider their options and decide whether or not to run again. The politics of campaigns and elections is discussed in the next chapter.

Chapter Four

The Electoral Context of Lawmaking: Nominations and Elections

Perhaps the most commonplace utterance heard in the General Assembly is: "The people of my district want . . . , therefore I am in favor of . . ." You can count on hearing legislators testify to the connections between their actions and their constituents' views every day that the legislature is in session.

One can be cynical about such statements, believing that "the people's interest" is held up as a shield for self-aggrandizement. Sometimes it is. There is no way to verify when a member truly seeks to reflect constituency preferences and when an action is prompted by other motives. What is certain is that legislators hold office only by the consent of the people. The privilege of serving has to be won and the status of veteran means that the privilege has been won more than once. Thus the cultivation of constituent support ranks high in the priorities of lawmakers. As Chapter One points out, one side of the lawmaker's job is to be an advocate for constituents—getting state services for them while preventing the state and special interests from hurting them. The practical incentive for constituent service is election and reelection.

SOME GENERAL CONSIDERATIONS IN ELECTORAL VOTING

Most Americans vote, and believe that it is good and appropriate to do so. Over the years the legal impediments to voting have become less and less restrictive. In the early years of the Republic voting was restricted to white male landowners over 21 years of age; the color, sex, ownership and age barriers have tumbled since then.

Eligibility

There are two steps necessary for a citizen to take part in elections—registration and voting. In order to vote, Illinois citizens 18 years or older who have resided in a place for 30 days have to register with the election authority: a city, county or election commission clerk. The citizen provides a name and address, shows two pieces of identification including the address, swears to their accuracy and signs the registration form. The voter is assigned to the precinct in which he or she resides, which is a subdivision of a ward or township. The registrant then must appear at the precinct polling place on election day, identify him/herself, sign for a ballot and vote. Election authorities are authorized to purge their books of registrants who have not voted within the previous four years. If a person will be away from the precinct on election day, there is a procedure for voting by "absentee" ballot shortly before the election. The rules are intended to allow registrants to vote only once in each election in the district where they live.

Critics of current voting laws focus on two concerns. Registration could be easier. Currently, any person wanting to register, or re-register, must personally fill out a form with an authorized election official at least 28 days before an election. Some people argue that the law should allow this to be done by mail or at every election precinct on election day. Proponents of the status quo argue that making registration that easy will increase the likelihood of fraud.

The second criticism is that elections could be more accessible. Traditionally, American elections are on Tuesday; for example, the first Tuesday after the first Monday in November in years divisible by four is the day Congress has chosen for presidential elections. However, it might be easier for people to take part in elections if they were held on weekend days, such as Saturday, Sunday or even both days consecutively.

Turnout

The law no longer makes voting an exclusive privilege. Gone are the days of male privilege, primaries for white voters only, literacy tests and poll taxes. Nonetheless, turnout and the number and nature of those who vote are some of the variables that make election outcomes difficult to predict. Turnout was the variable that confounded pollsters in the dead-heat contest between Governor Thompson and his challenger, Adlai E. Stevenson III in 1982.

Turnout is statistically related to socioeconomic status and education. Generally, those higher in status and education put a greater premium on voting than the poor and poorly educated. Also, those who trust political authorities "to do what is right" are likelier to vote than those who don't. Not surprisingly, those who are more educated and well off usually are more trusting, and almost always vote. Those on the low end of the trust, economic and education scales often do not vote, although these individuals constitute a potential electorate that sometimes comes out to vote when social and economic stress or conflict are high.

Voting turnout is calculated in relationship to two other numerical estimates. The larger of these estimates is the "voting age population." The U.S. Bureau of the Census makes authoritative estimates of the number of people who could qualify, by age and citizenship, to take part in a given election. Journalists and political scientists compare actual turnout to the voting age population. By that standard American voting is low, and has been declining. Nationally, U.S. voting participation was at

63 percent for the Kennedy-Nixon contest in 1960, but down to 52.6 percent for the Carter-Reagan election in 1980. There was a fractional upturn in 1984 to 53.3 percent. Voting levels were higher in Illinois than the national percentage for both years, 76 percent in 1960 and 59 percent in 1984; but the decline in Illinois over the period was even steeper (Everson and Parker, 1981; Everson, 1985).

Participation in gubernatorial elections in all the states for 1974-1980 compared to voting age population ranges from 67.3 percent in Utah to 23.3 percent in Texas (Bibby, Cotter, Gibson and Huckshorn, 1983, p. 63). Consistent with the Elazar typology (see Chapter Two), voting is highest in the moralistic states of the north, lowest in the traditionalistic states of the south and middling for the individualistic states that mostly lie between. Illinois was shown to rank 16th among the states with participation at 49.8 percent.

The second standard against which voting is compared is the number of registered voters. As noted, registration is a legal barrier to voting. Said differently, a person must put forth some effort to register before being permitted to enter the voting booth. In Illinois registered voters were 81 percent of the voting age population in 1976, and 77 percent in 1980 and 1984. Of the registered voters, the proportion actually voting in presidential elections has been about three-fourths—75 percent in 1976, 76 percent in 1980 and 77 percent in 1984. In off-year elections, however, the percentage is regularly lower: 52 percent in 1974, 57 percent in 1978 and 65 percent in 1982.

Turnout is clearly variable from election to election for a variety of reasons in addition to socioeconomic status and education. More voters turn out for presidential elections than for off-year elections. Of the actual voters, more vote for contests at the "top of the ticket"—president, U.S. senator, governor, other statewide elective offices—than for lower offices—state legislators, county officials and judges. In 1982, for example, the total of Democratic (Stevenson) and Republican (Thompson) votes for governor was over 3.63 million. The Democratic and Republican vote total for all state Senate seats was 3.55 million, and 3.47 for the House. Turnout is affected by partisanship, ticket splitting, personalities, issues, the political climate and the efforts of the candidates; all matters for further discussion.

Partisanship

A continuing characteristic of American elections is that the competition is led by volunteer organizations—the Democratic and Republican parties. Most people, in fact, usually think of themselves as Republicans or Democrats, a fact which has been documented nationally since 1952 by the Survey Research Center and Center for Political Studies at the

University of Michigan. But over that period the proportion of "party identifiers" has declined from 75 percent to a little over 50 percent of the people. The number of apoliticals—people who don't know or won't say which party they prefer—has not changed much: about 3-5 percent of the people. But those who call themselves independents have increased from fewer than 25 percent to nearly 40 percent of the people. The preferences of the party identifiers are highly uneven. Just over 33 percent call themselves Republicans. So the Democratic identifiers outnumber the Republicans nearly two to one.

The party balance in Illinois is more even than in the nation as a whole, and in statewide contests the parties are evenly matched. Although poll data on the partisan composition in the state are less precise than for the nation, one enduring measure of party competition was developed by Austin Ranney (1965, 1976). It focuses on three factors: proportion of party success, duration of party success and the frequency with which control of the governorship and legislature is divided between the parties. The Ranney index, which could range from 0 (totally Republican) to .5 (even party competition) to 1 (totally Democratic) has been calculated for three periods: 1946 to 1963, 1962 to 1973 and 1974 to 1980. Ranney and the later researchers (Bibby et al., 1983, pp. 59-96) were interested in the comparison of all states and in establishing categories and definitions for the scores of each state. These scores were differentiated into five categories, using only contests for state office, not the votes for the president or U.S. senators. The middle category, .3500 to .6499, indicates strong two-party competition. The scores for Illinois were in the competitive category for all three periods: .3847 for 1946 to 1963, .4245 for 1962-73 and .5384 for 1974-1980. Although competition has been close throughout the postwar era, it has gradually moved from Republican to Democratic advantage.

Although the partisan balance of voters is about even in the state as a whole, it is uneven in most electoral jurisdictions of the state. Chicago is heavily Democratic and elects nearly all Democratic legislators. Suburban Cook and the collar counties are Republican dominated and elect nearly all Republican lawmakers. Everywhere else the picture is mixed. There is Democratic strength in cities over 50,000 and in the southernmost third of the state. Elsewhere the prevailing identification is Republican. The enduring uneven distribution of partisans in this competitive state explains why redistricting has always produced such strident partisan wrangling. It is likewise the reason why most legislative districts tend to be relatively safe for one party or the other. The results of the 1982 gubernatorial election illustrate this distribution (see Map 4:1).

Democratic
(Adlai E. Stevenson won by 53% or more)

Republican
(James R. Thompson won by 53% or more)

Competitive
(Winner won by 52% or less)

Map 4:1   Distribution of Votes in 1982 Gubernatorial Election

Ticket Splitters

A growing election phenomenon is ticket splitting. When voters go to the polls they can vote "straight party," or go down the ballot voting for specific individuals, contest by contest. Voting straight is much easier. By making an X, or punching the modern day punch card ballot for one party alone, each one of that party's nominees from governor to county board member, gets one vote. In recent years, however, growing numbers of voters work their way down the ballot, supporting Republicans for some offices and Democrats for others—ticket splitting.

A rough way of measuring ticket splitting statewide is to compare the percentage of votes obtained by candidates of the same party for statewide offices. In 1982, while the gubernatorial election was a near tie, the Democratic candidate for attorney general, Neil Hartigan, had the largest percentage of the two-party vote: 65.9 percent. The Democrat with the lowest was the candidate for secretary of state, Jerry Cosentino, with 46.8 percent. Subtracting the smaller percentage from the larger, it can be deduced that the percentage of ticket splitters was at least 19.1 percent. This index indicated fewer than 5 percent ticket splitters in 1964 and 1968, but 16 percent in 1972, 31 percent in 1976 and 40 percent in 1978. With such growing ticket splitting evident, attractive candidates for an underdog party hope to win by attracting the support of ticket splitters.

But in legislative races the benefits of ticket splitting do not necessarily accrue to the underdog. Congressional research reveals that while the percentage of straight party voters has been going down, most of the defecting voters still vote for incumbent congressmen. Similarly, in state legislative elections voters are more likely to know or recognize the incumbent's name, and prefer that person to an obscure challenger. Incumbent legislators cultivate their constituents for precisely this reason. They handle problems the homefolks have with state bureaucracies and see to it that the district gets its share of projects, highways, services and jobs. So, ticket-splitting voters who recognize the lawmaker by name are likely to favor the incumbent.

Personalities, Issues, the Times

At election time the citizen makes two kinds of choices that are of much concern to candidates. The first is whether or not to vote; the second is which candidate to support. The voter's sense of duty about voting and strength of partisan identification are important to those choices. Also important to the voter's choice are personalities, issues, and the temper of the times.

It is easy after the fact to say that in the presidential race of 1984, Ronald Reagan's personality attracted more voters and votes than did Walter Mondale's. Many politicians have notable and attractive personalities and personal style. Several Illinois commentators suggested that in the 1982 gubernatorial contest Thompson registered higher on the personality index than Stevenson. But personality is not likely to be a strong guide to voters with regard to legislators. Legislators, even incumbents, have low visibility. The opportunities to see and directly compare rival legislative candidates are available, but require rather substantial initiative on the part of the voter.

A similar argument can be made about issues. Certainly issues are often important to voters, both stirring them to vote, and to vote for particular candidates. Issues are the common currency of exchange between voters and candidates. Candidates use them as topics on which they can present their preferences and ideas to the voters. Sometimes voters have specific concerns they want candidates to address. Other citizens are as interested in what candidates choose to discuss as they are in the views expressed. Citizens can respond with their votes to the candidates who are "right" on the issues.

Two factors prevent specific issues from being determinative in very many individual legislative contests. Most of the specific issues discussed in state legislative campaigns derive from the bigger, and usually partisan, matters argued by candidates at the top of the ticket. Legislative candidates rarely come up with novel solutions to issues like school aid, tax policy and new government services. Usually they take sides consistent with their party identification. Moreover, truly local issues rarely divide competing partisan candidates. If there is an issue about a local road, a bridge or a state park there is usually only one "right" and popular position to take. So competing candidates converge on the same position— both are for the district.

A variation, or exception, occurs when a challenger can find one or more issues on which an incumbent has previously taken a position that turns out to be "wrong," or unpopular. "He voted in favor of the tax increase." "She voted for a pay raise." Sometimes, too, the challenger can make the incumbent's record, integrity or personal life the overriding issue. A strategy that sometimes succeeds is for the challenger to argue that the incumbent has failed to be faithful to the constituency's regional interests. Downstate challengers have sometimes defeated incumbents for voting too often with Chicago or suburban legislative leaders.

The nature of the times affects election outcomes, even in legislative districts. Generally speaking, politics and partisanship are of scant interest for most people most of the time. (Who can imagine parents being unhappy because a son or daughter is dating someone from the "wrong" political party?) But if times are bad, with the economy sluggish, taxes up or the public processes in deadlock, there is a tendency for the voters to punish the incumbents at the top of the ticket—the president, the governor and other statewide candidates and their party. The "out" party and its candidates seek to provoke the anger and frustration of otherwise quiescent citizens to "throw the rascals out." When that happens, otherwise "safe" legislators, on the party ticket with more visible incumbents may suffer defeat.

The 1982 election illustrated this phenomenon. Illinois Republicans suffered conspicuously for the bad economy, then unresponsive to Reaganomics. Chicago turned out 16 percent more voters than four years before; a great many voted a straight Democrat ticket. Democrats won six of eight statewide contests (treasurer, attorney general, comptroller and three positions on the University of Illinois Board of Trustees), 12 of 22 congressional seats, 33 of 59 Senate seats and 70 of 118 House seats. Totalling all the major party votes for Senate and House races reveals that Democrats got 58 percent of the votes for all Senate seats and 57 percent of the votes for House seats, just like the 58 percent they got in the three statewide University of Illinois trustee votes. (Most political commentators in Illinois consider the trustee contests an election benchmark because they are devoid of personality and issue considerations.) An anti-Republican surge during bad times, in the first election after a reapportionment favorable to the Democrats, eliminated a number of Republican legislators. Under normal circumstances they would likely have been reelected. They were not defeated because of specific constituency issues, bad records as incumbents or offensive personalities. They were vulnerable largely because of events beyond their control and the actions of party leaders over their heads. They varied in their success at dissuading constituents from punishing them along with others higher on the ticket.

ELECTORAL HURDLES TO THE GENERAL ASSEMBLY

There are three phases to winning legislative office in a regular election: filing for nomination, successfully running in the primary election and winning the general election. The primary election is on the third Tuesday in March, every even-numbered year. Filing for office must take place between 99 and 92 days before that, in mid-December. The general election is the first Tuesday after the first Monday in November of the even-numbered years. The time between filing and the general election is almost a year.

Filing

Filing for a place on the primary election ballot is a partisan matter. A person declares him/herself a Republican or Democrat and a qualified voter in the legislative district where he/she wishes to be a candidate. The filing must be accompanied by at least 300-600 signatures of "qualified primary electors of the candidate's party in his legislative district" (*Illinois Revised Statutes*, 1984a). The law's specifics are intended to preserve a system in which the organized, major parties dominate the nominating and electing process. Although a candidate can obtain nomination as other than a Republican or Democrat, independent or minor party candidates rarely win office. Therefore, contenders with the greatest chance for success are those who try to win either the Democratic or Republican party nomination by winning the party primary. The number of signatures needed to get on the primary election ballot is not prohibitively large, but getting them can be a substantial chore. If a candidate has party support, getting the needed signatures with the help of party precinct workers is pretty easy. Usually, in fact, candidates file many more than the minimum number of petitions because some of the signatures may not be qualified, and it is newsworthy when a candidate shows up with boxes and boxes of signed petitions, showing early grass roots support. The State Board of Elections checks the legal qualifications of the candidates and their petitions, and about a month later certifies to the local election officials the names of persons qualified to run in the primary election.

The Primary

Many voters do not understand primary elections. In the past, party candidates were nominated at state, county and township conventions or caucuses. At best, these were partisan meetings of informed locals held to discuss issues and candidates rationally and thoughtfully. At worst they were rowdy circuses or clandestine meetings of insiders, in which bosses rammed a slate of favorites into nomination. Beginning in the 20th century, reformers, such as Robert M. La Follette in Wisconsin and Charles S. Deneen in Illinois, obtained changes in state laws to allow all registered voters to take part in making party nominations. These elections, called primary elections, determine which candidates shall run in the general election under the various party labels—Republican, Democratic or other. Primaries are conducted by public authorities and are open to all eligible voters. The key difference for the voter between the primary election, held in March, and the general election, held in November, is that in the primary a voter must declare his or her partisan affiliation before going into the election booth and there makes choices for that party only.

What really occurs at the primary election is that election officials conduct two parallel nominating elections at the same time—one for Democrats and the other for Republicans. Several candidates may have qualified by filing to run for specific offices—governor, county offices, legislative positions and the like—in each party. The primary is conducted to narrow down the choices to one candidate per office per party. If two or three candidates file as Democrats and are qualified for the House in a particular district, then the primary results determine which one will run as a Democrat in the November general election. A primary voter gets to take part in nominating party candidates for offices at all levels. At the same time, primary voters elect several party officials—ward committeemen (Chicago), township committeemen (suburban Cook), precinct committeemen (downstate), state central committeemen (by congressional district), delegates to presidential nominating conventions (in the presidential election years) and some others.

Because these are party elections, to make party nominations and to elect party officials, the voter must publicly request a ballot for one or the other party when coming to the polls. Election officials mark the poll book to show which party ballot the voter took.

Some voters take offense at the need to publicly declare for a party in order to receive a ballot. They feel that their party preference is a private matter, and should be made in the privacy of the poll booth. Once in the voting booth some primary voters are frustrated to find that all of the candidates they wanted to vote for are not on their ballot. Those candidates were in contests in the other party.

By voting in the primary election as a Republican or Democrat, the voter becomes officially identified with that party in the election records. Party officials then treat the voter rather like big corporations treat investors who own a few shares of stock. The voter finds him/herself getting mail and phone calls asking for campaign contributions and votes at election time.

The primary election rules do not require that the winner get a majority of votes; simply more than the nearest rival. What the winner actually wins is the party label for the general election.

One rarely used, exceptional procedure needs to be mentioned. It is possible for a candidate, who did not file for the ballot, to win the party label. That is done by "write-in" voting. A candidate can obtain the most votes by getting primary voters to write in his/her name on the ballot for a particular office. It is rare for a write-in to defeat candidates whose names are printed on the ballot as certified candidates. It does happen occasionally, however, usually when no certified candidate seeks nomination.

The General Election

At the November election voters may vote "straight," voting for every candidate at all levels in one party or the other. Others will split their tickets, voting for candidates of more than one party. The nominee, or write-in, with the highest number of votes for an office is the winner. This means "plurality rule," not necessarily "majority rule." It may be that because of the candidacy of persons from minor parties, independents or write-ins, the person with the most votes has fewer than half. With very rare exceptions the winners are Republicans or Democrats.

THE LEGISLATIVE ELECTIONS OF 1982 AND 1984

The 1982 legislative elections merit special attention for several reasons. First, the districts for both the House and Senate were redrawn pursuant to the redistricting requirements of the constitution. Second, House districts were established as single-member districts for the first time since 1870. Third, the cutback reduced the House from 177 to 118 members, providing a pool of incumbents more numerous than the number of available legislative seats. Fourth, the politics of redistricting left district lines unresolved until late in 1981, shortly before the deadline for candidates to file. Fifth, incumbents in the previous districts were allowed to run in new districts that contained any part of their former district. That meant they could shop around a bit for a district rather than being limited to the one in which they resided at the time of filing and running. Finally, dispossessed House members gave more than usual attention to the possibilities of moving to the Senate. The 1984 legislative elections provide some clues about the lasting impact of redistricting upon the decade of the 1980s.

There were many candidates for the General Assembly in 1982 who filed to be on the ballot. In the spring, the State Board of Elections published the candidates' names by district. There were 71 Republican and 85 Democratic candidates for the Senate, and 138 Republican and 153 Democrat candidates for the House. A few of these later dropped out before the primary election in March. There were no primary contests for "third party" candidates such as the Taxpayers or Libertarian parties.

The Primary

Tables 4:1 and 4:2 summarize a great deal of information about the legislative primary contests for the House. Although as many candidates may file in a particular district as can obtain the necessary signatures, in 1982 and 1984 neither party had more than four in any House or Senate district. In some districts there were no Democratic candidates and in

Table 4:1   Incidence of Primary Candidates per House District for the Illinois General Assembly: Percent of House Districts with Varying Numbers of Candidates, 1982 and 1984*

1982 Number of Republican Candidates	Number of Democratic Candidates 0	1	2	3	4	Total%	1984 Number of Republican Candidates	Number of Democratic Candidates 0	1	2	3	4	Total%
0	0.0	13.6	9.3	1.7	0.8	25.4	0	0.0	13.6	5.1	2.5	4.2	25.4
1	9.3	28.8	6.8	2.5	0.0	47.4	1	17.8	32.2	8.5	1.7	0.0	60.2
2	5.9	9.3	2.5	0.0	0.0	17.7	2	0.8	6.8	2.5	0.8	0.0	10.9
3	2.5	1.7	0.8	0.0	0.0	5.0	3	0.0	1.7	0.8	0.0	0.0	2.5
4	2.5	1.7	0.0	0.0	0.0	4.2	4	0.0	0.8	0.0	0.0	0.0	0.8
Total %	20.2	55.1	19.4	4.2	0.8	99.7	Total %	18.6	55.1	16.9	5.0	4.2	99.8

*Totals may vary from 100.0 due to rounding.

Source: *Official Vote Cast at the General Primary Election March 16, 1982.*
Official Vote Cast at the General Primary Election March 20, 1984.
Compiled by the State Board of Elections, State of Illinois.

Table 4:2   Incidence of Primary Candidates per Senate District for the Illinois General Assembly: Percent of Senate Districts with Varying Numbers of Candidates, 1982 and 1984*

1982 Number of Republican Candidates	Number of Democratic Candidates 0	1	2	3	4	Total%	1984 Number of Republican Candidates	Number of Democratic Candidates 0	1	2	3	4	Total%
0	0.0	8.5	10.2	3.4	0.0	22.1	0	0.0	20.0	0.0	5.0	5.0	30.0
1	8.5	25.4	6.8	3.4	1.7	45.8	1	5.0	40.0	5.0	5.0	5.0	60.0
2	6.8	10.2	5.1	3.4	0.0	25.5	2	0.0	10.0	0.0	0.0	0.0	10.0
3	0.0	3.4	1.7	0.0	0.0	5.1	3	0.0	0.0	0.0	0.0	0.0	0.0
4	1.7	0.0	0.0	0.0	0.0	1.7	4	0.0	0.0	0.0	0.0	0.0	0.0
Total %	17.0	47.5	23.8	10.2	1.7	100.2	Total %	5.0	70.0	5.0	10.0	10.0	100.0

*Totals may vary from 100.0 due to rounding.

Source: *Official Vote Cast at the General Primary Election March 16, 1982.*
Official Vote Cast at the General Primary Election March 20, 1984.
Compiled by the State Board of Elections, State of Illinois.

some, no Republicans. The number of candidates for each House and Senate district ranged from 0 to 4 in each party.

The numbers in the tables are percentages. Of all the possible combinations of Republican and Democratic candidates, a quarter to nearly half of the House and Senate districts had one Republican candidate and one Democrat candidate. Table 4:1 shows 28.8 for the House in 1982 and 32.2 in 1984. For the Senate, Table 4:2 shows that the parallel numbers are 25.4 for 1982 and 40.0 for 1984. In these districts there were no actual primary contests. One candidate ran to get the Republican nomination and another ran for the Democratic nomination, but there was no intra-party contest for either one. In 13.6 percent of the House districts (16 of 118) in 1982 and the exact same percentage in 1984, there was one candidate running for the Democratic nomination and no one running for the Republican nomination. In 9.3 percent of the House districts in 1982 and 17.8 percent for 1984 there was only one candidate for the Republican nomination while none ran for the Democratic nomination. Summing the number of these one-to-one and one-to-zero races shows that in 1982 there was no intra-party primary contest in 51.7 percent of the House districts and 63.6 percent in 1984. In the Senate districts, 42.4 percent had no contest in 1982 compared to 65 percent in 1984.

Another way of looking at Table 4:1 reveals similarities in the number of primary contests in the two separate years. The percentages for parallel types of races are not sharply different. The variation in two elections for the Senate, (see Table 4:2) is a bit greater, but in 1984 only 20 Senate districts were scheduled for elections.

Comparisons by party produce similar results. The totals at the bottom of the columns are for Democrats, and can be compared to the totals at the side for the rows of the Republicans. Except for the Senate in 1984, in about a fifth of the House and Senate districts there were no Democrats seeking nomination. For Republicans the proportion was a bit higher, closer to one-fourth. In both parties about half or more of the districts had one aspirant for the party nomination. Primaries with three or more candidates were rare in either party.

To summarize the data in tables 4:1 and 4:2, primary contests are commonplace, but not typical. Very few districts have contests of two or more candidates in both parties at the same time. The most commonplace situation is no contest in either party, but one candidate for each party's nomination.

Table 4:3 shows how competitive intra-party contests are. Few of those multicandidate contests were close. Winning requires a plurality: the candidate with the most votes wins. Comparing the winner to the next highest candidate can be calculated as a proportion. "Close" is defined as an instance where the winner's proportion was not greater than 3-to-2 over the nearest loser. Said differently, in the comparison of the two highest candidates, the winner had not more than 60 percent of the votes. The results show that about two-thirds of the contests are not close, but the percentage varies somewhat from one election to another and within the parties.

Table 4:3   Competitiveness* of Primary Contests with Two or More Candidates: By Party and Chamber in 1982 and 1984

| | Democratic Primary Contests | | | | | Republican Primary Contests | | | |
| | House | | Senate | | | House | | Senate | |
	1982	1984	1982	1984		1982	1984	1982	1984
Close	8	7	7	1	Close	16	8	4	1
Not Close	21	23	14	4	Not Close	16	11	15	1
Totals	29	30	21	5	Totals	32	19	19	2

*"Close" contests are those in which the winner had 60 percent or fewer of the total votes cast for the two highest candidates in the contest. All other districts with two or more candidates in the primary are considered "not close."

Source: *Official Vote Cast at the General Primary Election March 16, 1982.*
Official Vote Cast at the General Primary Election March 20, 1984.
Compiled by the State Board of Elections, State of Illinois.

These data only describe two elections, so our conclusions must be cautious. Although candidates are often fearful about the unpredictable nature of primaries, only about a third of the districts with multiple candidates produced close contests. When the number of close contests is compared to the large number of districts in which contests could occur, close primary elections are relatively rare.

Finally, it is not surprising to note that "write-in" efforts to obtain nomination were not very significant. In only a handful of districts were there noticeable numbers of write-ins, usually fewer than 100 votes. No outcome was affected.

The General Election

Table 4:4 summarizes information on the two-party competition for the House in 1982 and 1984. Table 4:5 is similar and reports on Senate competition. There is substantial rivalry in the general elections between Democrats and Republicans. The tables place every legislative district in one of six categories according to how high a percentage of the votes for Republicans and Democrats that the Democratic candidate achieved. The categories may be thought of as Safe Democratic (80+ to 100%), Democratic Dominant (60+ to 80%), Leaning Democratic (50+ to 60%), Leaning Republican (40+ to 50%), Republican Dominant (20+ to 40%) and Safe Republican (0 to 20%). The number and percentage of districts in each category are shown, followed by the district numbers. The reader may refer to the district maps in Chapter Five to see the partisan complexion of each district.

Table 4:4   Party Competition: Percentage of Votes Received by Democratic House Candidates by Districts, 1982 and 1984*

Type of District	No. of Dists.	Percent of Dists.	1982 District Numbers	No. of Dists.	Percent of Dists.	1984 District Numbers
Safe Democratic 80+ to 100%	28	23.7	2, 5, 6, 7, 9, 10, 11, 12, 15, 17, 18, 19, 20, 21, 22, 23, 24, 25, 26, 31, 32, 33, 34, 35, 36, 61, 111, 114	24	20.3	3, 9, 10, 15, 18, 19, 20, 23, 24, 25, 26, 31, 32, 33, 34, 35, 36, 71, 91, 92, 107, 111, 112, 116
Democratic Dominant 60+ to 80%	24	20.3	1, 3, 4, 13, 28, 29, 30, 47, 48, 51, 56, 68, 71, 74, 77, 78, 83, 91, 92, 101, 103, 113, 116, 117	27	22.9	1, 2, 4, 5, 7, 11, 12, 17, 21, 22, 28, 30, 51, 61, 68, 69, 74, 75, 77, 78, 83, 99, 101, 103, 113, 114, 117
Leaning Democratic 50+ to 60%	18	15.3	8, 16, 27, 52, 58, 69, 72, 75, 80, 85, 86, 98, 99, 105, 107, 108, 110, 112	16	13.6	6, 8, 13, 16, 27, 29, 47, 48, 56, 58, 72, 85, 86, 98, 108, 118
Leaning Republican 40+ to 50%	11	9.3	14, 37, 41, 46, 79, 84, 94, 96, 102, 109, 118	12	10.2	52, 76, 80, 84, 96, 97, 102, 105, 106, 109, 110, 115
Republican Dominant 20+ to 40%	29	24.6	38, 39, 40, 42, 43, 44, 45, 49, 50, 53, 54, 55, 57, 62, 63, 64, 66, 73, 76, 81, 82, 89, 90, 93, 97, 100, 104, 106, 115	19	16.1	14, 37, 39, 40, 43, 44, 49, 54, 55, 57, 62, 66, 70, 73, 79, 90, 94, 95, 100
Safe Republican 0 to 20%	8	6.8	59, 60, 65, 67, 70, 87, 88, 95	20	17.0	38, 41, 42, 45, 46, 50, 53, 59, 60, 63, 64, 65, 67, 81, 82, 87, 88, 89, 93, 104
	118	100.0		118	100.1	

*Percentage of votes obtained by the Democrat is calculated from the sum of votes cast for the Republican and the Democrat in each district.

Source: *Official Vote Cast at the General Election November 2, 1982*, and *Official Vote Cast at the General Election November 6, 1984*. Compiled by the State Board of Elections, State of Illinois.

Obviously, the party balance favored the Democrats in both 1982 and 1984. In the House there were 70 Democrat winners out of 118 in 1982 and 67 in 1984. This unequal division confirms a point made earlier. Although Democrats won most of the seats, there are still districts where Republicans are safe. Still, Democrats have substantial domination, because they won more than 40 percent of the districts with 60 percent or more of the votes. The Republicans had similar domination in less than a third of the districts. In the Senate, the number of races was smaller and

Table 4:5 Competition: Percentage of Votes Received by Democratic Senate Candidates by Districts, 1982 and 1984*

Type of District	1982			1984		
	No. of Dists.	Percent of Dists.	District Numbers	No. of Dists.	Percent of Dists.	District Numbers
Safe Democratic 80+ to 100%	13	22.0	2, 3, 4, 5, 6, 9, 10, 11, 12, 13, 16, 17, 18	5	23.8	4, 10, 13, 16, 49
Democratic Dominant 60+ to 80%	12	20.3	1, 7, 8, 14, 15, 26, 36, 39, 42, 49, 54, 56	2	9.5	1, 46
Leaning Democratic 50+ to 60%	8	13.6	24, 34, 38, 43, 46, 57, 58, 59	3	14.3	34, 43, 59
Leaning Republican 40+ to 50%	7	11.9	29, 35, 37, 48, 51, 53, 55	3	14.3	7, 37, 58
Republican Dominant 20+ to 40%	18	30.5	19, 20, 21, 22, 23, 25, 27, 28, 30, 31, 32, 33, 40, 41, 44, 47, 50, 52	8	38.1	19, 22, 25, 28, 31, 40, 52, 55
Safe Republican 0 to 20%	1	1.7	45	0	0.0	
	59	100.0		21	100.0	

*Percentage of votes obtained by the Democrat is calculated from the sum of votes cast for the Republican and the Democrat in each district.

Source: *Official Vote Cast at the General Election November 2, 1981,* and *Official Vote Cast at the General Election November 6, 1984.* Compiled by the State Board of Elections, State of Illinois.

the variation greater, but a similar Democratic dominance can be seen.

About a fourth of the districts for each chamber fall into the "leaning" categories. Knowing what we do about voter tendencies, these are the likeliest turnover districts. These are the ones in which the minority party candidate has a good chance to put together a winning coalition. The other side of this point is that in three-fourths of the districts the minority party candidates have very difficult, uphill battles to defeat the candidates of the dominant party. This suggests the difficulty for Republicans to capture majority control of either the House or Senate under the current district lines.

Finally, look at the district numbers for each category of consecutive elections. Shifts tend to be from one category of competitiveness to a neighboring one. Shifts of two categories, such as from Democratic Dominant to Leaning Republican, are very rare. They do happen, however, as with Senate district 7 (from Democratic Dominant to Leaning Republican) and House district 112 (from Leaning Democratic to Safe Democratic).

RUNNING FOR THE GENERAL ASSEMBLY

There is no typical candidate for the Illinois General Assembly and no typical campaign. Our remarks here, therefore, can only suggest some of the usual aspects of campaigns for the legislature. Filing activity occurs in December before the election year. A few candidates drop out shortly after filing their petitions. Most stay active for the primary, working especially diligently to attract support from known primary voters of their own party. That campaign reaches its peak in the first two weeks of March. The primary election then reduces the major party candidates to one per legislative office. Following the primary is a long period of little visible campaigning. From the 4th of July until the first Tuesday after the first Monday in November the public campaigns become increasingly visible, reaching a fevered pitch in competitive districts during the month of October.

Legislative campaigns vary according to situation, so let's imagine a downstate district which could be won by either party, which has no incumbent and contains no city over 50,000 in population. Such a district may very well attract two or more candidates in each party before the primary. These will be voluntary candidates, individuals who, with the support of some friends, family, neighbors and fellow workers, put together their own campaign organizations. Most or all of the workers are likely to be unpaid volunteers. Such downstate districts usually include all or parts of several counties, so the most significant party officials are the county party chairmen. Candidates often seek, and sometimes get, the endorsement of one, or more, party chairmen. Some chairmen, however, choose to stay neutral in such races, since their concern is more with county contests (sheriff, state's attorney, county board members, etc.). The legislative candidates are often on their own in obtaining help from active partisans, such as township and precinct committeemen. Some candidates ignore those "party regulars" altogether, running their own campaigns with bumper stickers, newspaper ads, door-to-door canvassing and Main Street politicking in the small towns. They round up their own volunteers, collect campaign contributions and nail up their own posters. Typically, such candidates do not create very big organizations. They do try, however, to get exposure in all sorts of existing organizations—union locals, Rotary Clubs, church groups, hobby clubs, parent-teacher associations, and the like.

The most important thing gained by winning a primary is the party label. After the March primary, the winners are official party candidates for the general election. The party regulars usually welcome the primary winners to the team of candidates seeking victory in November. Most downstate districts encompass several counties, so legislative candidates don't run with one slate of candidates. They run with several slates at the same time. Every four years there is the statewide slate of candidates—governor, lieutenant governor and the rest—as well as several county slates. The parties organize forums at which the legislative candidates appear, are introduced and given a chance to appeal for votes.

The label also means that the news media feel some obligation to cover the candidate. Newspaper editors usually interview all the candidates, featuring the major party candidates in their coverage area. As candidates tour the small towns, they drop in on local newspaper editors and local radio stations in hopes of getting some publicity.

With the party label there is also financial assistance. Sometimes county chairmen provide cash. The chairmen also include the legislative candidates in their advertising, and with the help of township and precinct committeemen, the legislative candidates' literature is distributed to the voters. The party regulars help candidates raise money—with fish fries, pancake breakfasts or whatever local events attract people, contributions and public attention.

Additional campaign assistance comes from legislative party organizations. The Republican and Democrat House and Senate caucuses each have a campaign committee. Each raises funds (on the order of $500,000 each) and provides some assistance and expertise to its party candidates. The money is usually expended on those races expected to be close. Sometimes veteran legislators, including leaders, help the novice campaign, as do candidates on the statewide ticket. Headliners, such as candidates for governor, attorney general and secretary of state, draw people and support to a legislative candidate's campaign events.

Campaigns in downstate cities such as Peoria, Kankakee, Champaign-Urbana, Quad Cities and Rockford include many of the activities mentioned above. In urban settings it is sometimes difficult for legislative candidates to connect with informal friendship networks that are so important in small towns. There are two typical solutions: one is canvassing, the second is a media campaign. Candidates use both.

Canvassing means going door-to-door, saying a few words, inviting voter support and leaving some literature. Many candidates do this themselves, week in and week out. Others depend on their volunteers and supporters. A variation on canvassing is meeting people at shopping malls and other public centers. In these outings campaigners learn who their supporters are, what issues bother people and who will need encouragement or help to get to the polls. Lists are made of people to be contacted again, especially by telephone during the last week of the campaign.

Generally, the more funds a candidate has, the more is spent on communication, including printed material, bumper stickers, yard signs, advertisements in newspapers and shopper weeklies, and on radio and television. The more urbanized the area, the costlier the newspaper ads and radio-TV time. Legislative candidates in downstate districts can perhaps afford some television spot ads, but for those in metropolitan Chicago, TV time is simply too expensive.

In the Chicago-dominated districts, legislative candidates have very low visibility. Campaign work in the Democratic party is the responsibility of the ward committeemen and their appointed precinct captains. These loyal campaign workers usually have jobs with the city, county or some other governmental unit. They maintain contact with the people of the district. Legislative candidates owe their slating, nomination and election support to the party organization. As part of the discipline of the organization, legislative candidates take part in various activities scheduled by ward committeemen and their precinct captains. Legislative candidates are members of a larger slate of candidates for whom the ward and precinct workers are expected to turn out the vote. At campaign events candidates for the General Assembly affirm their loyalty to other slated candidates both for the election campaign and in the governing phase to follow.

In the predominantly black constituencies of Chicago's west and south sides there have been a growing number of independent campaigns. Traditionally, blacks who were part of the regular Democratic organization held legislative offices. Increasingly, however, there have been independent black Democrats challenging the incumbents, and in some instances, capturing the Democratic legislative nominations, and winning election to the legislature. While tactics vary, such independent candidates have used black-dominated existing organizations such as churches, antipoverty and civil rights groups, news media and independent voter organizations to register and mobilize voters to defeat regular Democratic ward and legislative incumbents. In Chicago this is the most common kind of legislative competition. Often the independents add a moralistic tone to the competition when they challenge the business-as-usual politics of patronage and favors of the regulars.

Suburban Republicans vary in their degree of independence from county Republican organizations in Cook, DuPage, Will, Kane, McHenry and Lake counties. While these are relatively well-organized counties, legislative candidates and their workers and supporters are not as dependent on the party jobs and favors as is the case for the Chicago regular Democrats. Many of the workers are volunteers, attracted by some combination of Republican loyalty, citizen duty, perhaps a moralistic commitment to ideology or issues and personal desire for activity. Less dependent on the organization for financial rewards, these candidates and workers are more independent, undisciplined and "unbossed." Republican candidates in primaries and general elections vary greatly in how conservative, moderate or progressive their political attitudes are. The range and individualism of the candidates means that contests differ greatly in style and tactics. Voters have good incomes, are relatively well educated and independent. Many are ticket splitters and many are interested in specific issues. So, the survivors of these election processes feel they owe their loyalty to their own constituents and their own corps of election workers, rather than to a particular party organization.

CONCLUDING OBSERVATIONS

To understand the Illinois legislature and its members it is important to understand several aspects of Illinois politics. Statewide there is sharp and relatively even competition between the two parties. But ordinarily legislators represent districts drawn to favor one party or the other. Election after election most districts will remain in the control of one party or the other. Still, about 25 percent of the districts are competitive enough that the issues, the personalities of the candidates and the times may move enough voters in one direction or another to turn over control from one party to the other. Collectively, then, control of one or both houses of the legislature may go from one party to the other.

Even in the districts that usually elect Republicans or Democrats year after year, most are not firmly controlled by the party organizations. Instead, individual candidates build their own corps of supporters to win nomination and election. Most feel quite independent from party leaders or party control. They may be conservative, moderate, liberal or progressive, but their policy choices are largely to gain or keep majority support in their constituency. Underdog newcomers, willing to campaign hard and forge their own alliances, can win.

The exceptional portions of Illinois are Chicago and East St. Louis, where strong party organizations dominate many of the primaries and elections. Slating for the legislature is a reward for previous party service, and an opportunity to do legislative work for the party. Slated candidates do not have to worry about getting campaign workers and money for media. In return, those candidates take the party's directions seriously as they serve in the legislature. However, changes are occurring in the black-dominated districts of Chicago where the regular Democrats are increasingly challenged by independent candidates.

The interaction of this mix of partisan, ideological, ethnic and electoral pressures makes the legislative process fascinating and variable. Chapter Five examines the lawmakers.

Chapter Five

The People in Lawmaking: Members

The group of legislators that assembles in Springfield in January every two years is in many ways a unique collection of individuals. Compared to a cross section of the citizens of Illinois, they are older, better educated and more racially homogeneous. There are also many more males and more have professional occupations. They are a very politically oriented group. At a time when less than 60 percent of those eligible even bother to vote in Illinois general elections (Everson, 1985, p. 16), legislators are active members of political parties, often with many years of political activity behind them at the local, county, state and national levels. Each legislator is also the elected representative of a specific district which is different from all other districts. They will continue to be legislators only if their constituents reelect them. Once the legislature is in session, legislators take on additional political identities as leaders, committee members, House or Senate members and spokesmen for various groups and agencies.

A legislator's demographic and political identities will often reinforce each other, making legislative decisions easier. When a legislator's own policy preferences and those of his/her constituents and party leaders are all in agreement, a vote on an important and controversial bill will not be difficult to make. A conservative Republican who owns a small manufacturing company, considers himself pro-business and represents a solid Republican district would have no trouble casting a vote for a bill making it more difficult to qualify for workmen's compensation benefits, particularly when the bill is backed by his party leaders and the Illinois State Chamber of Commerce. But when the identity factors come into conflict, difficult decisions become even more difficult. A vote on the same workmen's compensation bill would present problems for a Republican legislator who was an attorney, viewed himself as a moderate and had been elected from a normally Democratic district with both labor and business support. In the sections that follow we will explore the various elements which make up the personal and political identities of the members of the Illinois General Assembly.

A DEMOGRAPHIC PROFILE

As the political cartoon (on p. 64) suggests, the phrase "an Illinois state legislator" is likely to elicit a variety of images, not all of them favorable. Winnowing fact from perception is not always easy, but an examination of the characteristics of the people elected to the General Assembly over the past 20 years reveals some interesting patterns, many

An Illinois Legislator, As Seen By...

A Chicagoan...   ...A DownStater

Reprinted by permission of Bill Campbell

at variance with the stereotypes pictured above. For example, only seven members (four percent) of those serving in 1983 listed "farmer" as their occupation. That figure is not much lower than the eight percent of those serving in 1963 who considered farmer their occupation. Over the last 20 years farmers have never constituted a great portion of the membership of the Illinois legislature. On the other hand, the percentage of members who consider themselves full-time legislators has risen from one percent in the Senate and four percent in the House in 1963 to 39 percent in the Senate and 48 percent in the House in 1983. Clearly the way members perceive themselves and present themselves to the public has changed tremendously. By looking at the characteristics of age, sex, race, education, occupation and length of service for the legislature that served in 1983, we can develop a profile of the modern General Assembly membership. By comparing this profile with that of 20 years ago, we see how the composition of the legislature has changed. The tables that follow are based on the *Illinois Blue Book 1963-64* and the *Illinois Blue Book 1983-84*.

Age

As can be seen from Table 5:1, of the members serving in the legislature in 1983, only 24 percent were under 40 years of age. Overall, the Senate was the older body with only 10 percent of its members under 40, compared to 31 percent under 40 in the House. The data from 1973 and 1963 are incomplete, but the national trend toward the election of younger state legislators over the last 10 years seems to have taken place in Illinois as well (Rosenthal, 1981, p. 31). Despite this trend, the average age of members in 1983 was in excess of 50 years, roughly the same as the 1980 U.S. Congress (Ripley, 1983, p. 95). There is also an interesting variance between the Republicans in the two chambers. In 1983 over 60 percent of the House Republican members were under 50 while over 60 percent of the Senate Republican members were over 50.

Table 5:1   Age of Illinois Legislators*

		83rd General Assembly (1983)						
		Democrats	(70)	Republicans	(48)	Total	(118)
House	Age	No.	%	No.	%	No.	%
	21-39	18	26	18	37	36	31
	40-49	20	29	12	26	32	27
	50+	32	45	18	37	50	42
		Democrats	(33)	Republicans	(26)	Total	(59)
Senate		No.	%	No.	%	No.	%
	21-39	2	6	4	15	6	10
	40-49	18	55	6	23	24	41
	50+	13	39	16	62	29	49
Total House & Senate Membership		Democrats	(103)	Republicans	(74)	Total	(177)
		No.	%	No.	%	No.	%
	21-39	20	19	22	30	42	24
	40-49	38	37	18	24	56	32
	50+	45	44	34	46	79	45

*Totals may vary from 100.0 due to rounding.

Table 5:2   Sex of Illinois Legislators

83rd General Assembly (1983)

House		Democrats	(70)	Republicans	(48)	Total	(118)
		No.	%	No.	%	No.	%
	Male	64	91	35	73	99	84
	Female	6	9	13	27	19	16

Senate		Democrats	(33)	Republicans	(26)	Total	(59)*
		No.	%	No.	%	No.	%
	Male	29	88	22	85	51	86
	Female	4	12	4	15	8	14

Total House & Senate Membership		Democrats	(103)	Republicans	(74)	Total	(177)
		No.	%	No.	%	No.	%
	Male	93	90	57	77	150	85
	Female	10	10	17	23	27	15

73rd General Assembly (1963)

House		Democrats	(87)	Republicans	(90)	Total	(177)
		No.	%	No.	%	No.	%
	Male	85	98	89	99	174	98
	Female	2	2	1	1	3	2

Senate		Democrats	(23)	Republicans	(35)	Total	(58)*
		No.	%	No.	%	No.	%
	Male	23	100	33	94	56	97
	Female	0	0	2	6	2	3

Total House & Senate Membership		Democrats	(110)	Republicans	(125)	Total	(235)
		No.	%	No.	%	No.	%
	Male	108	98	122	98	230	98
	Female	2	2	3	2	5	2

*Prior to the 1970 Constitution there were 58 senatorial districts.

Sex

In 1983, 85 percent of the members of the Illinois General Assembly were male. Twenty years earlier 98 percent of the members were male. Looking at Table 5:2 it is clear that the percentage of women elected to the legislature has risen over the last 20 years. There is also no question that the election of women in numbers that reflect their percentage of total population will not occur in the near future. The 15 percent figure for women members in 1983 is somewhat better than the national average for state legislatures. The best figures available indicate about four percent of all state legislators were women in 1970, while in 1980 the percentage had risen to 10 percent (Rosenthal, 1981, p. 90). By comparison fewer than five percent of the members elected to Congress in 1982 were women (Ripley, 1983, p. 96). The picture overall in Illinois is one of a steady increase in the percentage of women over the last 10 years, but of a legislature which is still an overwhelmingly male institution. The figures for Illinois for 1983 do show one interesting variation. While the percentage of women members in the Senate was approximately equal for the two parties (12 percent and 15 percent), 27 percent of the Republican members in the House were women compared to nine percent of the Democratic members. Overall, 10 percent of the Democrats serving in 1983 were women, while 23 percent of the Republicans were women.

Table 5:3   Race of Illinois Legislators

83rd General Assembly (1983)				73rd General Assembly (1963)			
House		No.	%	House		No.	%
	White	104	88		White	170	96
	Black	13	11		Black	7	4
	Hispanic	1	1				
	Total	118			Total	177	
Senate		No.	%	Senate		No.	%
	White	54	92		White	57	98
	Black	5	8		Black	1	2
	Hispanic	0	0				
	Total	59			Total	58	
Total House & Senate Membership		No.	%	Total House & Senate Membership		No.	%
	White	158	89		White	227	97
	Black	18	10		Black	8	3
	Hispanic	1	1				
	Total	177			Total	235	

Table 5:4   Education Level of State Legislators in Illinois*

83rd General Assembly (1983)

House		Democrats	(70)	Republicans	(48)	Total	(118)
		No.	%	No.	%	No.	%
	H.S. Diploma	17	24	4	8	21	17
	College Degree	28	40	25	52	53	45
	Graduate Degree	25	36	19	40	44	37
Senate		Democrats	(33)	Republicans	(26)	Total	(59)
		No.	%	No.	%	No.	%
	H.S. Diploma	6	18	2	8	8	14
	College Degree	12	36	17	65	29	49
	Graduate Degree	15	45	7	27	22	37
Total House & Senate Membership		Democrats	(103)	Republicans	(74)	Total	(177)
		No.	%	No.	%	No.	%
	H.S. Diploma	23	22	6	9	29	16
	College Degree	40	39	42	56	82	46
	Graduate Degree	40	39	26	35	66	37

73rd General Assembly (1963)

House		Democrats	(87)	Republicans	(90)	Total	(177)
		No.	%	No.	%	No.	%
	H.S. Diploma	38	43	28	31	66	37
	College Degree	19	22	26	29	45	26
	Graduate Degree	30	35	36	40	66	38
Senate		Democrats	(23)	Republicans	(35)	Total	(58)
		No.	%	No.	%	No.	%
	H.S. Diploma	6	26	6	17	12	21
	College Degree	5	22	8	23	13	22
	Graduate Degree	12	52	21	60	33	57
Total House & Senate Membership		Democrats	(110)	Republicans	(125)	Total	(235)
		No.	%	No.	%	No.	%
	H.S. Diploma	44	40	34	27	78	33
	College Degree	24	22	34	27	58	25
	Graduate Degree	42	38	57	46	99	42

*Totals may vary from 100.0 due to rounding.

Table 5:5   Occupation Listing for Illinois Legislators

83rd General Assembly (1983)

House		Democrats (70)		Republicans (48)		Total (118)	
		No.	%	No.	%	No.	%
	Full-time Legislator	38	55	20	42	58	49
	Lawyer	14	20	11	23	25	21
	Business/Finance	9	13	5	10	14	12
	Real Estate/Insurance	2	3	4	8	6	5
	Local Government	4	6	1	2	5	4
	Educator	2	3	2	4	4	3
	Health/Social Service	1	1	1	2	2	2
	Farmer	0	0	4	8	4	3
	Other	0	0	0	0	0	0

Senate		Democrats (33)		Republicans (26)		Total (59)	
		No.	%	No.	%	No.	%
	Full-time Legislator	15	45	8	30	23	39
	Lawyer	11	33	4	15	15	25
	Business/Finance	5	15	9	34	14	24
	Real Estate/Insurance	0	0	1	7	1	2
	Local Government	0	0	0	0	0	0
	Educator	1	3	1	4	2	3
	Health/Social Service	0	0	1	4	1	2
	Farmer	1	3	2	7	3	5
	Other	0	0	0	0	0	0

Total House & Senate Membership		Democrats (103)		Republicans (74)		Total (177)	
		No.	%	No.	%	No.	%
	Full-time Legislator	53	51	28	39	81	46
	Lawyer	25	24	15	20	40	23
	Business/Finance	14	14	14	19	28	16
	Real Estate/Insurance	2	2	5	7	7	4
	Local Government	4	4	1	1	5	3
	Educator	3	3	3	4	6	3
	Health/Social Service	1	1	2	3	3	2
	Farmer	1	1	6	8	7	4
	Other	0	0	0	0	0	0

73rd General Assembly (1963)

House		Democrats (87)		Republicans (90)		Total (177)	
		No.	%	No.	%	No.	%
	Full-time Legislator	5	6	2	2	7	4
	Lawyer	27	31	26	29	53	30
	Business/Finance	15	17	33	36	48	27
	Real Estate/Insurance	15	17	15	17	30	17
	Local Government	12	14	1	1	13	7
	Educator	2	2	2	2	4	2
	Health/Social Service	0	0	4	4	4	2
	Farmer	9	10	7	8	16	9
	Other	2	2	0	0	2	1

Table 5:5   (continued)

		Democrats (23)		Republicans (35)		Total (58)	
Senate		No.	%	No.	%	No.	%
	Full-time Legislator	0	0	1	3	1	1
	Lawyer	10	43	21	60	31	53
	Business/Finance	3	13	5	14	8	14
	Real Estate/Insurance	6	26	6	17	12	21
	Local Government	4	17	0	0	4	7
	Educator	0	0	0	0	0	0
	Health/Social Service	0	0	0	0	0	0
	Farmer	0	0	2	6	2	3
	Other	0	0	0	0	0	0

		Democrats (110)		Republicans (125)		Total (235)	
Total House & Senate Membership		No.	%	No.	%	No.	%
	Full-time Legislator	5	5	3	2	8	3
	Lawyer	37	33	47	38	84	36
	Business/Finance	18	16	38	30	56	24
	Real Estate/Insurance	21	19	21	17	42	18
	Local Government	16	14	1	1	17	7
	Educator	2	2	2	2	4	2
	Health/Social Service	0	0	4	3	4	2
	Farmer	9	8	9	6	18	8
	Other	2	2	0	0	2	1

Race

In 1963, only three percent of the members of the General Assembly were from minority groups. In 1983 the percentage had risen to 11 percent with 18 black members and one Hispanic member for a total minority membership of 11 percent. In 1980 Illinois had a non-white population of 18.9 percent, with 14.7 percent black, 5.6 percent Hispanic and 1.5 percent Asian (Legislative Research Unit, 1984a). The change to single member districts in 1982 and the 1980 reapportionment of the legislature do not seem to have adversely effected the trend toward more minorities and women being elected to the legislature (Everson and Parker, 1983, p. 16). Nationally the percentage of minorities elected to state legislatures has increased over the past 10 years, but still falls short of proportional representation. One study found in 1980 that blacks made up four percent of state legislators; although they constituted approximately 11 percent of the population (Rosenthal, 1981, p. 30). Table 5:3 compares the 73rd and 83rd General Assemblies. The Hispanic house member is the first one ever elected to the Illinois legislature. Over the previous 20 years only a small number of black Republican legislators have been elected, the last in 1976.

Table 5:6   Tenure of Illinois Legislators

83rd General Assembly (1983)

		Democrats	(70)	Republicans	(48)	Total	(118)
House		No.	%	No.	%	No.	%
	Freshman	16	23	13	27	29	25
	1-4 terms	39	56	27	56	66	57
	5 terms or more	15	22	8	16	23	19
		Democrats	(33)	Republicans	(26)	Total	(59)
Senate		No.	%	No.	%	No.	%
	Freshman	8	24	7	27	15	25
	1-2 terms	6	18	10	38	16	28
	3 or more	19	57	9	36	28	47
Total House & Senate Membership		Democrats (103)		Republicans	(74)	Total	(177)
		No.	%	No.	%	No.	%
	Freshman	24	23	20	27	44	25
	1-4 terms	45	44	37	49	82	46
	5 terms or more	34	33	17	23	51	29

73rd General Assembly (1963)

		Democrats	(87)	Republicans	(90)	Total	(177)
House		No.	%	No.	%	No.	%
	Freshman	9	10	22	24	31	18
	1-4 terms	55	62	41	46	96	54
	5 terms or more	23	27	27	30	50	28
		Democrats	(23)	Republicans	(35)	Total	(58)
Senate		No.	%	No.	%	No.	%
	Freshman	4	17	7	20	11	19
	1-2 terms	8	35	10	29	18	31
	3 or more	11	48	18	51	29	50
Total House & Senate Membership		Democrats (110)		Republicans (125)		Total	(235)
		No.	%	No.	%	No.	%
	Freshman	13	12	29	23	42	18
	1-4 terms	63	57	51	41	114	48
	5 terms or more	34	31	45	36	79	34

Education

In contrast to the characterization in the political cartoon featured at the beginning of this chapter, Illinois legislators have always been a well-educated group and have become increasingly more so over the last 20 years. Every member serving in 1963 and 1983 listed at least a high school diploma in their biographical sketches. In 1963, 67 percent of the members were college graduates. By 1983 that percentage had increased to 83 percent. This contrasts to the 16.2 percent of the adult population in Illinois who are college graduates (Legislative Research Unit, 1984a). The percentage of college graduates in state legislatures nationally is comparable to Illinois, while virtually every member of Congress serving in 1983 was a college graduate (Davidson and Olezsek, 1981, p. 101; Harris and Hain, 1983, p. 57). Looking at Table 5:4 we find that while the change in the percentage of college graduates in the Senate (from 79 percent in 1963 to 86 percent in 1983) has been moderate, the change in the House (64 percent in 1963 to 83 percent in 1983) has been more dramatic. The total percentage of members with graduate and law degrees has decreased somewhat over time, but still exceeds 37 percent of the membership.

Occupation

The data in Table 5:5 indicate how members characterize themselves. If they are attorneys, but list their occupation as a full-time legislator, then they are classified as a full-time legislator regardless of how little or much they may earn from the practice of law. As noted earlier, 20 years ago only three percent of the members considered themselves to be full-time legislators. In 1983, 46 percent of the members, including a majority of those in the House, called themselves full-time legislators. This change is the result of a number of factors: increased pay, greater time spent in session and the gradual increase in legislative activities assumed by those who consider themselves professionals in the modern Illinois legislature.

The second most prominent group represented in the legislature in 1983, and the most prominent in 1963 is lawyers. In 1963 60 percent of the Senate Republicans and over 36 percent of the total membership listed their occupation as lawyer. Twenty years later 22 percent of the members listed lawyer as their occupation. This figure underrepresents the actual number of law degrees held by members serving in 1983, but not by a great deal. The decline in the number of attorneys is often attributed to the change to a full-time legislature. When the legislature met only a limited amount of time, maintaining a law practice was not difficult, but with the increase in the time spent in Springfield and on constituent services, many legislators were forced to choose one career or the other.

One of the dramatic changes indicated by the occupation data is the overall increase in members who are lawyers or full-time legislators. In 1963 only 39 percent of the members were lawyers or full-time legislators. That figure exceeded 69 percent in 1983. Whether for better or worse, it is clear that there is less diversity in the occupational composition of the body. In 1963, 24 percent of the members listed business or finance as their occupation, 18 percent listed real estate or insurance, seven percent listed local government and eight percent listed farming. Among those members serving in 1983, 16 percent listed business or finance as their occupation, three percent listed local government, four percent listed real estate or insurance and four percent listed farming. What this means is that fewer people who identify their occupation as business, finance, real estate, insurance, local government or farming are being elected to the Illinois legislature. And many occupations are not represented at all. For example, no one serving in 1963 or 1983 identified themselves as blue-collar worker, labor official, housewife or student, and there were only a few health professionals and educators.

A national survey conducted in 1979 shows that lawyers make up about 20 percent of the membership in state legislatures while 15 percent of the members have business or finance occupations, 10 percent are educators, 10 percent are farmers and five percent are in real estate or insurance, four percent work for local government and three percent are housewives or students (Rosenthal, 1981, p. 27-28). Compared to other states the Illinois legislature serving in 1983 had approximately the same percentages of lawyers, business men and women, local government employees and real estate/or insurance agents; fewer than half as many farmers and educators and no students or housewives. Over the last 20 years all of these groups have lost numbers to the ranks of full-time legislators in Illinois.

Tenure

Another important dimension of a legislature is the experience of the members. What percentage are new? What percentage are seasoned veterans? The 1983 Illinois figure of 25 percent new members (Table 5:6) was about the state average for the last 20 years (Shin and Everson, 1979, p. 18), although it was up from the 18 percent figure in 1963. This means that when the legislature organizes in January of the odd-numbered year to begin a new, two-year session, approximately 25 percent of the members are new, a circumstance which complicates the legislative tasks of the leaders and members. Some turnover is healthy for any organization but significant turnover can adversely affect efficiency and effectiveness. This applies particularly to an organization like a legislature which relies heavily on informal rules and influence relationships for coordination and control.

At the other end of the spectrum are the veterans. If we define a veteran as a member who has served five terms in the House or three terms in the Senate, then veterans are legislators who have served at least 10 years and won at least three elections. The percentage of 10-year veterans in the 1963 legislature was 50 percent in the Senate and 28 percent in the House. In 1983 the percentage of 10-year veterans in the Senate was 47 percent, while in the House 19 percent of the members had 10 years of experience. In contrast to the roughly equal percentage of freshmen in the House and Senate over time, the Senate has consistently had a greater percentage of 10-year veterans. This is attributable to having to win three rather than five elections to become a 10-year veteran in the Senate and to the tendency of House members to run for Senate seats when the opportunity arises.

In 1983 the House was composed of 25 percent freshmen, 57 percent members with two to eight years of experience and 19 percent 10-year veterans while the Senate had 25 percent freshmen, 28 percent members with four to eight years of experience, and 47 percent 10-year veterans. While 25 percent of the members of the House and Senate are freshmen, the percentage of veterans insures that the norms and folkways of the institution are continued from one session to the next. The pattern suggests that only one in five House members serves more than 10 years while almost half of the Senate does. Additionally, over 58 percent of those serving in the Senate in 1983 had previously served in the House. These differences make the Senate a more experienced and stable body in comparison to the House.

Summary Features

The legislature that took office in 1983 varied greatly from the general population which elected them in several significant ways. The average legislator was over 50 years of age. Only 15 percent of the members were women and 11 percent were minorities. Over 83 percent were college graduates and over 69 percent considered their occupation to be full-time legislator or lawyer. Compared to 20 years ago, the current legislature contains more women and minorities and is better educated, somewhat younger, more oriented to the legislature as a profession and less occupationally diverse. But if the members had the same characteristics in the same proportion as the general state population, there would be more members under 40, 51.5 percent would be women, 18.9 percent would be minorities, about 16 percent would be college graduates, less than 20 percent would have professional occupations and more than 25 percent would be blue collar workers (Legislative Research Unit, 1984a).

There are also significant differences between the House and the Senate and between Democratic and Republican members. The Senate members as a group are older, more experienced, more male, less racially diverse and somewhat more occupationally diverse than are the House members. The Democrats as a group have more minorities and fewer women. The Republicans as a group are more diverse occupationally, less experienced and better educated. In terms of percentage of women, years of experience, age and occupation, the House Republicans are actually closer to the Democrats in both chambers than to the Republicans in the Senate.

Do these variances help us explain why the legislature votes as it does? Can we attribute the failure of the Equal Rights Amendment or decreases in the percentage of state support for elementary and secondary education solely to the demographic characteristics of the legislature? Obviously not. Legislative decisions, collective and individual, are more complex than simple correlations between votes and factors such as age, sex or occupation. First, a member does not have to be a union member, a banker or small businessman to understand these interests and represent them in the legislature. Secondly, not all members vote along the lines of their affiliations and backgrounds. Black members do not always vote the "right" way on "black" issues. The conflict over the creation of the Department of Human Rights in 1979 involved a dispute between black House members and black Senate members (Knoepfle, 1979, p. 27). Similarly, women legislators were consistently on both sides of the Equal Rights Amendment votes taken between 1974 and 1983 (Adkins, 1978, pp. 28-29).

But the basic profile of the legislature does have an impact on the legislative process. For example, a male-dominated legislature is likely to initially define questions of divorce and property settlements from the perspective of the husband. It should also be easier to make the case for more funding for higher education to a legislature dominated by college graduates than to one that is not. This does not mean that the legislature will always create divorce laws which favor the husband or fund higher education at the expense of public aid recipients. But the general characteristics of the members do create orientations and biases which affect the process, facilitating some outcomes and hindering others.

POLITICAL AND REGIONAL IDENTITIES

Party and regional identities help define and shape the legislative process. Members come to Springfield with certain personal characteristics and experiences. One member is a 59-year-old white male with a high school diploma who owns a small business, another is a 37-year-old black woman who is an attorney. In addition to these personal factors each member is elected as a Democrat or Republican from a specific district in a particular part of the state. Because the legislature is divided into two chambers and each is organized along party lines, members gain a group identity the moment they are elected: House Republican, House Democrat, Senate Republican or Senate Democrat. Members also have a general regional identity. While party, chamber and regional identities can hide as much as they reveal, they serve as initial benchmarks for gauging the actions of members. To say a member is a senator from the sixth legislative district provides some information; to label him as a Democratic senator and a Chicago "regular" provides a better, although still incomplete identification.

Regional Identities

In 1985 the Senate had 31 Democrats and 28 Republicans while the House had 67 Democrats and 51 Republican members. As expected, the members of these four delegations were not distributed equally throughout the state. Maps 5:1 through 5:6 illustrate the geographical distribution of the four party delegations. A short profile of each group and an analysis of its unifying and divisive factors will demonstrate the value and the limitations of party and regional identifications in explaining legislative behavior.

Senate Democrats. Of the 31 Democrats in the Senate, nine come from districts located wholly within the city of Chicago, eight come from Chicago districts that overlap into suburban Cook County and three come from suburban Cook County districts which border on or overlap slightly into Chicago (see Map 5:3). This makes 20 Cook County Democrats in all, although as we will see, it is fallacious to assume they or any other regional group are a monolithic voting bloc. Only one Democrat represents a district—Senate District 42—in the collar counties of DuPage, Lake, Will, Kane and McHenry. District 42 is in Will County and contains the city of Joliet (see Map 5:2). Two senators represent northeastern districts which border on the collar counties and two senators represent north and northeastern districts that include Rockford and Rock Island (see Map 5:1 and Map 5:2). These five members constitute a northern, mostly urban contingent of the downstate Democrats in the Senate. Looking at Map 5:1, we find two central Illinois Democrats (one representing a district containing part of Peoria), two southwestern Democrats (one representing a district containing East St. Louis) and two deep south Democrats. The downstate Democrats in the Senate represent a diverse set of districts with strong rural/urban and agricultural/industrial contrasts. There are no Democrats representing an east central district in the Senate.

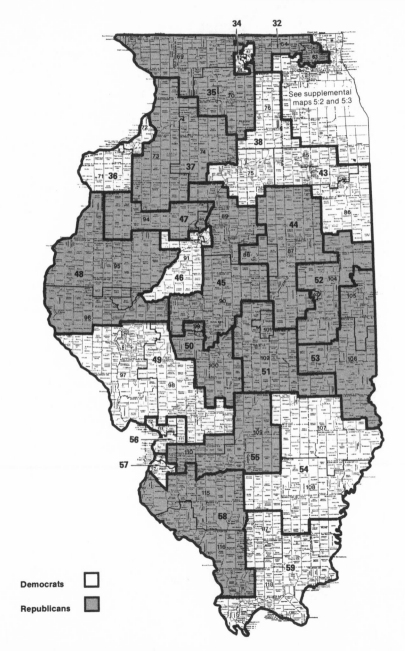

See supplemental
maps 5:2 and 5:3

Democrats

Republicans

Map 5:1   Legislative Districts of Illinois, Senate 1985

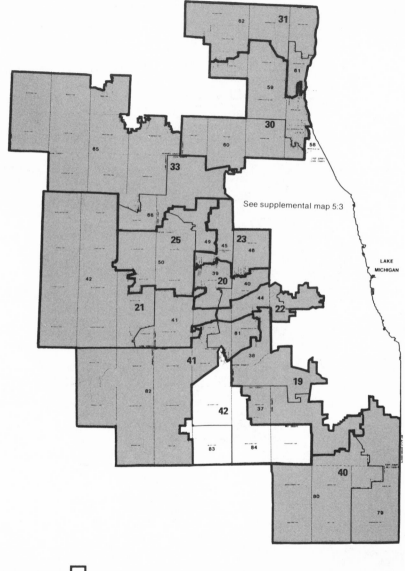

See supplemental map 5:3

LAKE
MICHIGAN

Democrats

Republicans

Map 5:2   Legislative Districts of Northeastern Illinois, Senate 1985

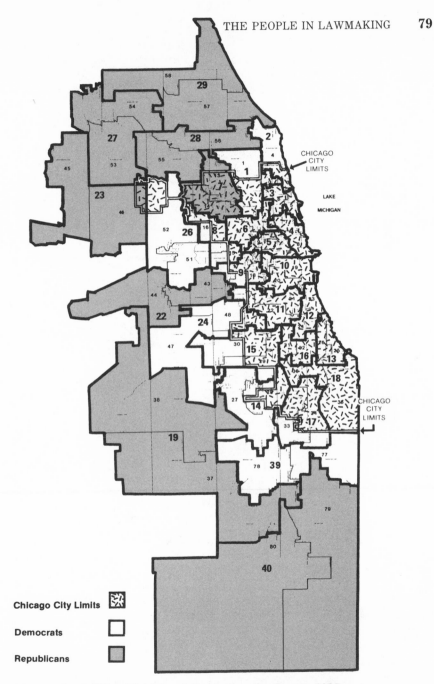

Map 5:3   Legislative Districts of Cook County, Senate 1985

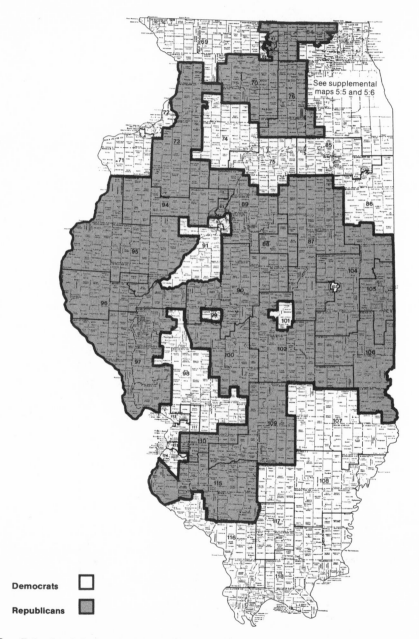

Map 5:4   Legislative Districts of Illinois, House 1985

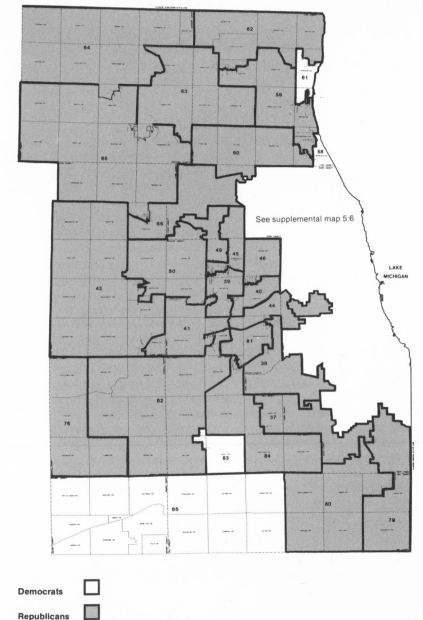

See supplemental map 5:6

LAKE
MICHIGAN

Democrats

Republicans

Map 5:5   Legislative Districts of Northeastern Illinois, House 1985

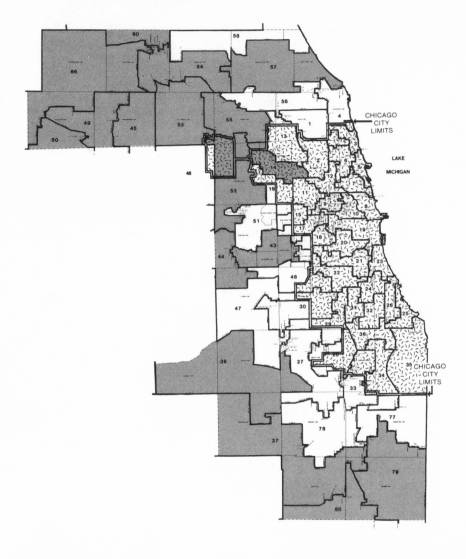

Chicago City Limits

Democrats

Republicans

Map 5:6   Legislative Districts of Cook County, House 1985

Senate Republicans. The largest bloc of Senate Republicans represents districts from the collar counties and suburban Cook County. There are 15 Republicans from suburban districts located wholly or primarily in suburban Cook, DuPage, Lake, Will, Kane and McHenry counties (see Map 5:2 and Map 5:3). One Republican represents a Chicago district—Senate District 7—which overlaps into suburban Cook County (see Map 5:3). The second group within the Senate Republicans is the 12 members representing downstate districts. Looking at Map 5:1, we find that two come from northwestern districts, two represent southern districts and the remaining eight are from central districts. As a group the downstate Republicans in the Senate represent a fairly homogeneous set of districts which are overall less urban and more agricultural than those represented by the downstate Democrats.

House Democrats. As with their Senate counterparts, Democrats from Chicago and Cook County form the largest group within the House Democrats. Of the 67 members of the delegation, 20 come from districts located solely in Chicago, 13 come from Chicago districts that overlap into Cook County and eight come from Cook County districts. All together there are 41 Cook County Democrats (see Map 5:6). Three Democrats represent districts in Lake and Will counties (see Map 5:5). These three added to the eight from Cook County districts constitute a suburban group of 11 members whose interests sometimes conflict with the 33 members from primarily Chicago districts. Beyond Chicago and the suburbs there are 23 downstate Democrats in the House. Looking at Map 5:4, we find six members from northern and northwestern districts, including districts containing Rockford and Rock Island. There are eight members from central districts including districts containing parts of Peoria, Springfield, Decatur and Champaign-Urbana. Finally there are five Democrats representing southwestern districts, including a district containing East St. Louis, and four representing deep south districts. As with the Senate Democrat profile, the non-Chicago representatives in the House are a diverse group of urban, suburban and rural districts, some with strong industrial bases and some with agricultural economies. There is only one Democratic member from the collar counties, one from an east central district and one from a west central district.

House Republicans. Of the 51 Republicans in the House 29 represent districts located wholly or primarily in the collar counties and suburban Cook County (see Map 5:5 and Map 5:6). One Republican comes from a Chicago district, District 14 (see Map 5:6). Looking at Map 5:4, we find that four members represent northern and northwestern districts while 14 members represent a group of central districts which run across the middle of the state from the Missouri to the Indiana border. There are also three members who represent southern districts. While the downstate Republican delegation is more widely dispersed in the House than in the

Senate, these house districts are also less urban, more agricultural and overall more homogeneous in comparison to the downstate districts represented by Democrats.

Regional Conflict and Coalitions

The regional groupings identified above do help in understanding how some decisions are made in the legislature. No regional group is large enough in either chamber to pass a bill by itself. Counting the regional identities without party labels in the Senate yields 18 Chicago, 19 suburban and 22 downstate members. No group has the 30 votes necessary to pass a bill, but any two constitute a winning coalition if they vote as a bloc. In the House there are 34 Chicago, 40 suburban and 44 downstate members. No group alone has the 60 votes necessary to pass a bill.

Because no single group can dominate, regional politics in the General Assembly is also coalition politics. Although Chicago has been the dominant region in the legislature for more than two decades, a coalition of downstate and suburban legislators has often been able to outvote those from Chicago. Toward the end of one spring session an education finance bill benefitting the Chicago School District was being explained by the Chicago Democratic sponsor. A downstate Democrat gained recognition and asked the sponsor if this was one of those bills where all the members from Chicago were going to vote on one side and all the other members were going to vote on the other. "I'm afraid so," the sponsor replied with resignation. When the vote was called, all the Democrats and Republicans from Chicago voted "aye," all the other legislators voted no, and the bill was defeated easily. Often the coalitions are more complex. For example, the elimination of the sales tax on food and drugs in 1979 involved a coalition of downstate Republicans and Chicago legislators who blocked the override of the governor's veto on the sales tax bill. Also in 1979, a coalition of downstate and Chicago legislators passed the state transportation package over the objections of suburban legislators (Everson and Redfield, 1980, pp. 12-13). There are times when the legislature acts as if it were comprised only of members from Chicago, downstate and the suburbs. When this happens party identifications are largely meaningless.

The current internal control of the partisan legislative delegations could be challenged by regional coalitions. While the Democratic speaker of the House in 1985 was from Chicago, downstate and suburban Democrats actually held a one-vote margin over the Chicago Democrats among the House Democrats. In the Senate the president was a Cook County Democrat who came from a party delegation in which the Chicago Democrats held only a two-vote majority over suburban and downstate Democrats. The long leadership fights in the Senate in 1977 and 1981 were largely regional conflicts among the Democrats (Galligan, 1977; Ross, 1981). The suburban Republicans have somewhat firmer numerical control over their downstate party members, particularly in the House. However, both the Chicago Democrats and the suburban Republicans need the cooperation of their party members from other regions to be effective.

Knowledge of regional politics contributes to understanding the legislature. But regional analysis has limitations. The problem with using a regional analysis to explain all legislative behavior is that members from a region do not always vote as a bloc. Within the city of Chicago the political interests of the various white ethnic groups, blacks, Hispanics and upper-class whites who live along the lake front have long been in conflict. This can be seen in voting patterns in Democratic primaries for mayor as far back as 1975 (Colby and Green, 1979, October), and more recently in the 1983 mayoral primary and general election (Green, 1983, August; Green, 1983, April) and in legislative votes on the statewide tax increase and a Chicago school property tax increase in 1983 (Parker, 1984). The Chicago Democrat label tells you something, but the knowledgeable observer wants to know more.

The suburban label also masks a variety of interests, although the conflicts are not as stark as those within Chicago. Suburban legislators represent established, high-income residential areas; older, changing towns which began as World War I suburbs of Chicago; and new urban areas which have doubled and redoubled in population since 1970. The economic and social problems of these areas differ, and suburban legislators will often be in conflict on specific bills. Districts in Cook and DuPage counties contain little open space; some districts in McHenry, Kane and Will counties have large rural areas (Colby and Green, 1979, February). There are also issue areas such as mass transportation, water pollution and economic development where the interests of the suburbs are more in line with Chicago than downstate.

As already noted, the term downstate as applied to everything outside Chicago and the collar counties is a most unwieldy umbrella. It covers business and manufacturing activities in the cities of Rockford, Rock Island-Moline, Peoria, Bloomington-Normal, Peoria, Kankakee, Champaign-Urbana, Springfield, Decatur, East St. Louis and Carbondale; the mining activities of central and southern Illinois; and the vast agricultural regions of the state. One of the interesting effects of the 1982 redistricting and cutback is the creation of a number of downstate districts which are completely urban in nature. Previously, most downstate districts which contained large cities also included rural areas as well. Defining downstate interests as "not Chicago" or "not the suburbs" is much easier than determining the common interests and goals which downstaters will or should pursue in the legislature (Colby and Green, 1978). In general the Chicago groups in the Democratic delegations and the suburban groups in the Republican delegations have been much more successful in articulating their interests and acting in a coordinated manner than have the downstaters (Peters, 1984b).

All of these factors of diversity make regional cooperation and coalitions much more difficult to organize and maintain than is widely assumed. Therefore, an understanding of legislative actions and outcomes has to be based on a number of concepts in addition to region. One of the most important is the impact of political parties.

Parties in the Legislature

In the late 1970s, when the House was controlled by the Democrats by one vote, 89-88, a controversial bill was being debated at great length along strict party lines. Finally a Democratic member rose to his feet and declared "We got 89, they got 88, let's vote!" There are times when the legislature does act as if party, not regional, considerations were primary. However, to get legislators to vote along strict party lines means bringing Chicago, suburban and downstate Democrats together in opposition to suburban and downstate Republicans. As the previous analysis indicates, this is not an easy task.

There are, however, a number of factors which encourage party cohesion among the members. First, because they have chosen to run under a party label there is at least a measure of issue and ideological agreement among party members. In addition, party loyalty is fostered by the direct financial and staff assistance in elections provided by legislative party leaders. Once in Springfield, party members sit on the same side of the chamber, work in offices next to each other, serve together on committees, elect a party leader, meet in party caucuses under the direction of the party leadership and are assisted by a staff controlled by the party leader. These circumstances and experiences build personal and professional relationships which significantly influence the members of a party delegation in committee and on the floor. An examination of the legislature's leadership and committee structures will illustrate these relationships.

Leaders and Followers. The 1970 Illinois Constitution in Article IV, Section 6 requires the speaker of the House and president of the Senate to be elected from the members of each chamber. The minority leader in each chamber is the leader of the party with the most members other than the party of the speaker or president. Given the regional makeup of the delegations in each chamber in 1985, it is no surprise that the speaker of the House was from Chicago, the president of the Senate was from a Cook County district that overlapped into Chicago and the minority leaders in each house were from DuPage County. These are powerful positions and the men who hold them exercise strong formal and informal influence over the legislative process. Each leader selects the rest of the leadership team, the committee chairmen (or minority spokesmen) and the party members for each committee. In the Senate, these choices are formally ratified by the Committee on Committees. The four leaders also control the partisan legislative staffs. The speaker and Senate president dominate the processing of legislation, assigning bills to committee and controlling the schedule, agenda and the flow of legislation on the floor. Each leader is heavily involved in raising campaign money and organizing and staffing the party's effort to win as many seats as possible in each election. As a result of these formal and informal powers, the legislative leaders are in the position to reward loyalty and service from members and, less frequently, to punish members who are not team players.

The four party leaders are not without rivals. Individual legislators exercise strong influence over particular regional, ethnic or racial groups. Party leaders outside the legislature have some impact, but compared to states like New Jersey or New York where local and state party organizations are very influential in the state legislature (Rosenthal, 1981, pp. 80-85), Illinois does not have many strong county organizations. The exception is the Cook County Democratic organization, although the lines of influence are now weaker and more ambiguous than in the 1960s and 1970s. When Richard J. Daley was alive, his dual position as Cook County Democratic chairman and mayor of Chicago gave him great control over the Cook County Democrats in the legislature (Rakove, 1975, p. 90-106). After Daley's death in 1977, the new Chicago mayor was not selected to also be county chairman. With these two positions currently in the hands of bitter political rivals, the Democratic leaders in the legislature are no longer faced with a unified Chicago delegation, controlled by one person (Green, 1984).

As we will see in Chapter Eight, the governor is a strong legislative actor in Illinois. But neither in informal power nor actual practice does Illinois' governor approach the legislative dominance of the governor in states like New York, New Jersey or Kentucky (Rosenthal, 1981, p. 251). The Republican leaders in the legislature have generally exercised considerable independence during the tenure of the current Republican Governor, James R. Thompson (1977-present). A recent example is the 1983 income tax increase battle. House Republican leader Lee Daniels offered the major alternative to the plan put forth by Governor Thompson; the final tax package was much closer to Daniels' proposal (Parker, 1984). Democratic Governor Dan Walker had even less influence over his party in the legislature during his term (1973-77). Much of this is attributable to the force of Mayor Daley's presence as a powerful legislative opponent during that time. Daley eventually engineered Walker's defeat in the 1976 Democratic primary (*Illinois Issues*, 1976, p. 24).

The configuration that exists is not one of a single Democratic or Republican Party artificially divided into two chambers, but rather four party delegations organized and largely controlled by each of the four party leaders. Looking at the parties in the legislature in 1985, it might have been over-stating the case to refer to these groups with labels such as the [House Speaker] Mike Madigan Party or the [Senate Minority Leader] "Pate" Philip Party, but this is closer to the truth than referring to the Democratic or the Republican Party in the legislature.

Beyond the four top leadership positions—House speaker, House minority leader, Senate president, Senate minority leader—are a number of secondary leadership posts. These are chosen by the leader rather than elected by the members, although the leaders do not have a completely free hand. Leaders incur obligations in getting elected to their posts and must acknowledge support in appointing their leadership teams. Seniority, loyalty, service and regional identities are also key factors in the selection process. A look at the make-up of the leadership teams in place in 1985 illustrates the importance the leaders place on regional and demographic balance when they make their choices.

In 1985 the Senate Democrats had three assistant majority leaders, two majority whips and a caucus chairman. Three were downstaters from central, eastern and southern districts and three were from Chicago districts. One of the Chicago leaders was black, none were women. On the Republican side in the Senate there were three assistant minority leader positions and a caucus chairman. These positions were filled by two suburban and two downstate senators. All were white males.

In the House in 1985 the majority Democrats had a majority leader from a west central downstate district and four assistant majority leaders who represented a Chicago, a northern downstate and two suburban districts. One of the assistant majority leaders was a black woman. There were also two whips and a caucus chairman. One was from Chicago, one from Cook County and one was a woman from central downstate. The Republicans had four assistant minority leaders, along with two whips and a caucus chairman. Of the seven, four were from suburban districts and three were from downstate districts. One of the Republican leaders was a woman.

The assistant leaders, whip and caucus chairman usually work closely with the leader to establish and maintain a team and party identification among the members. They provide important ties between the various groups within each delegation. The wise use of the leadership structure by a leader greatly enhances the organization and operation of the party delegation. Leadership identities can create strong cross pressures on members. For example, House Assistant Minority Leader Penny Pullen voted with great reluctance for the 1983 tax increase package which House Minority Leader Lee Daniels and the House

Republican policy caucus had played a key role in shaping. Her position as member of the minority leader's leadership team created an obligation to support a policy which went against her own convictions (Parker, 1984, pp. 86, 93).

It is not uncommon for legislative leaders to face conflicts between their role in the legislature and their role as a representative of a district (Fenno, 1978, pp. 215-224). In 1973, Republican Speaker W. Robert Blair worked with Democratic Governor Daniel Walker and Chicago Mayor Richard J. Daley in passing legislation creating the Regional Transit Authority. That program proved so unpopular with Blair's Will County constituents that he was defeated for reelection in 1974. Leaders can also become more closely identified with unpopular legislative decisions than the average member. In 1979 Governor James R. Thompson and Chicago Mayor Jane Byrne reached an agreement on a state transportation and Regional Transit Authority funding plan. When the plan failed in the legislature, Mayor Byrne publicly blamed House Majority Leader Michael Madigan for the defeat and suggested the potential hike in city bus fares be named after him (Adkins, 1979, p. 29). Any legislator can have serious reelection problems if constituents believe he/she is more concerned with what is happening at the Capitol than with what is going on in the home district. Leaders run a greater risk of being so criticized because their roles demand a statewide policy focus and a large time commitment to Capitol activities.

Committee Chairmen, Spokesmen and Members. The legislature has a system of committees which hears bills and reports them to the floor for consideration by the entire membership. The critical role of the committees in the legislative process will be explored in detail in Chapter Seven. Our concern here is with the role committees play in the party structure of the legislature. In 1985 the House had 24 standing committees and six select committees, while the Senate had 17 standing committees. Each committee is led by a committee chairman and a minority spokesman. These committee leaders are selected by the speaker and the minority leader in the House and the president and minority leader in the Senate.

These are important positions which are valued by the members. The chairmen, with or without consultation with the minority spokesman, post bills and conduct hearings. The chairmen and spokesmen consult closely with their party leaders about important bills, but exercise great influence over more routine legislation. Committee chairmen are able to establish a reputation for their expertise in particular policy areas. Being chairman of the House Agricultural Committee can be very beneficial to a member from a farming district at election time.

The four leaders also select the members of their party delegations who serve on the committees. All members, except those with leadership positions, will serve on two to four standing or select committees. Member preferences are accommodated as much as possible, but loyalty, service and seniority all play a role. The leaders use their power to appoint committee chairmen and committee members to create another set of obligations and relationships which help them maintain control over their party delegations. In this way the committee system serves to further rally the members of a party delegation around the leader.

The leadership posts and committee leader positions are critical parts of the party structures within the legislature. Once the appointment of the leadership teams and committee chairmen or spokesmen by the four leaders was complete in 1985, 56 percent of the House Democrats, 72 percent of the House Republicans, 74 percent of the Senate Democrats and 79 percent of the Senate Republicans had a position of some influence in the legislative hierarchy. This structure helps the leaders create party delegations and offsets district and regional loyalties.

House and Senate Identities

Just as the four party delegations take on separate identities, the two chambers of the legislature develop separate identities. The president of the Senate and the speaker of the House will often have different power bases and agendas even if they come from the same party. Because each chamber gives priority to its own business first, the majority and minority leaders in each develop close relationships. Relations within chambers are sometimes better than those between chambers. The committee work and floor session activities force the members of both parties to spend a good deal of time together, often in a cooperative atmosphere. Chamber loyalties can be seen in references on the House floor to the other body as "the House of Lords," or references on the Senate floor to the "zoo on the other side of the rotunda." These House-Senate conflicts often have a strong policy focus as well. The successful efforts in 1984 to reorganize legislative commissions is a good example of the House and Senate in strong conflict over the content of a policy decision. The alternatives were regarded not as the Democrat and Republican plans or Chicago and downstate plans, but as the House plan and the Senate plan (Peters, 1984a, pp. 25-26). Once the parties and regional groups in a chamber reach a consensus on a difficult issue, the tendency is for the members to remain united if there is a disagreement with the other chamber.

Member Caucuses and Groups

While district, party, regional and institutional identities cover most of the ways in which members think of themselves, they clearly do not cover all those which cut across party or chamber lines. To fill this void, a number of informal caucuses have been organized by members. The black members of the legislature belong to a long-standing black caucus, which elects a chairman, takes positions on some bills and tries to present a united negotiating front. In the past, conflicts between regular Cook County Democratic organization blacks and independent black Democrats have limited the effectiveness of the caucus, although this could change as the political situation in Chicago evolves. Another long-standing informal caucus is the women's caucus. As with the black caucus, members try to meet and agree on common goals and positions. There are some issues which split the women legislators along partisan or ideological lines, but the growing number of women in the legislature and the legitimization and acceptance of a women's agenda by political leaders have enhanced the effectiveness of this group.

Members also organize informal groups along ideological lines. A liberal-leaning democratic study group (DSG) has existed in both the House and Senate in some form since the early 1970s while the more conservative Republican members in each chamber have formed a variety of loose groups during the same time period. The most visible ideological group was a coalition of downstate and independent Democratic senators known as the "Crazy Eight," which was a liberal thorn in the side of the Chicago-controlled Democratic majority during the early and mid-1970s (Heinecke, 1976, pp. 21-23).

Interest Group and Agency Spokesmen

In addition to the various personal, party, district and group identities discussed here, many members are spokesmen for organized interest groups or experts on particular subject areas. These spokesmen and experts may hold committee leadership positions, but they need not. In the late 1970s one Republican House member was widely recognized as both an expert on insurance legislation and the spokesman for the major insurance companies. During a heated debate the Democratic majority leader asked that a question be put to the Republican spokesman for insurance. When it was referred to the minority spokesman on the insurance committee, the Democratic leader angrily suggested that minority spokesman was not the real Republican spokesman on insurance. In contrast, the minority spokesman for the House Counties and Townships Committee at that time was widely recognized as a spokesman for the township officials organization and as the leading House expert on township legislation. After the defeat, in 1984, of Representative Larry Stuffle, the

Illinois Education Association's spokesman in the House, there was widespread speculation concerning who the new IEA House spokesman would be. No real successor emerged during 1985.

Spokesmen relationships may also develop between members and state agencies and executive officers. As we will see in Chapter Eight, the governor and other executive officers usually work through their party's leadership rather than rank and file members. The governor also tries to maintain control over the interactions of agencies with the legislature. In spite of this, individual members often become spokesmen for particular agencies, protecting their policies and appropriations beyond what the governor is able or willing to do. A classic example is the late Senator John Graham's tireless support for the Illinois Department of Corrections during his tenure in the legislature. Similarly, a member whose district contains a state university can be expected to champion its cause before the legislature.

From the perspective of an interest group, it is a great advantage to have a member who will speak on its behalf on the floor, introduce favorable bills and amendments and talk to other members on an informal basis. For the member who is such a spokesman, the position provides influence, prestige and campaign support at reelection time. All of the major interest groups have friendly members whose philosophy fits their orientation and who can be counted on to promote their cause. A knowledgeable observer can sit in the House or Senate gallery and point out the spokesmen for groups such as the Chicago Park District, the insurance companies, teacher unions, the manufacturing interests, environmental groups, farm groups, higher education institutions, labor unions and so on.

CONCLUDING OBSERVATIONS

Legislators, like the rest of us, have personal, intellectual and occupational identities when they file for office. They acquire a political identity when they are elected from a district under a party label. In Springfield their district, regional and party identities are elaborated and often intensified as they pursue lawmaking, representational and policy goals. While these identities may be consistent and coherent across issues and time, they often jostle and collide. The result is a legislative body and a set of party delegations which at times vote along strictly partisan lines and at other times along regional or district lines. In some roll calls one can see the strong influence of interest groups, ideologies, race, sex or occupational background. There are times when conflicts occur between a unified House and a unified Senate. Other legislative outcomes can be explained only by invoking a combination of these loyalties. Because of these patterns and cross pressures the legislative process in Illinois is not easily explained. But as we look more carefully at the mechanics of the process and the roles of other legislative actors, we will find that the process is both comprehensible and predictable, regardless of how one judges the outcomes.

Chapter Six

Staffing The General Assembly

Spend a short time watching the Illinois legislature in action and you will learn that the members are not the only ones active in the process. Everywhere one looks there are members of legislative staffs: at the right hand of the leaders answering questions and receiving instructions; on the floor providing backup for sponsors and explaining amendments to members; in committee meetings working with the chairman and the members; and behind the scenes drafting and analyzing bills, researching issues and doing the thousand procedural things necessary to make the process run smoothly. The modern Illinois legislature has developed a number of large, specialized staffs to assist in its lawmaking and representational activities. In the last chapter we looked at the members who constitute the legislature. In this chapter we will look at the staffs who serve them.

TYPES OF LEGISLATIVE STAFFS

Because of the many different names given to the Illinois General Assembly's staffs and the variety of functions they perform, several points of clarification must be made. The legislature in Illinois does not have a staff, it has a number of staffs. They differ as to who controls them, who they serve and the functions they perform. A critical distinction is between support (also referred to as nonprofessional or clerical) staff and professional staff. The support staff consists of people with clerical, nonpolicy roles such as secretaries, pages and aides. Professional staff people have policy roles, do not perform clerical duties and usually have at least an undergraduate college degree. References to legislative staff by the participants in the legislative process almost always refer to the professional staff. The professional staffs of the legislature fall into four categories: personal member staff, partisan leadership staff, bipartisan legislative service agency staff and chamber staff. Prior to 1985 there was a fifth category, legislative study commission staff. Figure 6:1 shows the organization of the General Assembly's staffs in April 1985.

Personal member staff people are professionals who are employed by individual members and serve their interests. They work in the member's district or Springfield office and may be paid out of public or private funds.

Partisan leadership staff people are professionals employed by one of the four legislative leaders. They serve the interests of both the leader and the members of his party delegation, but their ultimate loyalty is to

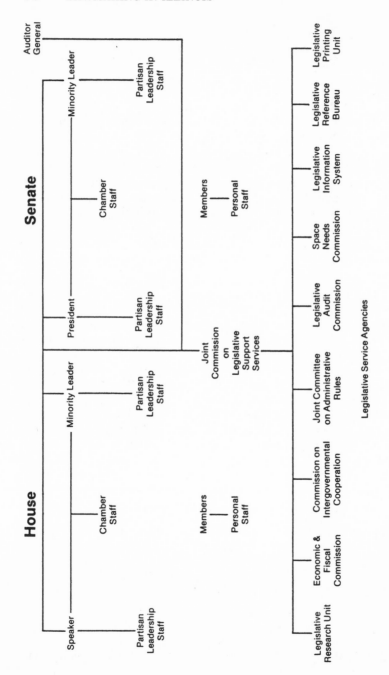

Figure 6:1   Organization of Professional Legislative Staff — 1985 (April)

the leader. The staff people present on the chamber floor or at committee hearings are usually partisan staff members.

Bipartisan legislative service agency staff people are professionals who are employed by one of the legislative service agencies. These agencies provide services for the entire legislature, not just one leader or chamber. The nine service agencies are governed by a joint committee comprised of the four legislative leaders. The service agencies also receive policy guidance from individual bipartisan boards of senators and representatives. These staff people are rarely seen on the chamber floor or at committee meetings.

Chamber staff people are professionals who work for one of the two chambers, performing bill-processing and record-keeping tasks. These staffs are hired by the clerk and assistant clerk of the House and the secretary and assistant secretary of the Senate. The chamber staffs operate in a bipartisan manner.

All legislative study commissions were abolished during 1984 and 1985. Legislative study commissions were set up to study one particular topic (i.e., education, children, agent orange). They employed professional staffs and were governed by bipartisan boards of legislators and, frequently, public members. These bipartisan boards were appointed by the legislative leaders. The legislative study commissions were less subject to leadership control than are the legislative service agencies. The reasons for abolishing these study commissions will be explored later in this chapter. Figure 6:2 shows the organization of the General Assembly's professional staffs in January 1983 prior to the abolishment of the legislative study commissions.

A Note on Commissions

The legislature did not abolish all commissions in 1984-85, only legislative study commissions. Four of the legislative support agencies have the word commission in their official titles, but they are legislative support agencies by virtue of their functions, governance structures and official designation as service agencies under the Legislative Reorganization Act of 1984. In addition, at any given time a large number of permanent and ad hoc gubernatorial and state agency commissions will be actively studying public policy questions. Legislative study commissions may have disappeared from the scene, but executive branch commissions are alive and well.

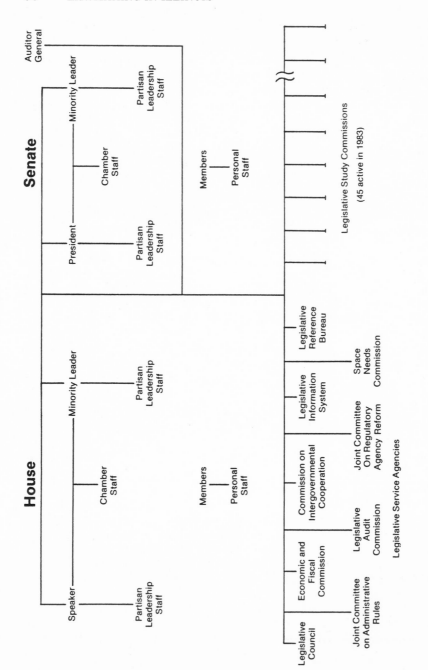

Figure 6:2   Organization of Professional Legislative Staff — 1983 (January)

THE DEVELOPMENT OF LEGISLATIVE STAFF IN ILLINOIS

Professional staff for the General Assembly is not a new idea. The first permanent legislative study commission was created by law in 1879, although the practice of creating these commissions through legislation did not become common until after the legitimacy of non-statutory legislative study commissions was successfully challenged in 1915 in the State Supreme Court (Illinois Legislative Research Unit, 1984b, pp. 68-69). The first legislative service agency, the Legislative Reference Bureau, was created in 1913 and three others, the Legislative Council, the Commission on Intergovernmental Cooperation and the the Budgetary Commission (now defunct), were created in 1937. The staffing pattern until the late 1960s was one of bipartisan legislative service agencies with small professional staffs, bipartisan legislative study commissions with a few professional staff, small chamber staffs and a few partisan staff assistants and legislative interns serving the legislative leaders and the committees.

As the legislature became a full-time and more sophisticated institution during the late 1960s and the 1970s, staffing patterns changed. When the Commission on the Organization of the General Assembly (COOGA) examined the legislature in 1967, it found no full-time, professional committee staff, no centralized bill tracking and data processing system, limited member support services in Springfield and in the district, inadequate appropriation and economic staff resources and too many independent legislative study commissions (COOGA, 1967). Ten years later a follow-up study (COOGA, 1977) found a legislature served by four large professional, partisan leadership staffs with individuals assigned to every substantive and appropriation committee. Revenue and economic analysis was provided by the Economic and Fiscal Commission and the movement of substantive and appropriation bills through the legislature was monitored by a data processing system under the direction of the Legislative Information System. One thing that did not change was the proliferation of legislative study commissions, which grew in number to over 40 by the late 1970s.

The reasons for the staffing changes of the 1960s and 1970s were many. During the 1960s in Illinois there were dramatic increases in the size of state government, the number of bills introduced in the legislature and complexity of issues faced by the legislature. It became impossible for individual members to read all of the bills and amendments before the legislature and to keep track of all of the programs of state government. The legislative leaders began to hire more professional staff to assist the leaders and members and provide support for the legislature's committees. Expansion of these staffs provided a source of independent, high-quality information that legislators needed to compete with the governor, the state agencies and interest groups for control of the legislative process.

A number of events and individuals stand out during the period of development from the early 1960s to the mid-1970s. In the early 1960s Senator Russell Arrington led the effort to expand and professionalize the legislature's staffs. An important part of that movement was the creation of a legislative staff intern program in 1961. This program helped introduce the idea of professional, partisan staff to the legislature and later provided a pool of individuals to fill staff positions. It is still in existence (see Appendix A). Representative Harold Katz was another leader in the professionalization and expansion of legislative staffs. He chaired the Committee on the Organization of the General Assembly (COOGA), which in 1967 issued a report providing an agenda for change. The shift in 1969 from biennial budgets, prepared by a commission of legislative leaders and executive branch representatives, to annual budgets prepared by the governor's Bureau of the Budget led to the creation of specialized appropriation staffs which provided systematic budget analysis for the legislature. Many longtime observers of the legislature regard the House Republican appropriation staff, put together by Speaker W. Robert Blair during 1970-74, to be the prototype of the modern partisan legislative staff in Illinois. Finally, the 1970 Illinois Constitution expanded the powers and responsibilities of the legislature, thus encouraging the expansion of legislative staffs.

Developments in legislative staffing between the two COOGA reports centered on policy analysis and bill-processing capability. There were significant increases in the legislature's effectiveness in both areas. Legislative staffs have continued to grow at a rapid rate and concerns with policy analysis and efficiency alone do not explain the continued expansion. The most important factors have been the desire of legislative leaders to increase the power of the legislature as an institution and the growing role of legislative staff in reelection and constituent activities.

A strong independent legislature and a strong staff go hand in hand. Jesse Unruh, former long-time speaker of the California Assembly and the driving force behind the development of the California legislature in the 1960s, is often quoted as saying, "Staff is knowledge and knowledge is power." Legislators want to make informed decisions on bills, but they also want to set agendas and control the political process. As more members became full-time legislators, and legislative leaders sought to realize the potential of their offices, the desire to increase the power of the legislature as an institution became greater. Legislative staff are properly viewed by the leaders and members as one of the chief means to that empowerment, and the number of staff members has increased accordingly since the second COOGA report.

It has become more difficult, time consuming and expensive to get elected and stay elected. Staff members produce the new ideas, bill drafts, policy analyses, position papers, press releases, speeches and letters, and perform the constituent services which enable members to serve and communicate with their constituents. As members and leaders have learned to use staff members more effectively in representation and reelection activities, the demand for their services has steadily increased. This has resulted in increases in the office allowances used by members to hire personal staff, increases in the size of the partisan staffs and increases in the specialization within the partisan staffs. The development of partisan staff units dedicated to issue development, constituent work and reelection activities was begun under the current House speaker, Michael Madigan, when he was House minority leader in 1980-82.

Today the Illinois legislature is served by leadership staffs employing over 200 professionals, and legislative service agencies employing at least 125 more. With the clerical employees of these legislative staffs, the chamber staffs of the House and the Senate and the Springfield and district office employees of the legislators, the total exceeds 750 people. While not the largest, the staff of the Illinois legislature is in the top ten in size nationally (Simon, 1979). Without this staff, the Illinois legislature could not process legislation effectively or make informed, independent policy decisions.

PARTISAN LEADERSHIP STAFF

In 1967 the General Assembly formally authorized staff assistants for the four legislative leaders. Each leader could have up to five staff assistants with individual salaries not to exceed $17,500 (a legislator's salary at that time). These staff assistants were " . . . to perform research and render other assistance to the members of [the leader's] party on such committees as may be designated" when the legislature was in session, and to " . . . perform such services as may be assigned by the party leadership" when the legislature was not in session (*Illinois Revised Statutes*, 1968). In 1969 the statutory limits on the number of leadership staff members and the level of their compensation were removed, but the concept of four partisan leadership staffs with equal resources was retained (*Illinois Revised Statutes*, 1970). Collectively, these four staffs (House Democratic staff, House Republican staff, Senate Democratic staff, Senate Republican staff) number more than 200 professionals. The directors of these staffs earn between $55,000 and $70,000 per year. While there are some variations in organization and the division of labor, these staffs all perform the same basic functions for their leaders and members. They can be divided into three categories: key leadership staff, committee staff and member service staff.

Key Leadership Staff

Legislative leaders shape strategy, set agendas and work schedules, negotiate agreements and generally advance their own political fortunes and those of their fellow party members within their respective chambers. Each leader has a few key individuals who work largely on these activities. These individuals may have impressive titles like chief of staff or unimportant sounding titles like assistant to the leader. Some live in Springfield all year, others come to Springfield only during the legislative session. All of them enjoy the personal trust and confidence of their leaders. These individuals represent and speak for the legislative leader; if the leader moves to a higher office they go along. If they work for the president of the Senate or the speaker of the House, they also have powers and responsibilities in relation to overall management and planning of the operation of their chamber and the legislature as a whole. (See Briggs, 1984, for profiles of the four partisan chiefs of staff in 1984.)

Committee Staff: Substantive and Appropriations

When committee members sit down for a meeting they have before them written analyses of the bills that are to be considered. These are prepared by the partisan legislative staffs. Republican members have analyses prepared by the Republican staff and Democratic members have analyses prepared by the Democratic staff. A majority of the professionals employed by the partisan staffs are assigned to committee work. Each staff will typically assign 15 to 20 people to the substantive committees and seven to 10 people to the appropriation committees.

A staff person who works for a substantive committee usually works directly with the committee chairman if his party is in the majority, or the minority spokesman if it is not. Staff members are responsible for analyzing bills that are heard by their committee and for preparing a written (usually one- to two-page) bill analysis for the leadership and the committee members. A typical analysis summarizes the existing situation, the proposed change, the reason for introduction, the implications of enacting the bill and the position of various interest groups and state agencies on the legislation. Staff members are also responsible for tracking their bills through the process and analyzing changes made in the bill by amendments offered on the floor or in the second chamber. Their work is usually supervised by a research or staff director. They are expected to work with legislators from their party who have bills before their committee, identifying potential problems and preparing corrective amendments. They are also responsible for the subject area of the committee they serve and will prepare legislation, do spot research, handle constituent problems and prepare press information for the leader or individual members concerning their policy areas.

Appropriation staff members are assigned to analyze the budgets of a group of state agencies. They are expected to monitor expenditures and programs for these agencies during the current fiscal year and to prepare an analysis of their budgets as presented by the governor in the budget message and introduced in bill form in early March of each year. Because agency programs and budgets do not change greatly from year to year, appropriation staff work is somewhat more predictable than substantive staff work. In contrast to the more independent work of substantive staff members, appropriation staff members work as a unit under the direction of an appropriation staff director who in turn works directly with the appropriation committee chairman or minority spokesperson. Appropriation staff members are also expected to prepare written analyses of agency budget requests for the next fiscal year. These analyses usually contain an examination of the agency's current expenditures and a discussion of any major changes in the proposed budget from the previous year's budget, highlighting any problem areas. Since appropriation committees usually assume that agencies ask for more money than they need, appropriation staff members are expected to recommend areas where budgets can be reduced and prepare appropriate amendments. As with substantive staff members, appropriation staff members will track their bills on the floor and in the second chamber and analyze amendments that are offered. They are also responsible for the general subject areas that their agencies administer.

Member Services Staff

Each staff has individuals who perform specialized services that are not directly related to the processing of legislation. These member service activities fall into four categories: press relations, constituent services, issue development and reelection activities.

Press Relations. The leader and the members have a strong interest in keeping the general public and their constituents informed about what they are doing. These activities are clearly part of the representation function of each member, but they also serve members' reelection interests. Each of the four staffs has a press staff that generates press releases, speeches, taped radio messages that can be used in news broadcasts, and informational booklets on topics of interest to constituents. Press staffs also provide training for legislators on how to handle themselves in radio and television interviews. In addition to providing services for their legislators, these staff members are responsible for general liaison activities with the electronic and print media.

Constituent Services. Another activity performed by partisan staff members is constituent services, usually referred to as casework. Members receive constituent complaints and requests personally or through their district and Springfield office staffs. Most are handled by the members' office staffs. Some of these requests are turned over to regular committee staff members, while others are referred to individuals on the partisan leadership staffs whose primary responsibility is casework. Depending on the leader, this can be an ad hoc or a systematically organized operation. On some partisan staffs, a staff person will be assigned to a group of legislators to assist in their casework and press activities. Leaders use their staffs to make their members more effective and responsive to their districts, which, of course, enhances the reelection chances of the members and the status of the leader.

Issue Development. All partisan staffs are involved in policy areas and issues. What makes issue or policy development staff members different from committee staff members is that they deal with particular policy areas and interest groups but are not responsible for analyzing legislation. These staff members are expected to identify solutions to problems and to develop issues that can be used to advance the power of the leader and the reelection of members. In doing this, they serve as liaisons to the key interest groups involved in their particular issue areas. Issue staff members are particularly valuable because they can be directed at a specific area or problem as the need arises. As with casework, these activities can be handled systematically or on an ad hoc basis. In 1985 three of the four partisan staffs had formally designated issue or policy development staffs.

Reelection Activities. Since the mid-1970s, there has been a growing tendency for leadership staffs to be actively involved in legislative races. Many staff members take unpaid leaves of absences and work full-time on election campaigns during the late summer and fall of election years. Because they are backed by a campaign organization and a political action committee controlled by the legislative leaders and because many are experienced campaign workers, these staff members are very valuable in legislative races. Some will even move into the districts they are assigned three or four months prior to the election. Once the election is over most staff members return to their legislative duties.

Organization

The four partisan staffs all provide services in the three areas just described: leadership, committees and member services. They vary in the degree of complexity and compartmentalization of their organizational structures. For example, since 1978 the House Republicans have made a conscious effort to integrate the substantive and appropriation staff functions, while the other three leadership staffs have maintained a basic structural division between them. In 1980 the House Democrats developed a separate unit to perform all the member services functions. The House

Republicans and Senate Democrats have recently developed separate issues or policy staff units which are similar to the House Democrats' issue development unit. Each of the partisan staffs in the Senate has a chief of staff, a research director responsible for the substantive committees and an appropriation director, while the two partisan House staffs have a chief of staff and a combination research and appropriation director.

These variations are largely a function of the leaders' organizational preferences. A separation of substantive and appropriation work reflects a traditional view of the process as a series of separate, identifiable tasks, while a concentration on member services staff indicates a focus on elections and political considerations. The amount of delegated power and responsibility determines the degree of decentralization within each staff.

LEGISLATIVE SERVICE AGENCIES

The legislative service agencies are organizations which provide support services for the General Assembly on a bipartisan basis. They were created by statute and until 1984 were governed by bipartisan groups of senators and representatives. Under the old system, these legislators set general policy and hired a director who was responsible for the day-to-day operations of the service agency's staff. Under the Legislative Reorganization Act of 1984, the four legislative leaders constitute a joint committee (the Joint Committee on Legislative Support Services) which sets general policy for the service agencies and hires the directors (Public Act 83-1257). Each service agency is also governed by a bipartisan group of six senators and six representatives which has specific policy or statutory responsibilities. These service agencies, which employ between 10 and 20 professionals apiece, perform one of three functions: policy development and analysis, bill processing or executive branch oversight. While the Office of the Auditor General is not technically a legislative service agency under the provisions of P.A. 83-1257, it is listed under this heading as an oversight service agency.

Policy-Oriented Service Agencies

Three of the legislative service agencies analyze and develop policy. They are the Illinois Legislative Research Unit, the Illinois Commission on Intergovernmental Cooperation and the Economic and Fiscal Commission.

The Illinois Legislative Research Unit (called the Illinois Legislative Council prior to the Legislative Reorganization Act of 1984) does research for members and other staffs. The Research Unit staff provides answers to questions covering the whole range of state and local government activities. The response can be verbal, a short letter or a more lengthy research memorandum, depending on the complexity of the question and the need for a rapid response. The Research Unit is divided into a general research staff and a science staff which deals with research on scientific or technical questions. The science unit is a resource not available to most state legislatures (Ahlen, 1983).

Under normal circumstances, the Research Unit staff does not analyze bills currently before the General Assembly. Rather, the work product of the Research Unit is usually more general in focus and is used by legislators and partisan staff members as background for developing legislation or support for positions on pending legislation. Although staff members get involved with pending legislation on an informal basis, the Research Unit is primarily a bipartisan research service.

The Illinois Commission on Intergovernmental Cooperation focuses on federal-state-local relations. The commission's staff assembles and maintains information on federal programs and analyzes their effect on state and local governments. The commission also serves as a formal clearinghouse for federal grant information and monitors the availability and expenditure of federal funds. The commission has an office in Washington, D.C., that tracks federal legislation and acts as a liaison between the state legislature and the federal government. The commission staff is directly involved with developing and analyzing legislation pending before the General Assembly, especially bills involving responses to federal programs and initiatives.

The Economic and Fiscal Commission performs a number of services for the legislature in the areas of revenue and taxation. The most important are periodic estimates of state revenues for current and future fiscal years. These estimates give the legislature a set of figures to compare with those provided by the governor's Bureau of the Budget. In considering the state budget the legislature may choose to accept the Economic and Fiscal Commission's estimates of expected revenues and appropriate accordingly. In the absence of these estimates, the legislature would be dependent upon the governor's estimate of expected revenues and the level of expenditure necessary to produce a balanced budget. The Economic and Fiscal Commission also provides an analysis of the impact of all taxation legislation which comes before the House and Senate revenue committees, and prepares impact notes on all legislation affecting long-term state debt and public employee pensions.

In the areas of revenue estimates, taxation bill analysis and debt and pension impact statements, the commission plays a more direct role in the process of considering and acting on pending legislation than does the Legislative Research Unit or the Commission on Intergovernmental Cooperation. But this involvement is primarily one of technical analysis provided on a bipartisan basis.

Process Service Agencies

There are four legislative service agencies that facilitate the processing of legislation in the General Assembly: the Reference Bureau, the Legislative Information System, the Legislative Printing Unit and the Space Needs Commission. In contrast to the other service agencies, these agencies do not play a policymaking role in the legislature.

The Reference Bureau's primary function is to draft legislation. All legislation must conform to constitutional requirements and be in standard bureau form. The Reference Bureau has a staff of attorneys that receives requests for bills and amendments from members, or a partisan staff person acting on behalf of members, and translates them into bills and amendments for introduction. The Reference Bureau prepares an official synopsis and digest of legislation and legislative action that are published and periodically updated during every session. The bureau is also responsible for reviewing existing statutes and suggesting technical revisions. The services of the Reference Bureau are provided on a bipartisan, "attorney-client" basis. Requests are handled confidentially. The bureau's objective is to draft the best possible bill regardless of policy content (O'Grady, 1982).

The Legislative Information System (LIS) operates the bill status and appropriation-tracking system through which the participants follow the daily, even hourly, progress of legislation. This is done through a computerized data base that is updated constantly and which can be accessed through terminals located throughout the Capitol complex. LIS also produces a variety of printed reports on a daily and weekly basis that provide information on specific matters, for example, all bills sent to the governor or all actions of a particular committee.

Prior to 1984, the Legislative Council ran the legislature's printshop. Under the new legislative service agency structure, the Legislative Printing Unit is a separate service agency with its own bipartisan board. The Printing Unit prints member newsletters, amendments, some bills and reports and documents from legislative service agencies, committees and commissions.

The Space Needs Commission is a planning and advisory body charged with finding and allocating space for the legislature and its agencies. It also oversees the rehabilitation of old buildings and the construction of new buildings in the capitol complex.

Oversight Service Agencies

The legislature's three oversight service agencies, the Joint Committee on Administrative Rules, the Office of the Auditor General and the Audit Commission, enable the legislature to monitor and evaluate the implementation of programs by state agencies. They provide valuable information about the executive branch to the legislature and like the policy-oriented service agencies become involved in legislation pending before the General Assembly. Another oversight service agency, the Select Committee on Regulatory Reform, was abolished in 1984.

The Joint Committee on Administrative Rules—whose acronym, JCAR, is pronounced "jaycar"—reviews and publishes all proposed state agency rules and regulations and conducts periodic reviews of all existing rules and regulations. These activities are carried out under the Illinois Administrative Procedure Act, which became law in 1977. While JCAR is concerned with the implementation of legislation by the executive branch, it becomes directly involved in the legislative process through the introduction of bills that seek to resolve conflicts between the committee and state agencies over the specific intent of previously enacted laws.

The post of auditor general is a legislative office created by the 1970 Illinois Constitution. Prior to that time the legislative did not have an independent source of information on the expenditure of state funds by the executive branch. The auditor general is elected by the members of the legislature for a 10-year term. His office is charged with monitoring the obligation, receipt, expenditure and use of public funds. Under the provisions of the Illinois State Auditing Act, the Office of the Auditor General conducts financial, compliance, management and program audits of all state agencies.

The Audit Commission works closely with the Auditor General's Office in overseeing the expenditure of funds by state agencies. The commission's staff provides the commission members with an analysis of the auditor general's reports. The commission may recommend legislative action to address problems brought to light by its staff or the auditor general's. The commission also makes general policy recommendations to the Auditor General's Office.

The Joint Committee on Regulatory Agency Reform, referred to as the Sunset Commission, was charged under the Regulatory Agency Sunset Act of 1979 to determine if various professions and businesses should continue to be regulated by state law. The act sets up a schedule for reviewing the various regulatory laws and either renewing or abolishing them. Sunset was abolished on September 30, 1984, under the Legislative Reorganization Act of 1984. The committee's work on the review of the state's public utility law was continued by the Joint Committee on Public Utility Regulation, which was abolished June 30, 1985.

PERSONAL MEMBER STAFF IN SPRINGFIELD

Every member of the General Assembly either has a full-time, year-round secretary located in the capitol complex or shares one with another member. These secretaries are paid from the budgets of the legislative leaders, but they work directly for the members. Prior to 1985 each member also received an office allowance of $17,000 per year. This money was usually used to set up and staff one or more legislative offices in their district, an arrangement which would be regarded enviously by legislators from many other states (Rosenthal, 1981, pp. 210-212). Legislation passed in 1984 (P.A. 83-1177) increased the annual office allowance for representatives to $27,000 and $37,000 for senators.

In contrast to states such as New York or California, Illinois legislators have almost no Springfield-based, professional staff hired by and loyal to the individual member. Prior to the 1984 increase most members could not stretch their office allowances far enough to cover the salary of professional staff in Springfield. When members in Illinois want a bill analyzed, research conducted, an appropriation amendment drafted or indirect reelection help such as an informational booklet prepared for their constituents, they have had to deal with a staff member employed by one of the partisan leadership staffs or legislative service agencies. These staff members do not have the same kind of personal loyalty and vested interest in the member's success as staff members hired and controlled by the member. In short, legislative leaders have control of professional staff assistance and have not been reluctant to exercise that control. This basic staffing pattern makes the Illinois legislature different from states with substantial individual-member staffs and helps shape the relationship between members and the legislative leaders. The 1984 increase in legislative office allowances could alter this relationship if a significant number of members hire professional staff people. This would give the members greater resources and more independence in making policy and getting reelected.

CHAMBER STAFFS

The chamber staff in the House is directed by the clerk and assistant clerk of the House while in the Senate the key officers are the secretary and assistant secretary of the Senate. They are chosen by the majority and minority party in each chamber. These chamber staffs have procedural, nonpolicy functions. They operate in a bipartisan manner, but the majority party exercises ultimate control.

The tasks performed by chamber staffs follow the steps a bill takes through the process. All bills and amendments are filed with them prior to their official introduction. They direct the printing and distribution of all bills and amendments. They also maintain bill rooms where the public can obtain copies of all bills and adopted amendments, and receive and post all notices of committee meetings. Once bills are heard in committee, they receive and report the official actions of the committees. They publish the daily legislative calendars of bills ready for floor action; they record the official roll calls on floor votes and transcribe the floor debates; and once a bill has passed, they incorporate any adopted amendments into it before it is sent to the other chamber or the governor. They transmit official messages to the other chamber. Finally, they publish a daily journal for each chamber, which is the official record of all legislative action.

LEGISLATIVE STUDY COMMISSIONS

Over the years the legislature created a number of permanent, policy-oriented study commissions. These commissions became a key feature of the legislature after a 1915 Supreme Court ruling raised questions concerning the status of legislative committees during the interim period between the spring adjournment of the legislature in the odd-numbered years and the seating of a new legislature 18 months later. The legislature's need to function on a continuous basis in important policy areas was met by the creation of legislative study commissions. Funds were appropriated to these commissions for member expenses and staff salaries. Both legislators and private citizens usually served on them as regular voting members. Initially, these commissions conducted hearings and studied issues during the periods when the legislature was not in session, producing packages of proposed legislation and policy reports (Legislative Research Unit, 1984b, pp. 73-74).

With the adoption of the 1970 Constitution, the legal power of the the legislature to function year-round was established beyond question. Since 1970 the legislature has averaged over 160 days in session every two years. Legally and practically, the legislature's regular committees and service agencies could have done the work done by legislative study commissions. Prior to 1984, however, all attempts to abolish study commissions and transfer their resources to the legislature's standing committees and service agencies were unsuccessful. Instead, the legislature regularly considered, and occasionally approved, the creation of new study commissions. Study commissions survived because they served the policy, influence and reelection goals of the legislative members. They provided the legislative members with a public forum and resources which they could use to influence policy and gain attention and prestige. They were also supported by interest groups because they gave special attention and focus to a policy area and members of these groups were often appointed to them.

In 1983 there were 45 study commissions employing over 100 professionals. Study commission staff members often analyzed pending legislation and formulated legislative proposals which were introduced by the commission chairman. Some study commission staffs were closely aligned with the chairman or other key members of the standing committee in their area and played an important role in the legislative process. Other commissions had little influence.

In the spring 1984 legislative session a successful effort was mounted to abolish the study commissions and transfer most of their functions and some of their resources to the legislature's standing committees and service agencies. These changes are contained in the Legislative Reorganization Act of 1984, which abolished all but seven of the study commissions on September 30, 1984. The remaining seven were abolished March 15, 1985. Under the same act the service agencies were continued, but under a new structure which gives the four legislative leaders control over the hiring of directors, the setting of policy and the approval of contracts and personnel. The compromise legislation was passed at the end of the 1984 spring session. It is still not clear what the final relationships between the service agencies and the leaders will be or how the various functions and resources of study commissions will be integrated into committee structure, the partisan leadership staffs and service agencies.

Among commissions abolished September 30, 1984, were the Legislative Investigating Commission, the Committee to Visit and Examine State Institutions, the County Problems Commission, the Data Information System Commission, the Transportation Study Commission, the Illinois Recreation Council, the Special Events Commission, the Labor Laws Study Commission, the Pension Laws Study Commission, the Agent Orange Study Commission and the Joint Condominium Study Commission. The seven study commissions which were abolished March 15, 1985, were the Commission on Children, the Commission on Economic Development, the Illinois Energy Resources Commission, the Commission on Mental Health and Developmental Disabilities, the Legislative Advisory Committee on Public Aid, the School Problems Commission and the Commission on the Status of Women. A successful effort was made at the end of the 1985 spring session to recreate these seven commissions as citizens councils within a Citizens Assembly (P.A. 84-15). While the exact function of these councils has not been established, their creation demonstrates the strength of their constituencies and they are likely to continue in some form (Emerson, 1985; Willard, 1985).

The success of the effort to abolish study commissions and reorganize the service agencies can be attributed to a number of factors (Peters, 1984a). The familiar litany of study commission patronage abuses, waste and duplication of activities had a strong basis in fact. When House Minority Leader Daniels proposed a sweeping reorganization in the name of efficiency, effectiveness and responsible administrative control, House Speaker Madigan joined the reform effort and quickly formalized the proposal into legislation. Sensing that some change in the system was inevitable, Senate President Rock and Minority Leader Philip proposed a more gradual phaseout of the study commissions and a less sweeping reorganization of the service agencies. Once the four legislative leaders had publicly committed themselves to change, what had begun as a recommendation for a one-year study of possible service agency and study commission reorganization became an almost inevitable tide of change.

The reorganization plan passed by the legislature was attractive to the legislative leaders for three reasons: it projected an image of cost-cutting efficiency, it consolidated power in the hands of the leaders and it will increase the effectiveness of staff. The payoff for the members is less obvious. The increase in members' allowances for hiring professional and support staff provides some compensation for the loss of study commission memberships and staff assistance. Serving as a committee chairman or member could become more meaningful if the power and money previously held by the study commissions are transferred to the legislature's committees.

WHO ARE STAFF?

Legislative staff are generally well-educated young men and women who work for the legislature a relatively short time. They all have college degrees; many have master's degrees or law degrees. While approximately 40 percent of those on the partisan and service agency staffs are women, none of the staff directors are women and only five of the 17 in assistant director positions are women. Most staff members are in their 20s and 30s and staff members over 40, even directors, are rare. There are few careerists, particularly on the partisan staffs. Of the 90 individuals listed as partisan committee staff in a March 1980 legislative directory, only 38 were still listed as staff members in an April 1984 directory (Illinois Legislative Council, 1980; Illinois Legislative Council, 1984). Of the 11 listed as staff, research or appropriation directors in 1980 only two were still holding those positions in 1984. In contrast, the service agency and commission staff members are a little older and stay a little longer, but careerists in non-supervisory positions are still unusual. The high turnover rate reflects the intense pressure and long hours common to legislative staff work (Rosenthal, 1981, pp. 226).

ROLE OF STAFF IN THE LEGISLATIVE PROCESS

One spring in the mid-1970s a House legislative leader walked into an appropriation committee meeting. One of the members was having a difficult time explaining the content of the amendment he was offering. Finally, in exasperation, he exclaimed, "There is no problem with this, it is an agreed *staff* amendment!" The leader turned to the staff person standing next to him and asked, "Have we really come to that?" While legislative staff members have not become independent actors within the process, their role has increased dramatically since the late 1960s.

As noted earlier, the partisan legislative staffs and service agencies now employ over 325 professionals. These individuals have a significant and growing impact on both the processing and the content of the legislation that passes the General Assembly. While there are occasional complaints by members, lobbyists, agency people and press members about the power of staff, the situation in Illinois does not approach those noted by Rosenthal (1981, pp. 228, 229) in California in the 1960s and New York in the 1970s where serious concerns were raised about the control of legislative staff members over the legislature. Nor is the General Assembly likely in the near future to develop a staff system like that of Congress. There the size and influence of members' personal staffs have led one observer to compare the congressman and his/her personal staff to a small, independent organization (Salisbury and Shepsle, 1981), and another to raise serious questions about the power of staff in the legislative process, calling them unelected representatives with more power than the legislators (Malbin, 1980). Neither concern applies in Illinois; still, legislative staff in Illinois are important and the role they play subtle and complex.

Control Over Legislative Staffs

Partisan staff members are leadership staff, hired and fired by the four legislative leaders. In 1985 the people who worked for the Democratic staff in the House answered the phone, "Speaker Madigan's staff."Calls to the other three staffs elicited similar responses. But because staff members work on the bills of individual members and usually work very closely with one committee chairman or minority spokesman, the question, "Who do you work for?"is not as simple as it seems. Staff members develop allegiances to a political party, individual members, committee leaders and staff directors, but ultimately they work for the legislative leader. While unusual, it is not unheard of for a member to publicly complain on the floor of the House or Senate about the fairness and adequacy of the assistance and information provided by the leadership staffs. Such complaints are more often expressed in private.

Prior to the reorganization of 1984, legislative service agency staff members were largely oriented towards policy and the General Assembly. Directors looked to the legislative chairman of their service agency as much or more than to the four legislative leaders. Service agencies had a great deal of independence from the legislative leaders and their partisan staffs. The lack of direct control by legislative leaders and the blurring of lines of responsibility were factors in the reorganization undertaken in 1984. Opponents of the reorganization cited the same relationships as a virtue of the system which should be retained. It is still unclear how much control the legislative leaders will ultimately exercise over the legislative service agency staffs, but the general expectation is that it will be much greater than under the previous system.

Interstaff Relations

In spite of the partisan organization of the leadership staffs, they do cooperate and share information. Because most bills are nonpartisan and routine, substantive committee staff members regularly share information within and between chambers. Similarly, the basic information necessary for an appropriation analysis is factual. Appropriation staff members will coordinate information requests and meetings with agency representatives. The staff directors work together to manage the legislature's schedule and work flow and negotiate on behalf of their leaders on highly partisan, political matters. This interaction and the sharing of the experiences of the typical spring session create friendships and understanding which ameliorate the natural rivalries of the partisan staffs. Because of the necessity to work together, there is even a tendency for staffs within a chamber to have closer relationships than staffs of the same party from opposite chambers.

Generally, the partisan staffs and the legislative service agency staffs have cooperative, supportive relationships. Partisan staff members can benefit from the research information and policy expertise of the bipartisan staff and bipartisan staff can benefit from the legislative information, policy expertise and political analysis of the partisan staff members. Similarly, the directors of these staffs have mutual interests and concerns. At times, tensions do exist between the leadership staffs and the policy-oriented service agency staffs. Leadership staff members sometimes view service agency staff members as politically naive researchers who produce material too general to be relevant to the needs of the legislators. Conversely, policy-oriented service agency staff members sometimes view the work of partisan staff members as limited by politics and time constraints. These opposed perceptions and attitudes make the distance between partisan staffs and policy-oriented service agency staffs greater than the actual distance between the Statehouse (where most partisan staff members are located) and the Stratton Office Building (where many policy-oriented service agency staff members are located) would suggest. Talk about people "across the street" sometimes has a very negative tone. These strains are part of the reason for the ongoing reorganization efforts begun in 1984 by the legislative leaders and their staff directors.

Life on a Partisan Staff

Ask partisan staff members why they stay with the legislature and they will tell you the work is interesting, exciting and satisfying. Ask them why they leave and they will tell you the hours are long, the pressures are intense, the work is often frustrating and there is little positive feedback or opportunity for advancement. Ask them where they are going and you will find they are usually taking a higher-paying position with the governor's staff, an agency or an interest group where they will use the skills and understanding gained from working on a partisan legislative staff.

The legislature is an exciting place to work. The stakes are high and the action varied. Staff members are usually right in the middle of it. It is exciting to know what will be in the morning paper (and what won't) and why. It is rewarding to see bills and amendments you have developed signed into law. For the person who wants to be involved with policymaking and politics, staff work is an excellent entry point. The list of legislators, agency directors and lobbyists who entered state government as partisan legislative staff members is long.

There is another side to legislative staff work. Just when a staff member has made plans for the weekend, his/her committee chairman will suspend the legislative rules and post an additional 10 or 20 bills for a Tuesday hearing, and that weekend will become two more regular work days. A downstater will want an amendment drafted to hurt the suburbs, a suburban member will want one to hurt downstate and the leader from Chicago won't want any amendments drafted at all (O'Grady, 1981).

A staff person with an advanced degree and several years experience in a particular subject area develops a professional identity with the policies and institutions of that area. At this point a professional, partisan staff person can feel tension between his professional and his partisan identities. The third time a bill he knows is a good idea goes down for reasons having nothing to do with its merits, he may ask why he bothered to do the research in the first place.

The month of June can mean 80-hour weeks, culminating in 16-hour days at the end of the month. While June 30 is the traditional end of the spring session, every session since 1970 has gone into the month of July. In 1985 the House was even in session on the 4th of July. At the end of the session, even the most enthusiastic and loyal staff person starts considering another line of work.

When staff members look at advancement within the legislature, they will see that just as there are only four leaders, there are only four chiefs of staff and four appropriation directors. Both the working conditions and the limited opportunities for advancement contribute to the high turnover in legislative staff members.

While some staff members leave for law school and a few seek elective office, most move on to jobs with the executive branch or private companies and associations. The governor and other constitutional officers have legislative liaison offices and program staffs where the skill and experience of former partisan staff members can be put to good use. Each state agency employs at least one legislative liaison. The Bureau of the Budget is another place where appropriation staff skills and experience can be a valuable asset. Private companies and associations that maintain permanent lobbying staffs in Springfield often hire people from partisan legislative staffs. For the staff person these jobs offer a less hectic, more secure, better-paying and often more personally rewarding way of life.

The Future of Legislative Staff

The most recent developments in legislative staffing in Illinois have been the creation and growth of member services staffs, the growing involvement of partisan leadership staffs in individual election contests, the movement to consolidate leadership control over legislative service agencies, the elimination of study commissions and the increase in office allowances under the direct control of individual members. These changes reflect the changing nature of the legislature. Once a strong policy analysis and bill-processing capability had been established through the changes that took place in the decade from the late 1960s to the late 1970s, the leaders and members were able to concentrate on developing their own agendas, independent of the governor or interest groups. As members and leaders continue to seek ways to increase their political power, legislative staffs will play a critical role.

The interest of members and leaders in developing legislative staff do not operate in complete harmony. The leaders want to establish control over the money and influence once held by the study commissions and to consolidate control over the legislative service agencies. Some members favor more influential and independent committees, which would challenge the power of the leaders. The increase in member office allowances, if used to hire professionals, will give the members greater independence in both policymaking and running for reelection. The members favor a more fragmented staffing system while the leaders would like to expand their control. Tensions naturally exist between the interest of rank and file members and those who lead and maintain the institution, and it is not surprising to find that recent developments in legislative staffing in Illinois reflect those tensions.

The Influence of Legislative Staff

The legislature as we know it would cease to function without partisan, service agency and chamber staffs handling the drafting, amending, analyzing, information gathering, digesting, scheduling, recording and coordinating activities which move bills through the process (O'Grady, 1981). In the 1985 spring session the legislature considered 2529 House and 1462 Senate bills. Over 2500 of those were introduced during a four-day period in early April. Without legislative staffs the legislature would have to rely on lobbyists and agency representatives for their information. As an institution, the legislature is much more powerful, efficient and informed because of its staffs.

It is difficult to provide an overall evaluation of the role of the legislative staffs in the areas of representation and reelection. Members use information and services from partisan, service agency and personal staffs to build relationships with their constituents and create a favorable image. They also use legislative staffs to give them an advantage over their election opponents. The use of staff in these areas continues to grow in importance. The systematic use of partisan leadership staff members—who are on unpaid leaves of absence—in legislative campaigns has become a regular pattern in Illinois. (They are, however, paid from campaign funds.) For the members, these skilled and highly motivated people are very valuable campaign resources. The leaders' use of their staffs in this manner creates obligations which give the leaders influence once the election is over and the legislature is in session.

The policy-shaping and decision-making role of the legislative staffs is also difficult to evaluate. Individual partisan and service agency staff members who remain in the same substantive or appropriation area for more than a couple of years and gain a reputation for competence and reliability become influential because they are called on for advice and are trusted to work out the details on difficult policy questions. Partisan staff members are also expected to handle routine bills without detailed consultation or supervision. They have the procedural and policy information and technical know-how to deal with situations where members and leaders do not have the time or information to deal personally with the details. This responsibility is delegated by members and leaders. Staff members vary on how aggressively they seek and use this power, but it flows naturally to them (O'Grady, 1981). The staff directors are also influential because of the power and responsibility delegated to them by the legislative leaders. While they do not have independent resources which allow them to pursue their own agenda without the implicit approval of the leaders, they have considerable freedom. Ultimately, power rests with the members who cast the votes and the leaders who hire and fire staff members. Part of the frustration of working for a legislative staff is that while staff members may believe they understand a problem and know how to solve it, they must always defer to the elected members and the leaders.

Overall, the skills and expertise of partisan and service agency staff members in policy areas and appropriations help legislators and leaders compete with the governor's staff, the agencies, the interest groups and the members and staffs of the opposition party. In the absence of the opinions of legislators, staff members, particularly those on partisan staffs, shape the legislature's responses to agencies, interest groups and constituents. Even on issues where members and leaders are actively involved and well informed, staff members help shape the options. Although the potential exists for the loss of control by the elected members in specific situations, staff members cannot abuse their power if they are to maintain credibility. Staff members who act contrary to the wishes of their leaders or members do not last very long. Legislative staffs have considerable influence, but no one seriously believes that they run the legislature in Illinois.

Chapter Seven
Lawmaking: Matters of Organization and Process
THE BASICS OF LEGISLATIVE ORGANIZATION

In the preceding chapters we have shown that members are expected both to represent—serve as the advocates and protectors of their constituents—and to legislate—pass bills to regulate the great range of social and economic relations between people and their government. These two functions of lawmaking regularly jostle each other, and sometime collide as members play one, then the other role. This tension in and between lawmakers is one of the many tensions and conflicts built into the legislative process. Some of these tensions have roots in the constitutions of the nation and the states. Constitutions do confer authority upon governmental units. But they also set restrictions on that authority. One of the basic premises of American constitutionalism stimulates a great many specific conflicts. That premise asserts that government has limited power over the inherent rights of people.

Constitutional Considerations

In the 18th century Americans developed a great love for constitutions. They wrote and rewrote the basic charters for their states and when they won independence from England they wrote the U.S. Constitution, which became the standard for western representative democracies. The prompting ideal was to preserve the rights and independence of citizens from encroachment by their government, to encourage groups of citizens to seek benefits through government, to balance the authority of the branches, or subdivisions, of government, and still afford that government enough unity, authority and resources to make its enactments stick. Some very big ideas run through this constitutionalism: limited government, inherent equality of citizens before the law, popular sovereignty, pluralism, separation of powers and federalism to name just a few.

Several of these ideas are subsumed under the notion, *limited government*. It means that Americans hold to the principle that governments may not do all that they could do, but only those things set forth in a written constitution. Americans consider constitutions to be the written limits upon government, and all American constitutions set forth rights of people that are inalienable: so inherent they can neither be given away by the people nor taken away by government. One of those inherent rights is that each citizen is *equal before the law* and has the right to a fair trial. The right to rule the community rests in the *sovereignty of the people*. All citizens have a right to vote and all can express their own opinion, and pursue their own version of life, liberty and happiness. In doing so, people may form groups—James Madison called them factions—to advance their cause or interests. *Pluralism,* the diversity of interests in society, Madison noted, would be the cause for factions. The multiplicity of interests would preclude a tyrannical majority because each particular faction would be balanced by others (*The Federalist Papers,* 1961, pp. 77-84). The U.S. Constitution helps citizens protect their equality by making key positions of authority elective, which forces those who are elected, especially legislators, to go back regularly to their constituents to renew their popular mandate.

The separation of governing institutions, that which is loosely referred to as *separation of powers,* is an enduring structural and organizational principle. Legislatures, large bicameral bodies of equals, make laws, impose taxes and appropriate funds for spending. Executives in a separate branch oversee the administration of the law and the collection and actual spending of the money. Judges conduct trials under the law, deciding issues between citizens or between the executive branch and citizens. While power is not so clearly separated, the branches and the people who exercise authority in them certainly are. Lawmakers cannot at the same time be judges or officials of the executive branch. Judges may not be fired by executives or legislators. Executives are not directly controlled by legislators or judges. Instead of "separation of power," American constitutions actually authorize power that is shared by separate institutions. This authority is constitutionally assigned to the government's branches, so interaction among them with regard to issues is a major part of politics. At various times sharing power takes form as conflict, bargaining, compromising and trading favors.

American government is characterized not only by its branches, but also by its *federalism.* Ordinarily people distinguish three levels of government: national, state and local. Legally, at least, the distinctions between the national government and the states are clearer than those between states and local governments. The first distinction, national from state, comes historically from the fact that the national government was preceded by the states. The U.S. Constitution asserts that power came from "We the people. . . ." But ratification was made by the states rather than by the people directly or as a whole. The U.S. government has the powers delegated to it, those implied thereby and the powers necessary to implement those delegated powers. States, on the other hand, have all the powers not denied them under the U.S. Constitution or under their own individual state constitutions. Indeed, states have broader general constitutional grants of power than does the national government and have comprehensive authority over local governments. In legal terms, cities, counties, school districts, towns or townships and the like are "creatures of the state" in a manner much different from the relation of states to the national government. For example, Illinois could limit Carbondale and Chicago much more broadly and authoritatively than the national government can limit Illinois, although the Illinois Constitution sets terms for sharing the state's power with local governments in its progressive "home rule" provisions (Art. 7). But the emphasis in intergovernmental relations is not necessarily on limiting power. Often it is on agreeing to arrangements for sharing. So, as noted earlier, politics manifests itself as compromise, exchange of favors and conflict across the levels of government.

The primary legal limits upon Illinois state government generally, and the General Assembly in particular, are contained in the Illinois Constitution. There are also constraints from the U.S. Constitution and laws: Illinois cannot conduct its own foreign policy or mint its own money, interfere in interstate commerce or deny the privileges or immunities of citizens of other states. But these are not highly limiting constraints. In any case, states are used to them. State governments are more sharply limited by their own constitutions. For instance, Article 9, Section 5 of the 1970 Illinois Constitution abolished the tax on the assessed value of personal property (a tax imposed on furniture, automobile and other personal belongings). Previously Illinois' personal property tax was enforced irregularly—collected annually in some of its areas, but not others. Since the adoption and implementation of the 1970 Constitution that tax is no longer constitutional in Illinois.

The state constitution limits taxation, state debts, the use of state funds for sectarian purposes and a variety of other practices. But like the U.S. Constitution, many of the limits on state government are intended to preserve the liberty of citizens from governmental interference. Some rights are traditional, like the right to due process of law in Article 1, Section 2. Others go beyond tradition like the prohibition of discrimination according to sex, in Article 1, Section 18, and the prohibition of discrimination against the handicapped in Article 1, Section 19.

The Direction of Constitutionalism

Illinois has had four constitutions: those of 1818, 1848, 1870 and 1970. Conventions were held in 1862 and 1920-22 at which constitutions were proposed, but the people did not adopt them. The 1870 Constitution reflected an era in which distrust for government was generally high, especially for the legislative branch. The limits placed upon the General Assembly were severe and in the 20th century its representation of the people became increasingly distorted by unequally populated districts.

The 1970 Constitution extended the rights of the people against interference by the state, but it also clarified and increased governmental flexibility generally and that of the General Assembly in particular. The 1970 Constitution provided for a tie breaker to end deadlocks in redistricting.

Article 14, Section 3 gives a very limited opportunity for the people to amend the Illinois constitution by initiative petitions. It allows only changes of "structural and procedural subjects contained in" the legislative article. This limited power, however, permitted a successful petition drive in 1980 that cut the size of the legislature and ended three-member House districts and cumulative voting. But the initiative cannot be used to limit the governor to two terms or to establish merit selection of judges. These and other amendments can only be proposed by the legislature or a state constitutional convention.

The constitution permitted the legislature's sessions to be continuous for two years at a time, as well as allowing continuous operation of its committees. It allowed the legislature to select its own leaders in both chambers. Under the old constitution the lieutenant governor was president of the Senate and could vote as a tie breaker in Senate decision-making, but the 1970 Constitution discontinued that intrusion of the executive into the legislature. The legislature is given increased power and discretion over taxation and state debt. The constitution provides the legislature its own officer, the auditor general, to examine expenditures and the operation of all state agencies to ensure that public funds are spent as the legislature directs. And, while the governor obtained a wider array of veto powers (to be discussed later), overrides were made much easier, both because the legislature operates continuously, and because overrides require only a three-fifths majority instead of the previous two-thirds. Last, the constitution gave local governments a broad grant of power and flexibility in "home rule" provisions. By doing so it removed from legislative consideration a host of local government matters, thus reducing a heavy load of local bills.

The constitution also assures that Illinois legislative processes shall be open to public view. Its formal operations are open, and always have been. But two significant new constitutional requirements are in place. One requires reasonable public notice of all meetings, including those of committees and commissions. Second, not only is there a journal of the legislature's activity describing its bills, amendments, actions and roll call votes, there is also a transcript of the debates which is available to the public. So citizens and journalists have broad access to legislative business both as it happens and after it is over.

The 1970 Constitution enlarged the General Assembly's capacity to govern, while assuring the people that they can monitor its activities and decisions, and even change its structures and procedures by initiating constitutional amendments to the legislative authority. This constitutional authority allows the legislature to be both progressive and responsive.

The Legislature in Relation to the Executive and Administrators

The system of separate institutions with shared powers makes for a rich array of contacts across those jurisdictional lines. The legislature is sometimes referred to as the first branch. In the constitution the legislature and its powers are described first, before those of the executive and judiciary. That preeminence is because of the centrality of the law in all of government organization and action. In Chapter One we mentioned that the laws of Illinois fill four huge volumes. The legislature's bills define the programs that the executive and agencies carry out. They set the taxes; spell out the structure, organization and powers of the agencies; appropriate funds so that government agencies may spend money; define the regulations which police enforce and which serve as the basis for court trials. The laws of the state, therefore, are the written instruments by which state government operates. That means the General Assembly is the central institution of state government and its lawmakers are at the heart of its politics.

Executives and administrators do not feel neutral about legislative matters. To the contrary, our governors and those they appoint as agency administrators to put laws into effect have always had strong feelings about the legislature's work. It is the governor who prepares the annual budget: the entire spending plan for all of state government. The governor speaks for and coordinates requests for new bills that originate in agencies such as the Department of Labor or the Department of Transportation. So the governor wants a great variety of bills to come through the legislature, including appropriations bills which permit expenditures.

Agency heads want things too. The Secretary of the Department of Transportation may want funds to build certain highways. The director of the Department of Conservation may wish to create a new state park. And sometimes those two will disagree about whether a highway should be allowed to go through a particular park. So the specifics of policymaking and administration can make the legislature an administrative battleground. Certainly agency directors keep a careful eye on what bills are before the legislature, and let their preferences on specific bills be known to legislators.

Interaction between legislators and administrators in Illinois has grown substantially in the last twenty years as the legislature has become increasingly interested in oversight. Legislators care how their laws are made operational and want reports from or about the people who are supposed to administer them. These include departmental reports, reports from legislative staff and testimony in committees. Sometimes they make on-site visits to departments and field offices. In addition, legislators have constituents who let them know—often by their complaints—in what manner agencies are putting laws into effect.

A recent innovation is the Joint Committee on Administrative Rules (JCAR). Established in 1977, it is a joint committee of both senators and representatives that has its own professional staff. Its task is to examine and review the administrative rules of all state agencies. JCAR's chief concern is whether or not agency rules are consistent with the authority assigned to it by the legislature. The agency should not go too far in regulation, nor should it fail to carry out the legislature's mandates. Sometimes JCAR has trouble getting administrative cooperation. When that happens, its members can introduce legislation to bring the recalcitrant agency into line.

The Legislature and the Courts

For the most part, relations between the legislature and courts are indirect. The courts do have an influence on law, of course, because judges must apply it in trials. In a tiny proportion of cases the interpretation made by a trial judge is challenged at a higher judicial level. The Illinois Supreme Court usually has the last word on the interpretation of state statutes and in determining the constitutionality of laws. While the courts' powers are significant and broad, most citizens overestimate the degree and frequency with which courts overrule or limit the discretion of legislatures. Moreover, if the legislature disagrees with a particular court's statutory interpretation, it can pass a new law to assert its intentions. Constitutional judgments are more difficult to change but the General Assembly can propose constitutional amendments that require the approval of the voters to become effective.

The legislature has a good deal of discretion in how it touches the courts and judges. The three-layered courts system—trial courts, the appellate division and the Supreme Court—is established in the constitution, along with a basic description of jurisdictions and the rights of the people to appeal its decisions. But much discretion is left to the legislature. The number of appellate judges, judicial circuits (districts) and trial judges is determined "by law," that is, by the legislature. While the legislature cannot reduce salaries of judges, it does determine their salary increases. The legislature also defines the procedures for electing judges. In its authority over criminal law, the legislature decides the seriousness of various kinds of crimes and specifies the punishments. The General Assembly, in short, controls many aspects of the legal environment in which judges and the courts operate.

One other point bears mentioning. Many legislators are lawyers, and some of them aspire to be judges someday. So there is a respectful concern among General Assembly members for the well-being of the courts and judges.

Legislative Structure—Bicameralism

Except for Nebraska, all state legislatures are bicameral: comprised of two chambers, or houses, of nearly equal power. This is a remarkable arrangement that stands in marked contrast to local governments with their unicameral legislative bodies—city councils, county boards, school boards and the like. It is probably a result of tradition, more than anything else. The unicameral Continental Congress was associated with the failure of the Articles of Confederation. The Congress, with its House and Senate, was established in the U.S. Constitution of 1787. In a unique compromise, the Constitution allowed representation of the people apportioned by population in the House, and equal representation of the states in the Senate with members selected by state legislatures. It was expected that the Senate would check and balance possible excesses on the part of the directly elected representatives. This check and balance role is rarely evident in state legislatures; today, no one would seriously argue that state senates are a conservative check on lower houses around the country. But there are real contrasts between the two houses that affect the legislative process. The key differences are between the chambers and the members: the chambers are unequal in size, and the members are unequal in status.

The House is bigger—physically bigger—with a larger chamber crowded with people and desks. Until 1983 there were 177 representatives, a ratio of three representatives for every senator. With this size difference, nearly all aspects of the legislative process in the House were larger, busier and more raucous. There were more bills, more resolutions, more amendments, more roll calls and more time spent on the floor. It was widely believed among House members that they worked harder than senators. It is unquestionably the case that the House was in session, that is, conducting public business on the floor, longer than the Senate. This was largely due to the fact that the larger number of House members introduced more bills.

Although the cutback reformers argued in 1982 that reducing the House from 177 to 118 would cut down House business, there was scant evidence of that in the reduced 83rd General Assembly. By the deadline for bill introduction in April 1983, there were 2,277 bills introduced in the House, compared to 2,012 by the 1981 deadline (Jurgens, 1983, p. 22). In 1985 there were 2,527.

Because the membership of the House is greater than that of the Senate, there is greater anonymity. There are more staff members, more hearings and more issue specialization among legislators. So there is less social and political intimacy among the House members. The very size of the House chamber—86 feet wide—means that members with seats at one side only occasionally cross way over to the other side. The center aisle separates the Democrats from the Republicans.

The higher activity level of the House is evident by its sound level. When the House is in session, it functions amid a low roar, a babble of voices. There is a sound system, of course, and the speaker has control over the microphones. So anyone recognized to speak can be heard. This simply means that members engaged in dozens of conversations around the room talk and laugh at a sound level needed for their conversations. Looking from the gallery, or across the chamber, the observer can only tell who is the recognized speaker by being familiar with names, voices and seat locations. When the dull roar gets too loud, the presiding officer strikes the gavel a few times, and the sound level diminishes for a while. But the buzz gradually picks up again.

By contrast, the Senate is more genteel, quiet and orderly. The dress code is more rigorously followed. None of the men—not even pages—come on the floor without wearing a coat and tie. Behavior is more subdued than in the House. Of course, in the heat of battle tempers do flare and voices rise, but disputes are typically resolved with more grace and courtesy than is typical in the House.

The chambers are nearly equal in powers, with the exception that the Senate must concur in the governor's appointees to positions in the executive branch. Senators do have higher status than representatives, however. The opportunities to become senator are fewer and they serve twice as many constituents. Their terms of office are longer. The movement of legislators from one chamber to the other is almost always from the House to the Senate. In 1982, 22 House incumbents ran for the Senate (13 were winners), but only one senator ran for (and won) a House seat. He was Steven Nash, one of the Chicago regulars who agreed to run to accommodate the changed circumstances in the city because of redistricting and the cutback. A greater proportion of senators are committee chairs or minority spokespersons. Because of the Senate's task of concurring on the governor's appointees, senators have more clout in patronage matters than representatives.

The rivalry between the chambers is usually friendly, and members of the one chamber kid the members of the other about the variations. House members call the Senate the "other" House. Senators refer to the Senate as the "upper" house. House members think that the specialization of labor in their chamber produces better crafted bills than does the Senate. Senators think that in making policy their chamber gives more regard to the "big picture" than the more fractious House. Shortly after assuming the speakership in 1983, Representative Michael Madigan (D-30, Chicago) commented on the meaning of the cutback, and in doing so, commented on bicameralism:

Madigan: I would hope that the House would not become another Senate because, in my experience, many times the Senate as a whole is just too insulated and not as populist as it should be.

Ross: You mean variety of viewpoints?

Madigan: I mean that in the past we always felt that the House was a reservoir of ideas; the Senate is just not as perceptive of new ideas as it should be (Ross, 1983, p. 9).

Two Political Consequences of Bicameralism: Checking Haste and Dividing Power

During the 1970 Illinois Constitutional Convention there was an hour of debate devoted to the proposition that the General Assembly consist of only one chamber. The proponents of unicameralism were granted a chance to make their case. While tradition may have been sufficient to defeat them, Dwight Friedrich, a former senator (and now a House member), offered the following example in support of a bicameral legislature:

> Now, it was said that nothing was ever developed in the committee [Con Con's Legislative Committee] which indicated that one house killed the bad bills of the other. Well, I can tell you that the senate killed a lot of bad house bills, and even once in a while the house killed a bad senate bill. That's not quite so frequent, but it does happen. I want to tell you one case that happened, and this is what can happen. Representative Norman Shade, who is a good friend of mine, when he first came down to Springfield introduced a very bad bill, in my opinion. It had to do with mechanic's liens. Well, Norm Shade was a fine guy and everybody liked him, and nobody ever said anything about the bill. . . . It got over to the Senate Committee on Judiciary. It had a short hearing in which Senator Groen told what a great guy Norm Shade was. It got exactly two votes, which is exactly what it should have gotten in the house. That's one of the finest examples I know of a second house killing a bad bill that came from the first (Sixth Illinois Constitutional Convention, 1972, Vol. 4, p. 2727).

After all were heard, the proposal for a unicameral legislature was defeated 65 to 18.

Many bills get scant attention until after they have passed one house. But the very fact that a bill gets out of its house of origin can generate interest in the press, among various lobby groups and agencies of government. Such interest often stimulates broader consideration of the implications of the proposed law and the resulting responses then get back to the legislators of the second house, who may modify or kill the bill. In a real sense, then, a bicameral legislature is a check against hasty legislation.

Some observers believe bicameralism is a check on any legislation.

Two houses just mean more barriers than one. Therefore two chambers are more conservative—more protective of the *status quo*—than one. That is a very difficult proposition to test. There is no doubt that many bills which pass their house of origin would not make it if first passage was final passage. Sometimes members of one house pass bills to use for negotiating purposes with the other house, for friendship, as the Friedrich example suggests, or for other political and social reasons.

A bicameral legislature constitutes a significant division of power. The power to legislate is extremely comprehensive. It provides the legislature the potential for controlling the elected executives—not just the governor, but also the secretary of state, attorney general, comptroller and treasurer. But the fact that there are two chambers complicates matters immensely. It sets up a natural rivalry between the president of the Senate and the speaker of the House. It creates the possibility that Democrats will hold a majority in one chamber while Republicans hold a majority in the other. (That was the case in the 82nd General Assembly, 1981-82.) Neither chamber can take final action on anything without the concurrence of the other. The division complicates negotiations by the governor, or other executives, but raises the opportunity for the executive to play one off against the other.

It is not so apparent to distant observers of Illinois politics, but is well-known among insiders, that large amounts of legislative effort go into inter-house rivalry and conflict. Elements of the two chambers are constantly in competition and conflict. Sometimes, in fact, chamber loyalty is higher than party loyalty. Even in 1983, when Democrats held a majority in both Houses, Democrats of the two chambers reacted differently to Governor Thompson's tax and budget proposals. Thompson's budget was proposed, and the appropriations bills were introduced, assuming no tax increase. In the Senate, bills with appropriations substantially above the governor's proposed level were moved for higher education. "In so doing, the Senate shifted to the House the onus to bring the higher ed bills in line with the doomsday budget" (Parker, 1984, p. 51). Meanwhile, Speaker Madigan, with the support of the Democratic majority in the House, refused to release the budget bills from committee until a tax revenue plan was agreed to, and the Republican governor had announced his plan for spending. Intercameral competition played a big part in the politics of the 1983 tax increase (see Parker, 1984, Chap. 3).

The competition extends to ideas for bills, hiring staff, controlling office space, overseeing executive agencies and supervising legislative service agencies. Each chamber protects its turf from incursion by the other. Typically, the Senate and senators fear the House and its representatives as the aggressors. Senators, outnumbered two-to-one, want equal representation on joint committees, but fear that even in those circumstances the representatives have more time to devote to their duties than senators, and will eventually capture control. Moreover, there is the persistent suspicion among senators that representatives are plotting to move up into the Senate at the first opportunity. In fact, neither fear is unfounded. The result of this competition is that the two chambers work separately on most policy questions. Because the Senate and senators feel a higher status, it is they who tend to be aloof, and to distance themselves from the House.

One aspect of bicameralism which may be of dubious value could be remedied by a unicameral structure. In the nation and the states concern is commonly expressed that the chief executive is "too strong." The legislature is the governor's main rival and the strongest check on executive power. An undivided legislature could devote energies now spent in intramural rivalry on the contest with the chief executive. Moreover, a unicameral legislature would have a single head, a leader who could speak on behalf of the entire legislature concerning the whole range of state budget and policy issues.

But the bicameral form has had remarkable resilience in Illinois and the other states. Although not beyond the reach of constitutional change, there is no apparent popular pressure for a unicameral legislature. The bicameral arrangement means that passing bills and appropriations is beyond the control of any single legislator. Illinois summitry takes an obvious form: the governor calls together the four party leaders from the two chambers for hard bargaining on issues of statewide significance.

BILLS, COMMITTEES AND THE BILL PROCESS

The General Assembly majors in handling bills. There are thousands of bills—most are only a couple of pages long, but others are more than twenty pages in length. Appendix B shows a specific example and indicates characteristics of form. It is important to know that while lawmakers are receptive to bill ideas from all sorts of people, it is only the lawmakers who may introduce bills and amendments to bills. That is an absolute monopoly. The governor, bureaucrats and the lobbyists may not introduce bills or amendments. To do so, they must work with lawmakers.

Bills, Amendments and Resolutions

Ideas for bills come from a variety of places. A legislator may have an idea to solve a particular problem. Constituents often write their legislator explaining some concern, and end by saying literally, or in effect, "There ought to be a law to . . . ." It is a regular part of a lobbyist's job to think about legislation that benefits his or her interest group—the realtors, the chiropractors, the bird lovers or the people on public assistance. Agency administrators are frequently sources for bill ideas.

So too are editors of newspapers and various policy experts around the state.

Bill proposals to lawmakers vary in the degree of their refinement. Constituents and newspaper editors are usually the source of basic ideas for bills, not for their specific legislative language. Agencies and interest group lobbyists, on the other hand, often propose very specific terminology. Either way, the lawmakers have access to professional assistance for turning rough ideas or specific legal language into a properly formulated bill. The Legislative Reference Bureau (LRB) has a professional staff of legal experts who draft bills. It is a technical requirement of the General Assembly that a bill may not be introduced until its legal form has been approved by the LRB. On the other hand, LRB in no way limits the contents of bills. If a lawmaker asks for a bill to change the executive branch by establishing three lieutenant governorships, the LRB director would doubtless tell the member that such a bill, if enacted, would be declared unconstitutional upon challenge in the courts. Nonetheless, if the member insisted on having such a bill, LRB would draft it. As a staff agency, the LRB serves, but does not limit, the actions of members.

Amendments for bills are handled very much like bills. Members ask LRB to draft them. Many are very brief, but some constitute a substantial rewriting of a bill. Amendments too may only be introduced by lawmakers. Obviously, amendments are meant to change the substance and effect of a bill; often, therefore, the sponsor of an amendment may be an opponent of the sponsor of the bill to be amended. Because LRB does the drafting for both sponsors, it is important that its work be professionally competent, and unbiased.

A great many, probably most, amendments are "friendly." That is, they make a change in a bill that eliminates a loophole, or sharpens its effectiveness. Often, in fact, the sponsor of a bill later proposes amendments to remedy problems noted by others after the bill is introduced. Acting on bills and amendments is the primary work of the legislative process.

Lawmakers also deal with resolutions. Resolutions do not have the authority of the law. There are House, Senate and joint resolutions. Some of them are for internal purposes, such as to set the time and date of adjournment or to change the rules of procedure. A few are earnest "memorials" or messages to public officials not under the legislature's control—such as the president or Congress. Constitutional amendments, both for the state or the United States, are handled as joint resolutions. But the great bulk of resolutions are congratulations or commendations to people and organizations. Usually they are non-controversial and symbolic. For example, the state champion basketball teams usually visit the legislature and go home with both House and Senate resolutions marking their accomplishments.

Types of Bills

The constitution distinguishes three types of bills: revisory, appropriations and substantive. *Revisory* bills are a special class because they are exempt from the general rule that a bill must deal with a single subject. Revisory bills are not controversial and do not initiate a policy change. Ordinarily, they make technical corrections throughout the state statutes. For example, if an agency is given new responsibilities and its name is changed, a bill to change all statutory references to reflect the new name can be done with a single revisory bill.

"Money is the critical ingredient of government, largely determining whether abstract policies get translated into concrete services and action. In so far as the legislature can exercise control over the flow of funds, which come mainly from the taxpayers and go mainly to the departments and agencies of government and to the state's localities, it exercises power" (Rosenthal, 1981, p. 285). The General Assembly spends money with *appropriations* bills, which specify the dollar amounts that may be spent by agencies. These bills do not contain "substantive language"; that is, they have no statutory content. This prevents appropriations bills from being used as vehicles for policy goals other than spending authorizations. Although the governor proposes a comprehensive budget each year for state spending (to be discussed in Chapter Eight), the amounts recommended for various agencies are put into specific appropriations bills with legislative sponsors. Of course, lawmakers also propose their own spending ideas in appropriations bills, or they may propose amendments to the governor's recommendations. These bills and amendments constitute a major part of the legislative task each year.

Most bills are *substantive:* they are written provisions that spell out the regulations of the state over its people and organizations. There are three kinds of substantive action. The first is a new law. It does something not previously provided for in the state's statutes. Consider a hypothetical example. At this writing there is no such organization as the Illinois Authority Commission on Laser Research Regulation. But a bill to establish one, give it a purpose and specify its structure and organization could be written and passed. Every session legislators propose such new laws.

Most substantive bills amend existing statutes. Hundreds of bills are proposed, for example, to "amend the Revenue Act" or the Pension Code, the Liquor Control Act or the thousands of other acts already on the books. These bills to amend may completely change the existing act, or just make a slight revision.

Another kind of substantive bill is a *repealer.* To repeal simply means wipe out a previously existing provision of the statutes. Horse racing, which is legal in Illinois under the provisions of the Horse Racing Act, could be made illegal by a repeal of the existing act. A bill to repeal simply specifies the existing acts or sections thereof to be eliminated, and the date when the repeal becomes effective.

Substantive Bills by Difficulty

Bills vary according to difficulty in winning passage. So far we have referred to types of bills in a technical sense. Perhaps a more useful typology, but one that is not easy to define exactly, sorts bills into major bills, middling bills and assembly line bills.

Major bills are those that make major changes in the existing law. Some are new acts, but many are amendatory bills that are important though brief. Typically, major bills are controversial. Because they are far-reaching, such bills provoke diverse and strong opinions among people and organizations around the state. They get continuing attention in the media. Examples are: income tax increase, changing unemployment benefits, changing the school aid formula, making seat belts mandatory, changing the Regional Transportation Authority and the Chicago Transit Authority (RTA-CTA), increasing controls on hazardous waste, substantially changing the criminal code or establishing an elected commission to review utility rates. Legislative leaders take sides, as does the governor on such important bills. Usually the sponsors of such bills are highly uncertain about whether or not the bills will pass, knowing only they are in for a long fight. Sometimes there are two or more basic versions of the bill, introduced by competing sponsors. The two political parties may present rival views on the issue, or there may be competing bills from regional interests, such as Cook County versus downstate.

Assembly line bills are the other extreme. A great many bills make minor or technical changes to existing laws, or formalize a practice which has been going on in an agency for a long time. These may include member proposals to carry out a pet project in the home district, or make a change in statutes to benefit a state agency or a local unit of government. Such bills are highly specific, and written to satisfy a particular need without offending other interests. The following paraphrase of a bill summary is an illustration: "Amends various Acts regarding vandalism of traffic control signs, devices, structures and related subjects."

Between these two extremes are the middling bills. They may set up or change an agency program without basically changing the agency. Middling bills are significant enough in effect to provoke both support and opposition from the public and organized groups, but are not likely to create substantial conflict between the governor and legislative leaders.

There may be partisan bias to the issue, but chances are there is support and opposition from both parties. Media attention will be occasional or brief. Examples include a bill to get a flood control project approved, to change regulations over financial institutions (banks, savings and loan, credit unions), to give senior citizen exemptions from certain fees and costs of state services, to regulate the use of asbestos in building materials, to enlarge the enterprise zone program for depressed areas, to end mandated physical education in schools. A sponsor cannot be sure such a bill will pass; in fact, when introducing the bill, the sponsor may not be certain who all the potential supporters and opponents will be, or how hard they will fight. But only a small percentage of legislators will pay much attention.

The Context of Committees

As the backs on a football team depend on their blockers to make scoring possible, so theoretically, at least, legislatures depend on their committees to sift, screen, revise, refine, weed, prune, shape, develop, dismiss, amend, gut, chop and rewrite bills. Because the Senate has 59 members and the House has 118, not everyone can have a say on every bill. The standard method for a large group of people to efficiently handle its business on many matters is to divide into smaller work groups with specific responsibilities. For legislatures, that means committees.

Illinois legislative committees come in three kinds. There are standing, select and service committees. Standing and select committees deal with bills. Service committees handle matters of internal operation in each chamber. During the 84th General Assembly the House had 24 standing committees, six select committees and two service committees. The Senate had 17 standing committees and three service committees. The House had increased the number of its standing committees by four over the 83rd General Assembly. The Senate left its standing committees unchanged. The names of the committees appear in Figure 7:1. Each house establishes its own committee structure for every General Assembly. But there is a good deal of carry-over from one biennium to another. The standing committees "stand" for the two-year term, and their main job is to hold hearings and make recommendations to the chamber on each bill assigned to them.

In both the Senate and the House one of the service committees is the rules committee. Each of the rules committees considers the body of rules by which its chamber operates. Each can recommend additions, changes and deletions. Ordinarily a rules committee is not busy but occasionally "the rules" are controversial. For example, after the 1970 Constitution, House and Senate rules have required a three-fifths majority

SENATE 31/28*		HOUSE 67/51*	
Agriculture, Conservation & Energy	8/5	Agriculture	9/7
Appropriations I	12/9	Appropriations I	15/12
Appropriations II	12/9	Appropriations II	12/9
Education — Elementary & Secondary	10/9	Cities and Villages	8/6
Education — Higher	6/4	Consumer Protection	9/7
Elections and Reapportionment	6/4	Counties and Townships	8/6
Executive	11/8	Elections	10/8
Executive Appointments, Veterans Affairs		Elementary and Secondary	
and Administration	10/7	Education	12/10
Finance and Credit Regulations	8/5	Energy, Environment and Natural	
Insurance, Pensions and Licensed		Resources	8/6
Activities	7/4	Executive	9/7
Judiciary I	6/4	Financial Institutions	12/9
Judiciary II	7/4	Higher Education	11/8
Labor and Commerce	6/4	Human Services	8/6
Local Government	7/4	Insurance	9/7
Public Health, Welfare and		Judiciary I	9/7
Corrections	7/4	Judiciary II	8/6
Revenue	7/4	Labor and Commerce	14/11
Transporation	7/4	Personnel and Pensions	4/3
		Public Utilities	6/4
(Service Committees)		Registration and Regulation	7/5
Committee on Assignment of Bills	2/1	Revenue	9/7
Committee on Committees	6/4	State Government Administration and	
Rules	6/4	Regulatory Review	11/9
		Transportation and Motor Vehicles	11/9
		Urban Redevelopment	5/4
		(Select Committees)	
		Aging	9/7
		Economic Development	9/7
		Local School District Reorganization	7/5
		Small Business	11/9
		Veterans' Affairs	5/4
		World's Fair 1992	12/9
		(Service Committees)	
		Assignment	2/1
		Rules	11/7

*Numbers indicate party balance: Democrat/Republican.

Figure 7:1   Standing Committees: 84th General Assembly

to approve amendments to the U.S. Constitution. The Equal Rights Amendment to the U.S. Constitution was considered at various times in the House and Senate, usually with majority support, but never with a three-fifths in both chambers in the same year. The three-fifths rule became an issue in both chambers. By the beginning of the 83rd General Assembly, after the time for ratification of ERA had expired, the House changed its rule on consideration of amendments to the U.S. Constitution, and only a constitutional majority is needed there to ratify (60 votes instead of 71). The Senate has continued to require three-fifths. The rules committee also considers motions to change rules and it can exempt bills from certain procedural deadlines. The party leaders in each house serve on the rules committee and maintain a system of rules that protect leadership control over internal processes in both chambers.

The Senate Rules Committee, in addition to the duties mentioned, has a traffic cop task in the second year of each biennium. A key provision in Rule 5 says that in that year all bills introduced in the Senate during the regular session shall be referred to the rules committee. The practice of the rules committee is to refer to the Senate Committee on Assignment of Bills only appropriation bills implementing the budget, administration bills and bills deemed by that committee to be of an emergency nature, or to be of substantial importance to the operation of government. The makeup of the rules committee, typically consisting of six leaders from the majority and four from the minority, simply means that Senate leaders can control what bills will receive committee attention in the second year of the biennium.

In both chambers the committees on assignment decide which standing and select committees get what bills. Jurisdictions for the committees that handle bills are not formal, not highly detailed in the rules; although the revenue and appropriations jurisdictions are specifically mentioned there. Nearly all the bill referrals made to standing and select committees by the committees on assignment are routinely made without questions or disagreement. In occasional cases, the sponsor of a bill may request that a bill be re-referred if that sponsor feels that his/her bill has been sent to an inappropriate or unfriendly committee. The assignment committees usually respect the sponsor's wishes, but because the assignment committees are arms of the majority leadership, occasionally assignments are made over the objections of a sponsor in order to honor the wishes of the speaker of the House or the president of the Senate. Assignments can be appealed to a majority decision in either chamber, but that is a step that is rarely taken and that almost never succeeds.

The Senate has a third service committee called the committee on committees. It has ten members, six from the majority and four from the minority. It formally appoints senators to their standing committee assignments. Usually the leaders of both parties serve on this committee, and in practice each party assigns its own members to the standing committee. In the House there is no committee on committees. The rules authorize the speaker and the majority leader to make all committee assignments, each for his or her own party.

The House select committees are a rather new phenomenon. The House rules of the 83rd General Assembly say, "For purposes of these rules, the Select Committees shall be treated as standing committees"

(*Handbook*, 1985, Rule 16C, p. 196). It appears that they consider relatively narrow or short-term problems. For example, in 1985 there was a World's Fair Committee. Its job disappeared when the legislature would not fund further planning for the Fair. The permanence and significance of select committees remains to be seen. The Senate does not have any select committees.

The size of standing committees and party ratio of members is a determination of the party leaders, approved by a majority of the membership in each house. The key rule of practice is that the majority party has a majority on every committee if it wishes. House rules limit the total membership of committees to no more than 35 members, but that rule, carried over from the 177-member chamber, is not a significant limit. The Senate has no limit. For the 84th General Assembly the largest House committee, Appropriations I, had 27 members and the smallest, Personnel and Pensions, had seven. Senate committees varied in membership from 10 to 21 members.

Party ratios in committees roughly reflect the party balance in each chamber (see Figure 7:1). For the 84th General Assembly, Democrats in the Senate outnumbered Republicans 31-28, a ratio of about 10-to-9. Actual committee membership ranged from 12-9 (Democrat-Republican) down to six-four. Democrats maintained a two or three member advantage on all standing committees. In the House, Democrats controlled 67-51, a four-to-three ratio. The members on standing committees varied from 15-12 down to four-three.

The party balance in committees is a further instrument of party control of the chamber. Chamber organization and rules are determined by majority vote. A key meaning of "party control" is that the majority party has the votes to establish the rules and the committees. By setting committee balances and assigning members, the majority assures itself enough votes on each committee to control the outcome of all committee actions.

The typical number of committee assignments, including select committees, for House members is five. Nearly all senators have four. Recent changes have slightly reduced the average number for senators, while the Cutback, combined with added House select committees, have raised the number of committee assignments for House members. Almost 20 percent of the House assignments, however, are to select committees whose work load is relatively low.

Committee Assignments

Consistent with the idea of party balances, assignments to committees are a partisan matter. The Democratic and Republican leadership teams in each chamber have control over which members are assigned to what committees. Committee assignments reflect leader discretion. Put differently, part of the attraction for seeking to be a party leader is to obtain control over committees and committee assignments. Committee assignments, including appointments as chair or vice chair (majority) and minority spokesman, can be rewards or punishments for previous party loyalty or, following contests for the party leader positions, consequences for being on the winning or losing side.

While partisanship and party infighting affect particular committee appointments, there is a basic routine that takes place at the beginning of each new General Assembly after the leadership teams are in place. Members fill out a request listing their committee preferences. In the House, the speaker formally makes committee assignments for the majority party and the minority leader for minority party members. The leaders determine assignments, taking into account their own needs to retain party control on the one hand, while satisfying member preferences on the other. Making committee assignments is a big job. In the 84th General Assembly the House established 397 positions on its standing committees, with an additional 94 more on the select committees, for a total of 411. The majority Democrats made 277 assignments to its 67 members, leaving the minority Republicans with 214 for its 51 members.

As noted earlier, Senate rules formally provide for a committee on committees to make assignments of members to standing committees. Although the committee on committees (itself counted among the service committees) consists of six members from the majority and four from the minority elected by the Senate, it is the leaders who are elected to the committee on committees. After the Senate determines who shall be president of the Senate and the minority chooses the minority leader, the assistant leaders are named and each side slates its choices on the committee on committees. The outcome is like that in the House, and the Senate party leaders control assignments. The Senate task is not quite as big. In the 84th General Assembly, 227 standing committee positions were assigned to 59 Senators, 137 parcelled among 31 in the Democratic majority, and 90 apportioned to 28 Republicans.

In both chambers member committee preferences vary a great deal. Some lawmakers want to be in on the action of the money committees—appropriations or revenue. But, as noted in Chapter Five, members come from a variety of backgrounds and have varied previous experience. A member with business experience in insurance might consider an assignment to an education committee to be a dreadful assignment, while a slot in the insurance committee would be perfect. On the other hand a former school teacher would find the education assignment very attractive, while insurance would be a bore. For most legislators the House Select Committee on Veterans' Affairs would be considered a worthless assignment,

Sidelight on Bill Screening by the Illinois General Assembly

The first comprehensive study of the Illinois General Assembly, written by Steiner and Gove (1960), pointed out the deficiencies and weaknesses of the legislature's committee system. The data presented here are drawn from recent research by Everson (1984).

An effective committee system is expected to do several things:

- handle all bills — a bill should not be allowed to bypass the committees;
- prevent bad bills from getting to the floor;
- develop, amend and shape legislation into effective bills for floor consideration;
- obtain the respect of the other members, so that overturning the committee's bills will occur only rarely;
- anticipate policy needs and problems rather than just react to bills after introduction.

While bills no longer bypass the committees, the basic criticism of General Assembly committees is that they let too many bills get to the floor. The committees do too little shaping of legislation, and they rarely anticipate future needs.

Nonetheless, Illinois committees are changing and gradually showing increasing marks of effectiveness. Table 1 shows that the percentage of bills getting "do pass" and "do pass as amended" recommendations has been going down over time, especially in the House.

Table 2 shows that *of the bills acted on,* very large percentages are recommended favorably. Few bills are killed outright; those not acted on are simply held in committee.

The shaping function of committees can be inferred from Table 3. The statistics vary from year to year, but about a third of the bills that are approved in committee are recommended with amendments. Nonetheless, many of those amendments were made by the sponsors, not imposed by the committees.

The numbers help to describe the general picture. The committees do some filtering and shaping, but not a great deal. Some committees, particularly the money committees, do more than others. But the committee system does not infringe very much on the prerogatives of sponsors, who often argue with committees, not about the merits of a bill, but about their "right" to have their bill heard by the "whole house." The very crush of bills that get to the floor helps to insure the power of the party leaders, especially the majority leaders, to manage members by using their power to hold bills hostage and work out exchanges with the minority, the other house and the governor.

Table 1   Bill Screening: Average percentage of bills reported favorably from committee,* 1960s to 1980s

Decade	House	Senate
1960s	81	83
1970s	63	62
1980s (1981-1983)	46	65

*The percentages are total bills sent to committee divided by bills receiving "do pass" and "do pass as amended" recommendations for the various sessions of the decades.

Table 2   Action on bills: Percentage of favorable committee action, 1979-1982

Year	Number of bills acted on in committee	Number reported favorably	Percent
1979			
House	2,615	2,084	77
Senate	1,639	1,487	90
1981			
House	2,162	1,481	70
Senate	1,564	1,483	95
1983			
House	1,633	1,192	73
Senate	1,544	1,523	98

Table 3   Shaping legislation: Bills approved and amended in committee

Year	Total bills approved in committee		Total bills voted "do pass as amended" in committee		Percentage amended	
	House	Senate	House	Senate	House	Senate
1979	2,004	1,487	782	449	39	30
1981	1,481	1,483	584	576	39	39
1983	1,192	1,523	423	402	36	26

but taking care of veterans' legislation was Representative Lawrence DiPrima's primary concern from the time he was first elected to the General Assembly in 1962 until he retired in 1985. Often members seek positions that will help them get reelected. Rural legislators seek the Agriculture Committee while those from the inner city may want Human Services or Urban Redevelopment. So tastes clearly vary a great deal among members about what constitutes a good assignment.

Moreover, committees change in their importance over time. The House Public Utilities Committee has, in years past, been thought of as a dull and minor committee. But the energy crisis and rocketing utility rates has made it the focus for controversial legislation. The House Insurance Committee was recently the site of controversy when efforts were made to resolve the insurance liability crisis. However when these issues decline in importance, the committee's activities become more humdrum.

Partisan Committees

Some committees are important as arenas for partisan conflict, and party leaders are especially careful to put dependable loyalists on them. One is the labor and commerce committee. Both chambers have such a committee, and it often pits the Democrats, as spokesmen for unions and working class interests, against Republicans, advocates for business interests and a management point of view. Another is the elections committee (called elections and reapportionment in the Senate). Because statewide elections are close in Illinois, and each party has regions of relative strength and weakness, any changes in election rules are viewed from a partisan perspective. Not only that, Illinois partisans believe in party organization, so both Republicans and Democrats are wary about do-gooders and advocates of nonpartisanship trying to "reform" the electoral process.

A third pair of partisan committees are the executive committees, one for each chamber. This title does not limit them to matters having to do with the governor or any of the other executives elected statewide. Each is better understood as an all-purpose partisan committee. For example, a bill to change the governance of the O'Hare International Airport in Chicago would likely go to the executive committee. O'Hare Airport is part of Chicago's turf, thus its governance could be changed only with the willing consent of the Chicago Regular Democrats. But O'Hare's clientele is especially the suburban professionals who live around the city, whose residence patterns and land values are affected by the airport—and that is suburban Republican turf. So any tinkering with the airport governance would probably be handled in the executive committees, not the House and Senate transportation committees, which might otherwise be expected to have such jurisdiction.

Finally, the appropriations and revenue committees are strongly partisan. This is not meant to suggest that these committees never act unanimously or with bipartisan majorities. More often than not there is bipartisan cooperation. Rather, it is important to understand that state spending priorities, and restraints on spending, are important party issues. The appropriations committees, therefore, are arenas for such conflict. Similarly, the revenue committee deals with tax legislation—who shall pay, how much and with what loopholes. In recent years, there have been two appropriations committees in each chamber, named Appropriations I and Appropriations II. Each chamber has a single revenue committee. Money issues are the basic stuff of partisanship. As a result, party leaders usually assign to such committees partisans who know and will speak for party positions on spending and taxation.

In general, the other standing committees are less partisan. Again, this is a matter of degree, and a partisan wrangle can easily break out on issues related to agriculture, banking, the environment, or matters handled in other committees. But expectations about partisanship are lower in these standing committees.

How a Bill becomes a Law in Illinois

At first glance (see Figure 7:2), the process appears to be beyond comprehension. It is not, and hundreds of bills move through the process every biennium. This figure was prepared by the General Assembly's Legislative Research Unit, and it accurately indicates the decision points and the procedural options. We will explain key points on the well-traveled route that bills follow, but will not go into detail about all the many possible parliamentary problems which a bill can face. Note that Figure 7:2 is divided into two sides, "First House" and "Second House," not House and Senate. Procedures are the same, but at any given time political considerations may be very different. We will limit discussion in this chapter to the steps that are necessary before the bill goes to the governor.

1. *First Reading and Committee.* It is important to understand that bills "belong" to their sponsors in Illinois. Bills don't pass unless a legislator "carries" them. First the sponsor carries an idea for a law to the Legislative Reference Bureau to be drafted. The sponsor files the bill with the clerk of the House or secretary of the Senate and the bill is "read the first time"; in fact, only the title is read, i.e., "An Act to authorize police officers to organize and bargain collectively with their public employers." The bill is printed and goes to the committee on assignment, and it is assigned to a standing committee. Typically the sponsor knows where a bill will be assigned, but sometimes this is fuzzy. When sponsors are unhappy with assignments, they can request a different one, and may or may not get it.

Once a bill is referred to a committee, it is on the committee's calendar. Partisan staffs for the majority and the minority each prepare a written analysis of the bill (see Chapter Six). There are deadlines for committee action that must be respected, but a bill is not "heard" until the sponsor asks for the hearing. It is up to the sponsor to bring in witnesses or information about the bill. In the meantime, lobbyists and those interested in the bill may contact the sponsor indicating support, opposition or the desire for amendments. Committees have regularly scheduled meeting times, so when the sponsor wants his/her bill "called," the sponsor must notify the chair of the committee several days in advance of the meeting. During the committee meetings the chair calls the bill, and the sponsor has the opportunity to speak in behalf of the bill. Sometimes the sponsor has witnesses who advocate the bill's benefits. Opponents may speak too. Anyone may fill out a "witness slip," indicating a desire to testify. Lobbyists often fill them out simply to indicate whether they are for a bill or opposed to it. At the end of this consideration, which may take two minutes or two hours, the committee usually acts on any proposed amendments and a "do pass" motion. Consideration is usually brief, and on assembly line bills, the chair may jocularly warn a sponsor, "The less you say, the more votes your bill will get." That message just means, "Don't waste our time and we will reward you with a 'do pass' motion."

Frequently, a sponsor's presentation will provoke questions about the effects of a bill. If a sponsor does not know the answers or the answers are unsatisfactory to the questioners, the committee gets uncomfortable. A savvy sponsor then asks that the committee "hold the bill," i.e., not act for or against it. Responsibility rests with the sponsor to iron out the problems and have that bill "called" again later. Committees rarely vote a "do not pass" motion; but it does occur when an insistent sponsor presses for a bill which most members clearly oppose.

Bills of middling importance get more committee attention than assembly line bills. The sponsor takes the initiative, explaining the bill and bringing witnesses. Often the sponsor has done a great deal of work on the bill, including the cultivation of lobbyists favoring or opposing the bill. Lobbyists often negotiate with the sponsor concerning amendments before the bill is heard in committee. If the sponsor is willing to accept the amendments, the lobbyists then pledge their support for the bill.

When a middling bill is called in committee it is common for the sponsor to immediately move the adoption of the amendments previously agreed to with lobbyists. Committees routinely approve these. The bill is heard, the sponsor explaining and defending the bill as amended. Opponents may appear, with amendments of their own, or merely to seek defeat of the bill. If the sponsor fears defeat, or wishes the bill to be further amended, negotiations may take place then and there. Sometimes

HOW A BILL BECOMES LAW IN ILLINOIS

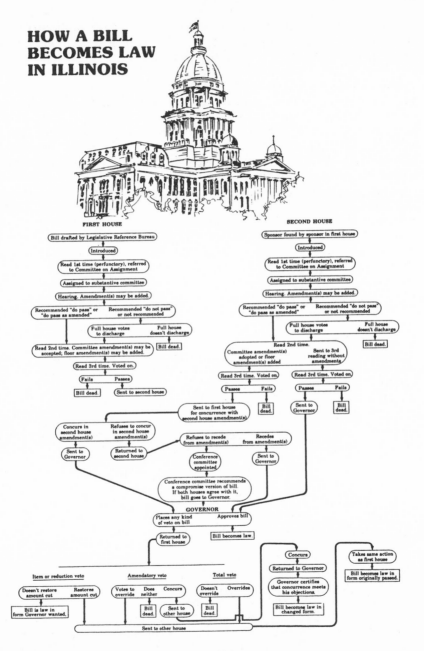

FIRST HOUSE

Bill drafted by Legislative Reference Bureau

Introduced

Read 1st time (perfunctory), referred to Committee on Assignment

Assigned to substantive committee

Hearing. Amendment(s) may be added.

Recommended "do pass" or "do pass as amended" / Recommended "do not pass" or not recommended

Full house votes to discharge / Full house doesn't discharge

Read 2nd time. Committee amendment(s) may be accepted; floor amendment(s) may be added. / Bill dead.

Read 3rd time. Voted on.

Fails / Passes

Bill dead. / Sent to second house

SECOND HOUSE

Sponsor found by sponsor in first house

Introduced

Read 1st time (perfunctory), referred to Committee on Assignment

Assigned to substantive committee

Hearing. Amendment(s) may be added.

Recommended "do pass" or "do pass as amended" / Recommended "do not pass" or not recommended

Full house votes to discharge / Full house doesn't discharge

Read 2nd time.

Committee amendment(s) adopted or floor amendment(s) added / Sent to 3rd reading without amendments

Bill dead.

Read 3rd time. Voted on. / Read 3rd time. Voted on.

Passes / Fails / Passes / Fails

Sent to first house for concurrence with second house amendment(s)

Bill dead. / Sent to Governor / Bill dead.

Concurs in second house amendment(s) / Refuses to concur in second house amendment(s)

Sent to Governor / Returned to second house

Refuses to recede from amendment(s) / Recedes from amendment(s)

Conference committee appointed / Sent to Governor

Conference committee recommends a compromise version of bill. If both houses agree with it, bill goes to Governor.

GOVERNOR

Places any kind of veto on bill / Approves bill

Returned to first house / Bill becomes law.

Concurs / Takes same action as first house

Returned to Governor / Bill becomes law in form originally passed.

Governor certifies that concurrence meets his objections.

Item or reduction veto / Amendatory veto / Total veto

Doesn't restore amount cut / Restores amount cut / Votes to override / Does neither / Concurs / Doesn't override / Overrides

Bill is law in form Governor wanted. / Bill dead. / Sent to other house / Bill dead.

Bill becomes law in changed form.

Sent to other house

Reprinted by permission of the Legislative Research Unit

the bill is held, and the sponsor negotiates outside the committee with opponents. Occasionally, amendments are voted onto the bill contrary to the sponsor's wishes. Most bills are reported "do pass" or "do pass as amended" by the committee; sometimes no action is taken and they are simply held in committee; rarely are they recommended "do not pass." Legislator reciprocity is a common courtesy: if a member insists on getting a bill to the floor for consideration, it will be voted "do pass" or "do pass as amended" even by committee legislators who will later vote against it on the floor. This norm of reciprocity means that legislative committees in Illinois are not always effective at sifting, screening and refining bills.

Major bills are not necessarily treated differently in committee, but how things will turn out is less predictable. Major bills are sponsored by party leaders or lawmakers who are in their third, or higher, biennium of service. The hearing goes easily if there is bipartisan agreement on the substance of the bill by the leadership. Then, for example, the speaker and the minority leader may personally testify for the bill. If the parties disagree, the majority can always get its version out of committee. Sometimes the majority lets the minority get its bills out. Sometimes it does not. The rival leadership teams "play games" with one another on such matters, and hearings do not always reveal the reasons for their tactics.

Depending on what is at stake, and what interests are involved, hearings on major bills can be used to get public attention for a point of view. Lobbyists for major groups may testify at length before a committee even when they know that no one's vote will change. For instance, on a bill for a Citizens Utility Board (CUB), utilities lobbyists for natural gas and electric power companies knew they could not stop the bill in committee. But they could not silently accept the blame for rising utility rates, so they stated their case, hoping at least for some newspaper coverage of their point of view.

Few bills are overtly killed in committee. This is in contrast with Congress, which kills most bills in committee. In the legislature most are reported to the floor "do pass" or "do pass as amended." Less than one in 10 bills is recommended "do not pass." Typical committee deaths occur in two ways. One is when the sponsor kills his/her own bill. If, after the bill is referred to a committee, the sponsor does not request a hearing and action, the bill simply dies at the deadline for reporting of bills from committee. Such quiet and inconspicuous deaths are routine. The second is when bills are "held" in committee, or not voted out with a recommendation "do pass" or "do not pass." In the House the "held" bills die on the committee's deadline for reporting bills. In the Senate such bills are reported "without recommendation," and "tabled" without ever actually being voted down. Such a death usually means the sponsor could not get enough votes to get the bill out, or would not agree to amendments desired by others. In the House a sponsor may ask that the bill be put on the committee's "interim study calendar." That is death with dignity. Perhaps, in fact, study will occur, but usually not. But such placement means that the bill can be carried over from the first to the second year of the biennium.

One more point: although the rules provide that committees have the right to write, or rewrite bills, thereby making the bills the product of the whole committee, it is rarely done. Bills belong to individual sponsors. Committees help sponsors improve bills, but committee members assume relatively little collective responsibility at the floor consideration stage for the bills that they recommended "do pass" in committee.

2. *Floor consideration in the First House—Second and Third Reading.* Each chamber gives a bill three readings. The first automatically follows introduction. The second comes after a "do pass" recommendation from a committee. The bill is put on the second-reading calendar of the house. Second reading is the amendment stage, and the amendment stage only. On an ordinary legislative day there is a long list of bills on the calendar for second reading. The presiding officer proceeds down the list of bills. If the sponsor is willing to defend his/her bill, it is called for consideration of amendments. If the sponsor is not ready, or not present, the bill is passed over, but it stays on the calendar for second reading.

In the House, only amendments that have been filed with the clerk, printed and distributed to every member, may be acted on. In the Senate amendments need not be printed in advance unless requested by five or more senators. Committee amendments added in the Senate must be adopted on the floor. Routinely that is done by voice vote, but on the request of two members is done by roll call. In the House amendments adopted in committee may be challenged and knocked off the bill at second reading, but failing that committee amendments are part of the bill.

In both houses after committee amendments have been handled, amendments may be offered from the floor. Often small refinements are made via amendment by the bill's sponsor. These are invariably adopted with little controversy by a voice vote. Sometimes amendments offer substantial changes to a bill. The sponsor of the amendment explains it and appeals for support. Other members are recognized to oppose, or ask questions. If controversy persists, a member may "move the previous question," a parliamentary action that can cut off debate on the amendment. This parliamentary move cannot be debated. If adopted by a two-thirds vote, the sponsor of the amendment gets to make closing remarks and the amendment is voted on. A majority present and voting is necessary to adopt an amendment. The vote may be by voice. But if the outcome is in doubt, or several members request it, the vote is taken on the electronic voting machine. Such record roll calls are recorded in the journals of each house. When all amendments are disposed of, the bill is considered to have been read the second time and is ordered to third reading by the presiding officer.

The consideration at third reading is to decide only on passage of the bill as amended. On third reading no amendments are allowed. It must take place at least one legislative day after second reading. The sponsor of the bill is recognized to present its contents and argue for its passage. For the assembly line bills, discussion may go very quickly. For middling or major bills, it may be an occasion for sharp debate, but it is unusual for such debate to consume as much as an hour. The time limit on each member is ten minutes in the House, and five in the Senate. It is rare for House members to press the time limit, and unusual for a dozen or more members to take part in debate on a particular bill. The Senate, in contrast to its national counterpart, is not a place of unlimited debate. Its actions are even more brisk than in the Illinois House.

Some aspects of the Illinois bill process are of particular interest. Sponsors vary in their skill at presenting bills. Assembly line bills will likely pass unless the sponsor botches the presentation—shows him/herself unable to make clear that the bill "merely" solves an existing problem in the law, but doesn't affect other seemingly related matters. This occasionally happens when a sponsor explains matters in too much detail, provoking someone to ask questions which the sponsor cannot answer. A sponsor with a clear, crisp explanation of what the bill will and will not do has an excellent chance of getting his/her assembly line bill passed.

On middling matters a good presentation by the sponsor is crucial. The sponsor needs to convince the members that most segments of the population (farmers, coal miners, elderly, etc.) will benefit, or at least not be hurt by the bill. Often middling bills, such as a bill to change required contents in graded milk, may pit dairy farmer profits and improved product quality against consumer and retailer desire for low prices. Different legislators will support or oppose different facets of the bill. Debate may last an hour while questioners note the implications of the bill's various provisions. If too many doubts are raised by the time of the roll call, the needed 60 (House) or 30 (Senate) yes votes for the required constitutional majority may not be there to pass the bill.

While voting is still open—the presiding officer intones, "Have all voted who wish? Have all voted who wish?"—the sponsor may ask for "a poll of the absentees." With the presiding officer's permission, the clerk calls the names of those not on record. It is a coded request by the sponsor—"please, colleagues, give me a few more votes." Often the sponsor that is about to lose will request "postponed consideration" before the presiding officer announces the result. In the House a bill with 47 votes or more (but less than 60) is then postponed. In the Senate a motion to postpone consideration is usually given courtesy approval whenever requested by the sponsor. When the sponsor asks for postponed consideration, it is like asking for time out in a basketball game. The bill stays alive, and the sponsor may be able to do enough homework or repair work to get the bill passed at a later date. A bill can only be postponed once in each house, and, having been postponed, the bill is in danger of dying by deadline.

A common practice of good debaters is to explain the technical issues on a bill with colorful analogies and metaphors. For example, in a debate on amendments to increase appropriation bills above amounts in the governor's budget, and before the legislature had approved taxes sufficient to fund the appropriations, one legislator insisted his colleagues had the cart before the horse. "In fact while they are getting that cart out there, the horse has retreated way back into the woods." Sometimes the metaphors get a bit mixed, as an interview with Speaker Madigan revealed: "Maybe I'm charming when charm is called for and maybe I'm rather cold when I'm telling some legislator who has fed at my trough for a long time that it's now his turn to bite the bullet" (Ross, 1983, p. 11). A Democrat, opposing an anti-labor bill with a Republican sponsor, used his favorite critical adjectives: "This bill is both invidious and insidious."

On the big bills the casual observer cannot always tell from the debate who is going to win. Often the questions become partisan and the tone is harsh. There are belittling remarks and charges of hypocrisy. Sometimes, apparently small points in a bill are picked over and criticized by speaker after speaker. Sometimes the sponsor will seem unresponsive to these challenges. Finally, someone moves the previous question, debate is over, and on a partisan vote the majority beats the minority. In such cases the outcome was a foregone conclusion. The minority knew it would lose, so its efforts were mostly symbolic and rhetorical. The majority may not even respond to the objections when it is confident that it has the needed votes.

3. *Action in the Second House.* As Figure 7:2 shows, the steps in the second house, which can be either the House or Senate, are the same. But a few observations are needed concerning second house consideration.

The original sponsor needs to get a sponsor in the other house. As has been noted, the impetus for actions must come from the sponsor in committee or on the floor. Sometimes getting the second house sponsor is a problem, and it is more likely to be a problem for a representative who must find a sponsor among only 59 senators. Members, therefore, cultivate connections across the rotunda. On the other hand, sponsor control from the first house is maintained. A bill cannot be taken for second house sponsorship by a member not acceptable to the first house sponsor.

As indicated before, a bill can pass the first house with little notice from potential opponents. But opponents have a second chance at all stages of action in the second house—committee, second reading and third reading—to defeat or amend the bill. Proponents (lawmakers and lobbyists) have to stay on top of developments, making sure they have answers and arguments to defeat any new objections or ground swells of opposition. Participants keep an eye on news reports and editorial columns for new objections or support.

Second house treatment of assembly-line or middling bills sometimes reflects intermember or interhouse relations. The rivalry of House and Senate has been noted. It is considered stealing if a representative or senator sponsors a duplicate, or near duplicate, of a bill sponsored by someone else without the originator's permission. Out of courtesy to its own members, the House or Senate may just sit on such a stolen bill after first passage in the other body. When the two houses are controlled by different parties, the opposing majorities commonly take bills hostage in the second house. Whether big bills or middling, the point is usually to force negotiation and compromise on major legislation. Even when one party holds majorities in both houses, the president of the Senate and the speaker of the House and their respective leadership teams do not always agree on everything. Holding bills can be a tactic to force negotiation, or to crystalize public opinion against rival proposals.

In Illinois the Senate has, more consistently than the House, acted to keep the second year of the biennial session a time of limited business. The Senate has dealt mainly with budget related bills—appropriations and taxes—and a few exceptions allowed by its rules committee. The House has held hearings and passed a much wider variety of bills, which then died on the Senate's agenda. Whether or not this pattern will persist remains to be seen.

4. *Conferences and Concurrences.* A bill cannot go to the governor unless it has been passed in exactly the same form by both houses. Because second house amendments are commonplace, especially on middling and major bills, there has to be a method for reconciliation.

There are several possibilities. The first house can concur with second house amendments. This is common, especially if the first house sponsor is willing. That failing, the first house refuses to concur, sending the bill back to the second house. The second house can recede from—in effect, drop—the amendments it put on the first house's bill. That is not unusual, but less common than concurrence. That failing, a conference is necessary.

A conference committee is a temporary committee to deal with only one bill. It consists of two halves—five members from the Senate and five from the House. House custom and Senate rules require three from the majority and two from the minority from each chamber. Senators are named by that chamber's committee on committees, but House members are named by the speaker and minority leader. Each chamber delegation has a chair, but the chair of the conference committee is named by the presiding officer of the chamber from which the bill originated. Normally the House and Senate sponsors are appointed to the conference committee.

Conference committees have wide latitude. Senate rules say, "The report . . . shall be confined to the subject of the bill or resolution referred to the committee, but shall not be otherwise limited by the scope of the disagreement between the two houses" (*Temporary Rules*, 1985, Rule 43, E1). House rules are silent on this point. The conferees work out whatever agreement can obtain six votes, although in most instances more than the minimum number approve. Usually the conferees are there to work out a compromise between the versions that have both passed one house; there is a positive bias toward making a deal that can get concurrence from both chambers. Sometimes conference committees become the arena of negotiation for major legislation late in the session. Major legislation that failed to pass at an earlier stage of the session is inserted into minor bills, or "shell bills," very late in the session, often by conference committees. Sometimes formal actions stop for negotiations by the top leaders of both chambers (and may include the governor or his/her staff). Upon the completion of these negotiations, several conference committee reports are filed on a variety of subjects that were all taken into account in the "cutting of the deal."

The action in each chamber on a conference committee report is equivalent to final passage, so it is done with a roll call vote. A constitutional majority is necessary in each house—60 in the House, 30 in the Senate—to send the bill on to the governor. If the conference report fails to pass in either house, the bill dies. Because House and Senate rules do not limit the latitude of conference committees, the only real check on them is the willingness of members in either house to vote down such conference committee reports. In practice, conference committee reports are usually adopted.

To this point we have described conference committees as combined groups from the House and Senate that actually meet, pound out an agreement and write a report. Sometimes they do just this, giving public notice of their meeting, and having an actual session that is open to the public.

But conference committees normally conduct business late in the legislative session, when bills have passed third reading in both houses, i.e., in the last couple of weeks of June. Literally dozens of such conferences may be going on at the same time. In actual practice, ten legislators rarely sit down together in a negotiating session. Typically the House and Senate chairs work out an agreement that they believe most conferees will sign. Then the partisan staffers write out the details in a report that gets passed around for signatures by a majority of conferees. Procedures are flexible, to say the least, when end-of-the-session pressure builds up at the end of June. The obvious check on these bicameral negotiations is the fact that final passage by constitutional majorities must be gained separately in both chambers.

5. *Death by Deadlines and Rules*. The General Assembly and its bill process can be understood as "deadline driven." In the 1960s and before, the legislature conducted nearly all its business during the first six months of the year following an election. Whatever had not passed by June 30 was dead. Then legislators adjourned *sine die*, Latin for "without day," meaning that unless the legislature were called into special session, that membership would conduct no more legislative business. Under those circumstances there was one big deadline—June 30. Typical news coverage in Illinois would show legislators literally stopping the chamber clock, while the chambers worked on into July 1 to break loose the logjam of bills.

Now both the House and Senate have a detailed list of deadlines in their rules. There are deadlines for the introduction of bills, for the reporting of bills out of committee and for passage on third reading in the house of origin. Similarly, there are deadlines for committee reporting and for passage on third reading in the second house. Rules permit carrying a bill from the first year of the biennium into the second year. Under the 1970 Constitution the General Assembly does not adjourn "without day" until immediately before the beginning of a new biennium. The General Assembly is a continuous body, and its committees can hold hearings and conduct investigations year-round up to the very day a new biennium begins.

The deadlines help the members and leaders pace their progress each year. Each deadline thins down the load of bills. Bill sponsors, sometimes purposely or because of the press of other business, see their own bills tabled for failure to make a deadline. Technically tabling bills by deadlines (actually killing them), is a functional necessity for the legislature. It is less of an embarrassment to most sponsors to explain to a constituent that a bill was tabled because of a deadline than to admit it could not attract enough votes in committee or on the floor to be passed. Members often leave doomed bills on the calendar, not asking for a vote on them.

The result is the same, but the defeat is less personal. Death by deadline is a humane form of slaughter practiced repeatedly on both middling bills and little bills that missed assembly line passage. More often, but not always, the big bills are killed at the floor stage—third reading or conference committee report.

Deadlines are part of the rules, and can be suspended with three-fifths majorities (71 in the House, 36 in the Senate). Ordinarily, suspension means that the party leaders can make exceptions in either chamber, but only with each other's consent. Thus there is the basis for negotiation, compromise and cooperation—as well as conflict—between the two chambers. Leaders in the House hold Senate bills from passage until the Senate passes House bills, and vice versa. Bills are held hostage in order to force bargaining. Deadlines really give tactical advantages to the party leaders. Members often vote for their leader's position lest the leader take hostage a bill that the member may be sponsoring. The possibilities for trading favors because of deadlines are innumerable.

CONCLUDING OBSERVATIONS

There are a great many details of procedure that we have left unmentioned. What we are describing here is a process with clear rules, basically fair to all, but with definite advantages to the majority party members in each chamber. It is a process in which bill sponsors and party leaders are especially important, but one in which committees and committee support are of rather modest significance.

A great many bills pass easily. This is especially true of minor bills that close this loophole or fix that detail. Few bills are killed outright on a third-reading roll call, but many perish without getting that far. They are tabled, or languish on the calendar with "consideration postponed," never again to be called by the sponsor. And a great many bills pass one house on the push of an originating sponsor, but then suffer death with dignity under the second house deadlines. So the legislature seems a soft touch, passing most bills that are called by their sponsors on third reading with comfortable margins. Yet that is the end, not the beginning, of a winnowing process in which more bills die than pass.

There are many decision points for action on bills. Controversial legislation, therefore, whether minor, middling or major, can be buffeted at numerous points. Interest groups and the general public get time to indicate support or opposition. Major bills inevitably pass with the support of the majority party which controls at all the checkpoints. But if one party does not control both chambers and the governorship, or if it cannot maintain party unity, the majority will have to "cut a deal" with the minority. And the dealing is complicated by the legislature's bicameral structure. The structure and rules for legislative action make the legislature an arena for building and testing public policy consensus.

Most of the General Assembly's visible activity is the consideration of bills of minor or middling importance. The deadlines, the rules including provisions to make exceptions and the strong procedural powers of the party leaders make the legislature an important arena for ratifying major policy decisions that have been negotiated late in the session outside the limelight of public debate. To the frustration of many in the news media, the final contents of major bills are often worked out in negotiations between the party leaders of both chambers, often with the participation of the governor's office. The crucial decisions are frequently made in backrooms, hallways, whispered floor conferences and telephone calls. Commitments are exchanged between the House and Senate leaders to pass bills that have been held hostage. Then the leaders call their party members into caucus and privately discuss the agreed-upon exchanges. If the leaders have their members' confidence and support, agreements are confirmed all around. Then members troop back to the floor, where the action moves quickly, sometimes unceremoniously, to formally pass what the leaders have negotiated.

The bill procedure encourages passing bills. It imposes few public defeats upon bill sponsors. Even in major controversies the emphasis is not on killing bills, but on compromise. A great deal of legislation dies in face-saving ways by deadlines and omission, but leaders serve members by seeing to it that everyone gets "something." This flow of benefits sustains the leaders and the members and keeps the system working.

But the flow of benefits sometimes produces abuses of power. For the most part the rules call for a deliberative, public process, with public hearings, three readings in each chamber and considered debate. Yet rules allow, and leaders cooperate with conference committees that sometimes insert brand new provisions into bills by means of a conference report. Typically these reports are adopted out of members' loyalty to their leaders rather than because of the persuasiveness of the legislation. Members follow their leaders because the leaders make sure members get their share of minor and middling bills for the constituents back home. One consequence of this reciprocity is that statute books are crammed with detailed legislation on every conceivable subject—probably more laws than the people of Illinois need.

Chapter Eight

State Leadership for Lawmaking: The Executives and Bureaucrats

In 1982, Robert Howard, a former Springfield correspondent for the *Chicago Tribune*, wrote an analysis of the Thompson versus Stevenson campaign for *Illinois Issues*:

> Each party nominated its best man for one of the nation's more important off-year elections. Republican James Robert Thompson, 46, a former law professor and federal prosecutor who was born of middle-class parentage on Chicago's west side, is running for an unprecedented third term on a record of having kept state government solvent and orderly during six difficult years. The Democratic challenger, a man of unusual political credentials, is Adlai Ewing Stevenson III, 52 on October 10, the millionaire son of a governor and great-grandson of a vice-president who two years ago gave up 10 years' seniority in the U.S. Senate to seek a new career in Illinois. Theirs is not a friendly contest for control of the executive branch of a major state. Each runs as an activist who has confidence in himself and who challenges the policies, promises and potential of the other (1982, p. 6).

Why would a U.S. senator with a winning election record leave that prestigious office to challenge an incumbent for the governorship of Illinois? Stevenson said, according to Howard, that he left the Senate because "in government the action is in the executive branch and increasingly in the states" (p. 6). The outcome, now history, was certified 20 days after the election as a victory for Thompson by a mere 5,074 votes. Even that outcome was unsure until the Illinois Supreme Court decided that no recount of the ballots would be granted (*In re Contest of Election*, 1983).

What makes the stakes for executive leadership in Illinois so high? If the governorship is so important, how does the governor affect lawmaking in the General Assembly? Our chief interest, of course, will be in the governor's executive leadership, but we will look as well at the other elected executives and the bureaus and bureaucrats under them.

LEADERSHIP AND THE GOVERNOR

Adlai Stevenson III is right. The action center of government is in the executive branch, and increasingly the action is in the states. And undoubtedly the preeminent position is governor. The governor has the tools of authority to make things happen—to propose the budget, to exercise the veto and to appoint heads of bureaus and personal staff. The governor is not *the* controlling leader of the state—there are too many checks and balances on the office's powers. But no other official controls the governor—not the speaker of the House, not the president of the Senate, not the chief justice of the Supreme Court, not the attorney general, not the U.S. senators and not even the president of the nation. These and others, like interest group directors, social critics, newspaper editors and political party leaders may rival the governor in certain circumstances, but on the broad range of issues subject to state control, the governor is number one.

Visibility

The governor can get public attention whenever it is desired. In media-conscious American culture, visibility—if marshalled properly—enhances power. Because the governor can make things happen, the media professionals pay close attention. The governor can pack a press conference on very short notice. When the governor wants to avoid attention, staff members can inconspicuously release the news. By contrast, when a state legislator or an interest group lobbyist calls a press conference, only a handful of newspeople come. Even committee chairs do not attract much attention. Legislative leaders (especially if they are not of the governor's party) can get substantial attention, but they rarely get headlines or extended TV time for their ideas.

If the governor is for budget reductions, who will speak for more spending? If the governor wants public employee unions, who will argue the case against? And if the governor vetoes an important bill, who is the spokesperson for the majorities in the two chambers that passed the bill? The answer is, "That depends—perhaps many people, but maybe nobody." In Illinois except in rare circumstances no single rival spokesperson can compete with or preempt the governor on a majority of public issues.

Obviously, the governor uses the media for political purposes. Little assembly line bills move easily through the legislature. But if the governor points out that Senator Smith's bill provides loopholes for a hometown industry in Smith's district that are "not fair" to the state, Smith's little bill becomes a significant issue which the press and other legislators can no longer treat as an assembly line bill. On the other hand, the governor can sometimes kill an idea by just ignoring it. For example, a few legislators and interest groups pushing for an increase in liquor taxes (sometimes characterized as "sin taxes") are unlikely to be successful without the governor's active endorsement.

All politicians know how important the scope of a conflict is. Like E. E. Schattschneider (1960, p. 2), they know that "the number of people involved in any conflict determines what happens." Some propositions become "too public" to pass. The governor's visibility allows some management (but not control) of the scope variable. Consequently, interest groups, legislators, social critics and the whole gamut of political activists lobby the governor for help in increasing or decreasing the scope of conflict on issues they consider important.

Policy Promotion

The governor plays a vital role in the lawmaking process. Although ideas don't become law without going through the legislature, the governor can do a great deal to knead the ideas into shape for passage and to encourage the legislators to vote positively. In fact, kneading is one of the governor's biggest jobs.

The governor is expected to have priorities for state policies. Every state has enduring problems, and every governor is expected to focus on some more than others. Moreover, the issues are complex. Consider these examples.

1. *What to do about mass transit and roads?* Mass transit, an enduring problem in greater Chicago, refers to trains and buses in and out of downtown Chicago, as well as transit service in the city and around the suburban towns. The downstate cities have transit problems too, but of a much smaller dimension. Downstate is especially concerned about decent roads and bridges. The entire state needs more and better highways and highway maintenance. How much should be paid for by users—bus and train riders, car and truck drivers—and how much should be paid from general revenues?

2. *What level of assistance should go to schools and universities?* According to the 1970 Constitution it is a state goal to obtain "the educational development of all persons to the limit of their capacities." Furthermore, "the State has the primary responsibility for financing the system of public education" (Art. 10, Sec. 1). The implication is that state assistance to local schools should increase while local property taxation for public schools and community colleges should go down. Where and how should the funds be directed? According to need? To enhance quality? Toward remedial education of the culturally deprived or for the gifted? What about mandates: required courses in physical education, driver training and citizenship? Should the curriculum emphasize basic skills or social living courses? Should higher education assistance go to state universities, or to the students who then may choose whether to go to private rather than public institutions? Should public universities be equivalent in quality and support, or should the University of Illinois be funded as a world-ranking university at the expense of Western Illinois, Chicago State and others?

3. *What is the state government's role in economic development?* Should it provide resources to stimulate (subsidize) industry? Because the

cost of doing business and employing labor is affected by unemployment compensation rates, what rates should the state establish? How strict will the government be about hazardous wastes, pollution and utility rates? How about enterprise zones with low taxes for new industries in the cities? Will encouragement go to smokestack, heavy industry or to "high tech," service industry?

4. *How will the state deal with dependent populations?* Public aid, mental health care, aid to dependent mothers and children, care for handicapped and disabled and expenditures for prisons are examples of maintenance costs for people who produce little or no "return on investment." But these expenditures are the earnest money of civility in an era of enlightenment. What level of support is just? What forms or levels of support induce continued dependence? Do ceilings on support, training, policing, counseling and rehabilitation really reduce dependency? Or do state service programs really serve the professional, salaried state employees more than the dependent people?

5. *Who will pay and how much?* State government does not produce wealth. It protects and regulates society so the people can be productive. Part of that productivity goes to state government by way of taxes and fees for service. All the questions about the quality and kinds of service mentioned above imply costs. Some costs can be paid by users. Hunters pay license fees, defraying part of the costs for the Department of Conservation. College students at state universities pay tuition, but that only covers roughly a quarter of the cost of their education. Fuel taxes and vehicle license fees pay a big part of maintaining a system of transportation. The rest of government expenses are paid from general revenue—generated mostly by the state's income and sales taxes. Are the taxes fair to high, medium and low income people? Should users pay more and the general public less? Are tax rates competitive with those of surrounding states?

These and other perennial questions require the governor to think about priorities and programs. But that thinking must be politically pragmatic. The urban poor are concentrated in the cities, especially Chicago and East St. Louis, which are dominated by Democrats. The corporate headquarters of major business enterprises are in downtown Chicago and some of the surrounding suburban areas. Downstaters—Democrats and Republicans—are not ideological about their politics, but they question the purposes and prudence of the Chicago machine, and the compassion of the suburban well-to-do. So the governor must make political calculations about what proposed policies will accomplish, what will pass and who will benefit. Moreover, the policy game has qualities like the game of pick up sticks. It is hard to pick out one without disturbing the others. The interdependencies of Illinois issues make it difficult to predict what will pass and what will not.

But the governor, armed with great staff resources and constitutionally granted tools (more on these below) can formulate policy proposals based on carefully reasoned priorities for the perennial problems. The formulations do not have to be brand new ideas. The trick is to put together this for prisons, that for environmental protection and something else for economic development. Policy formulation is followed by policy promotion: the process of advocacy by press conferences, speeches to business leaders and labor groups, correspondence with interest group leaders, luncheons with legislators and conferences with party leaders. The governor's efforts range from public appeals to one-on-one persuasion and combine visionary promises of a brighter future with threats to "help me or I'll veto your bills." The governor does not do this alone. Many others may be called on to play a part—the lieutenant governor, the directors of departments, the head of the Bureau of the Budget, executive directors of sympathetic interest groups. The governor's leadership lies in the effectiveness with which the variety of actors in smaller roles are effectively coordinated.

Why the drive to promote policy? Certainly to fulfill expectations and to make good on campaign promises. Chief executives rarely stay in office as much as a decade. Governor Thompson is only the second governor in Illinois history to win a third term. So the time is short, and the possibility of higher office (the presidency?) is only viable for someone noted for accomplishments. The need to be recognized is significant. The following is from an interview with Thompson in late 1979.

> [Ross]: You have an excellent reputation for fiscal responsibility. What is your single, biggest goal for the next three years? Thompson: I want to be able to leave a record behind that people could point to and say, "Hey, when Jim Thompson was governor he accomplished a, b, c, d and e." I want a future citizen of the state of Illinois, for example, to walk through a state park and say, "Hey, Jim Thompson built this when he was governor"; or take a family for a drive down a safe highway and say, "Hey, Jim Thompson built this when he was governor"; or I want a foster kid to be able to say 10 years from now, "Hey, my life was changed because of the care I got when Jim Thompson was governor." I want to be able to point to concrete achievements—I don't mean just "concrete"—but achievements in social services, in conservation, in transportation, that people will remember this administration for through the years" (Ross, 1980, p. 13).

Governors promote policy to make a record.

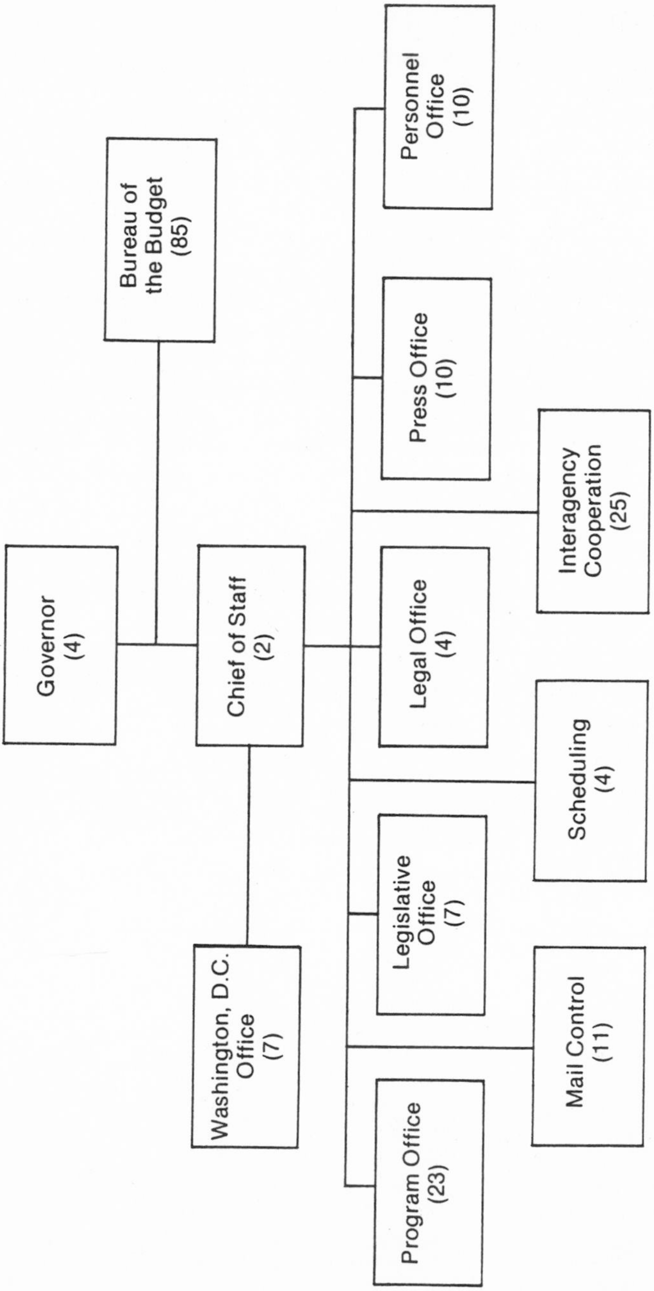

*Numbers in parentheses indicate total staff (professional and clerical) associated with each office in 1982.

Source: Carlson, 1982, p. 18

Figure 8:1   Organization of the Governor's Office*

The Role of Staff

Considering the weight of responsibilities, it is not surprising that the governor's office has the biggest, and usually the best, staff under the statehouse dome. Figure 8:1 offers a structural diagram of Thompson's staff as of 1982, which numbered about 200. These staff are especially relevant to the governor's policy leadership. They serve to gather and refine information, weigh alternatives, implement decisions and carry out negotiations in the governor's name. Most important, the hundred members outside the Bureau of the Budget serve at the governor's pleasure. Talented, mostly young, they have personal or professional connections with the governor or someone else on the staff. This is often in marked contrast with "cabinet" appointees or agency heads who have spent a career and earned a reputation in a policy area. The latter have ties to the bureaucracy, the industry or the interest groups affected by the department or agency. Staff, on the other hand, are loyal to the governor only. They look good only when the governor looks good.

The degree to which the governor compartmentalizes the staff and marks off clear jurisdictions varies. For example, there is not a rigid caste system in Thompson's office. Four units of Thompson's staff are especially relevant to the governor as policy promoter: the program office, the legislative office, the press office and the Bureau of the Budget.

A veteran staffer of the Thompson administration listed these activities being performed by professionals in the program office (Carlson, 1982, pp. 17-19):

— Providing program and policy advice to the governor.
— Monitoring legislative activities within an area of responsibility including occasional lobbying and extensive analyses of bills for gubernatorial action after passage by the General Assembly.
— Working on appointments to major boards and commissions.
— Recruiting directors and top agency staff (in conjunction with the governor's personnel office).
— Answering questions from the press, particularly in specialized areas where the press staff would have little knowledge or experience.
— Dealing with certain kinds of citizen complaints.
— Facilitating dealings with agency heads and other members of the governor's staff.
— Providing timely information to the governor and other staff members on agency programs and activities.
— Answering mail that requires more than a routine response from a state agency but not the personal attention of the governor.
— Assisting in the writing of speeches and press releases.

The legislative office functions substantially as the governor's lobbyist. The staffers help develop the governor's bills from position papers authored by the program staff. They secure good legislators as sponsors, and monitor bills in the legislative process according to whether they are perceived as good or bad for the governor's program interests. They secure needed committee witnesses—agency people or experts—for the bills that the governor wants passed. Keeping in touch with sponsors of the governor's bills also means helping sponsors react to any amendments that may be proposed in committee or on second readings.

A big part of this job when the legislature is in session is keeping in touch with members, especially those of the governor's party, but also with anyone in sympathy with the governor on a particular legislative item. The governor's lobbyists keep in constant touch with the party leaders and their staffs, as well as the many agency liaison people. They let the governor know when and whom to contact personally. Communication is not one-way. The legislative office lets the governor know the wants, needs and wishes of particular legislators. In addition, the legislative office is often in touch with county chairmen and politicians throughout the state, lobbying legislators indirectly through their friends and political contacts in the home district.

The main task of the press office, headed by a press secretary, is to enhance the public image of the governor. Because the public gets most of its impressions about the governor and his/her administration through the print and electronic media—newspapers, magazines, radio and television—the press secretary, typically a veteran reporter, is expected to be a media specialist. Organizing media events is an important part of the job. For example, when the governor is ready to push a new program, the press secretary arranges a public setting and notifies the press that the governor will make a statement. Summaries of the program and how it will work are released to the media. Appropriate agency directors are brought out for the occasion. Sometimes spokesmen from favorably affected interest groups are present. There will be photo opportunities and time to ask questions. If a crisis arises, the press secretary must be able arrange a press conference quickly and/or present an explanation of the problem, clarify the governor's opinion and indicate what response the governor intends to make.

The staff members in the press office handle myriad other public relations tasks, including the writing of the governor's speeches. The staff also assists reporters in getting information about many aspects of the executive branch. Sometimes the press office arranges a "fly around" so the governor can conduct a series of press conferences in the larger cities (major media markets) on a single day. Special attention is given to major events such as the annual State of the State speech in February and the budget message in March. All such efforts confirm the fact that governors take public relations very seriously. A study of the Ogilvie administration in 1971 revealed that during the month of June, Governor Ogilvie devoted 27 percent of his busy schedule to matters of public relations (Michaelson, 1975, p. 113).

The Bureau of the Budget (BOB) is the governor's major staff unit. It is large and highly professional. Its director, deputy director, planning director, general counsel and the top analysts for specific policy areas—administration and safety, economic development, education, health and social services—are in sensitive positions. Many of these professionals, however, serve as careerists and will stay on the job despite turnovers of governors within one party or from one party to the other.

A recent essay highlights the activities of the BOB:

> For a concentrated period of six months each year, the BOB performs a staff function to the governor by assisting in the 'development' phase of the executive budget. In general, this effort entails an examination of the program needs of the state (as defined by its code departments, the governor's office, and the General Assembly) and the fiscal or monetary impact associated with delivering the services required to meet those needs. . . .
>
> The BOB's second major activity, the line function, is performed as it assists the governor in the 'execution' phase of the executive budget. Here, the BOB exercises a stewardship role by directing and coordinating (and occasionally controlling) the rate at which revenues and expenditures are provided to/by the departments of state government (Bazzani, 1982, p. 41).

The BOB has a pivotal role in helping the governor determine the annual spending plans for nearly 20 billion dollars a year. It analyzes state and national economic trends in order to forecast the revenues that various taxes will produce, and what state services will cost. It evaluates agency requests, and helps the governor translate his policy goals into efficient procedures that the agencies can put into effect. It assists by analyzing the fiscal impact of policy in legislation so the governor can make veto decisions after the legislative session.

Staff members are the people consulted most by the governor when new solutions are needed for old problems, when crises arise, when revenues fail to live up to projections or when the governor wants to change the direction of public policy. Staff are not supposed to be widely known, make headlines or leak information to the press. They are there to make the boss look good, and they won't be around long if their actions make the boss look bad. Staff may fight and disagree among themselves about what constitutes wise, right and good public policy, but those fights are kept confidential, and once the boss's decision is announced, dutiful staff get behind it. These are the people to whom the governor delegates problems raised by legislators. Sometimes, therefore, they work directly with legislators, or with legislative staff. Similarly, they are often in contact with department directors and agency personnel, but for the most part those operations do not have much impact on the relations between the governor and the legislature.

One other staff member is secondary to the substance of policy promotion, but helps obtain support for policy development and execution: the governor's patronage chief. In the good old, bad old days there were thousands of unskilled and semi-skilled government jobs that were filled by partisan appointment. Every sweeper, telephone operator and elevator attendant was a political worker or had a political sponsor, often a relative. Civil service, new legislation, job descriptions, merit boards and court decisions have brought about a new era. Practically every employee of the state now must fulfill qualifications in the form of education, experience or test results. But, as Richard J. Carlson notes, "Despite these changes, there is a strong expectation among activists of both parties that job openings in state government should be filled by members or friends of the party in power. It is the job of the governor's patronage office to attempt to meet these expectations" (1982, p.28).

The patronage chief keeps track of agency vacancies and pushes the hiring of qualified job candidates who also have political credentials. There are also a great many positions filled by gubernatorial appointment. Many appointments are to advisory boards, regulatory bodies and review commissions. Most of these positions pay no salary but are nevertheless prized by those appointed. For example, the members of the prestigious governing boards of the state universities (except for the University of Illinois, whose board members are nominated by state party conventions, and elected at-large in the state) are appointed by the governor.[1]

Instruments for Policy Promotion

The governor can use a variety of means and methods to carry out the task of policy promotion. There are crucial constitutional and legal powers which encourage informal communication, as well as negotiations.

The constitution provides that, "The Governor, at the beginning of each annual session of the General Assembly and at the close of his term of office, shall report to the General Assembly on the condition of the State and recommend such measures as he deems desirable" (1970, Art. 5, Sec. 13). In more popular language, the governor before a joint meeting of the House and Senate, gives an annual "State of the State" address. Governors take this occasion seriously. It is a media event, and the speech is broadcast around the state on radio. Excerpts—with the key dramatic lines—are put on the television news. Typically, the governor treats the speech as a keynote address, giving a basic outline of what problems should be solved in the coming session. A governor whose party has clear control may give a highly partisan speech, or claim credit for past accomplishments. If the party balance is close, or held by the opposition, the speech is likely to be conciliatory or emphasize bipartisan concerns.

The speech does sketch priorities. Legislators and the press consider the speech carefully because it usually embodies the governor's policy agenda. They look especially at the proposals on the perennial issues to get an idea of what will be ignored as much as what the governor will emphasize. Shortly after the speech, bills to implement the governor's current concerns—so called "administration bills"—are delivered to friendly legislators for introduction on the governor's behalf. Only rarely does the governor have any difficulty lining up a sponsor. In fact, sometimes the governor's staff must distribute sponsorship carefully so as to please a variety of legislators who want to "carry" the governor's bills. The 1983 tax bill was not one of these. Democrats insisted that Governor Thompson get someone from his own party as sponsor. Volunteers were not apparent, so Thompson negotiated for some time before the Senate Republican leader, James "Pate" Philip, accepted the dubious honor and duty of carrying the governor's income tax increase bill (Parker, 1984, pp. 45-46).

A similar, but more focused, annual speech is the governor's budget message. The constitution requires the governor to prepare and submit a budget including ". . . the estimated balance of funds available for appropriation at the beginning of the fiscal year, the estimated receipts, and a plan for expenditures and obligations during the fiscal year of every department, authority, public corporation and quasi-public corporation of the State, every State college and university, and every other public agency created by the State. . . " (Art. 8, Sec. 2a). By law the budget is due each year on the first Wednesday in March. The usual emphasis is on the fiscal changes in the past year and new directions for the coming one. The governor sharpens the priorities announced in January, sometimes as a result of changes in fiscal trends and sometimes in response to political pressures evoked by the State of the State address. The budget message is accompanied by three bound volumes, some 800 pages of detail from the Bureau of the Budget precisely estimating expected income, telling how money was spent in the past year and specifying how the governor proposes to spend it in the coming year. The budget books are public documents that are available each March from the governor's office. Promptly thereafter copies are available in libraries around the state.

Shortly after release of the budget, the governor's staff prepares the appropriations bills for all the agencies (about 80) and gets sponsors for them—usually legislators from the governor's political party. The governor's people like to get sponsors who have a positive interest in the agency or its programs. Somebody concerned about toxic wastes may want to sponsor the appropriation for the Environmental Protection Agency. The bill for the Conservation Department may be taken by someone interested in parks and wildlife. The Southern Illinois University appropriation probably will be sponsored by a legislator whose district contains one of the two main campuses. The governor's staff gets help from agency liaison staff in identifying interested sponsors (more on agency liaison staff in Chapter Nine).

The governor often says he welcomes different viewpoints from legislators concerning how much should go for this or that function of government, but that the legislature "ought not to change the bottom line unless they change the revenues." Bottom line refers to total state expenditures. As noted before, lawmakers are representatives and feel duty bound to get their district's shares—and more, if possible. The governor often permits legislators to fight among themselves about which districts will get what, as long as every spending increase is accompanied by cuts somewhere else. On the other hand, if lawmakers want to spend a higher total, the governor insists that the legislature must raise taxes to cover increased expenditures. This is consistent with the constitution's requirement that, "Proposed expenditures shall not exceed funds estimated to be available for the fiscal year as shown in the budget" (Art. 8, Sec. 2a). However, a dubious practice that is occasionally resorted to is to raise revenue estimates and hope that the money will be available when the time comes to pay the bills.

During the legislative session the governor's legislative staff keeps in constant touch with the progress of the governor's bills and appropriations. The staff works with sponsoring legislators as well as legislative staff, particularly with the partisan staff of the governor's party. There are times when the governor gets directly involved with pushing bills: timing speeches about issues, negotiating compromises with the legislative leaders, and exchanging commitments, favors and patronage appointments for votes. Necessarily, the governor remains in Springfield during most of June because so many issues are decided in that pressure-packed month.

The governor's veto authority constitutes a powerful instrument for policy promotion. Prior to the 1970 Constitution, only four vetoed bills were overridden between 1871 and January 8, 1969 (Netsch, 1970, p. 177). The 1970 Constitution struck a somewhat different balance between the governor and the legislature by enlarging the governor's veto options and making legislative overrides easier to obtain. The basic veto power is accompanied by some fine tuning options: the *item veto*, the *reduction veto* and the *amendatory veto*. (See Figure 7:2 in the preceding chapter.)

Veto is a Latin verb form that translated literally means, "I forbid." In our shared-power governments, presidents and governors have veto powers (only North Carolina, of the 50 states, provides no veto power to its chief executive). The Illinois governor has 60 days to consider every bill or appropriation passed by the legislature. The governor may approve the bill by signing it, and it becomes law. The governor may veto the bill, and return it to the legislature. A bill neither approved nor vetoed becomes law automatically at the end of the 60 days. A vetoed bill is not dead. It is returned to the house of origin, which has 15 days to pass it again, but by a constitutionally required three-fifths margin (71 in the House; 36 in the Senate). The second house likewise has 15 days. If both pass the vetoed bill by the required three-fifths, the bill becomes law despite the veto. If the first or second house fails to pass the vetoed bill by three-fifths, it is dead.

The *item veto* gives the governor more control over specifics in an appropriation bill than that enjoyed by the president of the United States. The governor can veto a piece of the bill, an item, rather than, as the president must, an entire appropriations bill. For example, the Pollution Control Board has an annual budget of about $1.2 million. The governor can veto its equipment budget: a few thousand dollars for technical equipment, typewriters, filing cabinets, etc. If this seems like a minor control, it allows a governor to control two possible tactics for mischief otherwise available to rivals. Legislators may want to add funds to a budget by increasing appropriations. The governor can counter by vetoing an item. Defeating such steps by the governor requires three-fifths of the membership in both houses to override. By the same token, agency heads, who might try to "run around" the governor and BOB to get higher appropriations from the legislature, can be punished with an item veto of funds needed in the agency.

A sharper tool than the item veto is the *reduction veto*. The governor can selectively reduce one or more items in an appropriation bill. So the Pollution Control Board appropriation for equipment could be cut by half, or by some specific amount. Such a bill is returned to the legislature. A majority in each house is necessary to restore the reduced item to its original amount. Unless it is so restored by the legislature, the reduced appropriation becomes law.

The 1970 Constitution also gave the governor a fine tuning tool for substantive legislation, called the *amendatory veto*. The governor can return a bill to the legislature with specific recommendations for change, language that would amend the bill. The legislature has choices. If it accepts the governor's revisionary language by a majority in each house, then the governor certifies the bill and it becomes law as amended. If the governor does not certify, the bill is returned as a vetoed bill, requiring

71 votes in the House and 36 in the Senate to override. On the other hand, if the governor returns the bill with revisions but the legislature does not accept them or take further action, the bill dies.

Table 8:1 illustrates the interaction of the governor and legislature with regard to the governor's veto options. 1983 was the first session year after an election, and the legislature handled a full range of proposals. In that year nearly 1300 bills passed both houses, of which 58 percent originated in the House. Of that number, 918 were simply signed into law by the governor. But about a fourth, 351, were vetoed in whole or part by the governor. The plain message of the data is that very few of the governor's vetoes were overridden by the legislature. Most of Thompson's amendatory vetoes were approved by the legislature. The item or reduction vetoes were used sparingly, with six being overridden.

Numbers never tell the whole story. During the 1981 session the economy was changing rapidly—economic activity in the state slowed down, and revenue estimates were increasingly pessimistic. Thompson's fiscal year 1982 budget, presented in March, proposed to spend $14.9 billion. During the appropriations process Thompson reduced his request to $14.8 billion; the legislature subsequently passed $14.6 billion, and the governor used his veto to eliminate another $382 million. That year reduction vetoes were used as a tool to reduce the state's contribution to its employees' retirement funds by an average of 38 percent in all regular appropriations. That move alone, which obtained legislative acquiescence, cut $183 million from the budget.

Another note of explanation is needed about vetoes in full, the governor's veto of an entire bill. It is not uncommon for similar, even identical bills, to be sponsored by two or more legislators at one time. Several bills that the governor vetoed in 1983 were duplicates of bills already passed and signed. Sometimes the governor plays a bit of politics, signing a bill sponsored by someone from the governor's own party and vetoing the duplicate sponsored by a member of the opposition.

Unquestionably, the veto tools of the governor are of major significance in the legislative process. Often a governor can achieve a desired result simply by threatening to use one of the veto tools. The reduction veto and the amendatory veto permit the governor to make pinpoint changes in legislation. Of course, the reduction veto allows change in only one direction—the governor may only cut appropriations, not add to them—giving the governor the muscle to hold the line on the budget.

The power to amend the language of the bills offers great freedom to the governor. This latitude has created a recurring political controversy, namely, how far may the governor go in changing a bill? According to a legislative staff expert:

Table 8:1   General Assembly Enactments and Gubernatorial Vetoes: 1983

	Bills originating in the Senate	Bills originating in the House
Bills passed by the legislature and signed by the governor	359	559
Bills vetoed in part and/or appropriations reduced; legislature concurred	7	1
Bills vetoed in part and/or appropriations reduced; vetoes overridden	3	3
Bills vetoed in full; vetoes overridden	11	15
Amendatory vetoes concurred by legislature and certified by the governor	62	64
Amendatory vetoes overridden by the legislature	8	12
Bills filed without governor's signature	0	0
Total bills passed to become public acts	450	654
Bills vetoed in full, not overridden	69	81
Amendatory vetoes not accepted by the legislature	8	7
Total legislative enactments passed by both houses	527	742

Source: *Laws of the State of Illinois, Eighty-third General Assembly, 1983,* Office of the Secretary of State, pp. iv-ix. There were 1104 public acts in 1983.

. . . the Illinois Supreme Court has stated that the Governor may not, under the guise of an amendatory veto, propose a completely new bill to the General Assembly, change the fundamental purpose of the bill, or make "substantial or expansive changes" in it. However, the Governor may make more than technical corrections; indeed, a proposed constitutional amendment to restrict the Governor's amendatory vetoes to technical corrections and matters of form was rejected by the voters in 1974. The court in these cases upheld amendatory vetoes, agreed to by the General Assembly, which (1) reduced the rate of the additional corporate income tax that partially replaced the personal property tax from 2.85 percent to 2.5 percent and (2) made several changes in an urban renewal bill which the court described as minor requirements" of the bill (Miller, 1983, pp. 33-34).[2]

Those are rather loose restrictions. It is typical to hear arguments in the legislature, when vetoes are being considered, asserting that the governor has abused the amendatory veto authority. (For both sides of the issue, see Sevener, 1985.) Most often these objections come from legislators in the party opposing the governor. Until the constitution is changed with regard to the amendatory veto, the major limit on the breadth of the governor's amendatory veto power is the legislature's power not to approve them.

The veto powers allow the governor to take members' bills—major or minor—hostage. Bills that particular lawmakers got passed by colleagues may be minor as far as the state is concerned—an appropriation for something back home, for instance—but they are significant to the lawmakers as representatives of their constituents. As the end of the session nears, the votes of these legislators may be needed by the governor to achieve passage of the governor's program. The governor then can threaten to veto a member's pet bill unless the support for the governor's bills is provided.

Compared with governors in other states, Illinois has given its governor strong powers of *appointment*. The constitution provides that:

> The Governor shall nominate and, by and with the advice and consent of the Senate, a majority of the members elected concurring by record vote, shall appoint all officers whose election or appointment is not otherwise provided for. Any nomination not acted upon by the Senate within 60 session days after the receipt thereof shall be deemed to have received the advice and consent of the Senate. The General Assembly shall have no power to elect or appoint officers of the Executive Branch (Art. 5, Sec. 9a).

The governor appoints all the directors of executive ("code") departments. Code departments are established by law, and staffed almost entirely by personnel under the civil service code (*Illinois Revised Statutes*, 1986b). In several departments assistant directors are similarly appointed. Typically, deputy directors and below are civil service personnel. As noted earlier, the governor also makes hundreds of appointments to boards, commissions and advisory bodies. All these require Senate approval.

The governor's staff for patronage and appointments regularly reviews the qualifications of potential appointees. Often names are suggested by legislators, particularly senators, and lobbyists for interest groups. Whether the job is for pay, or honor, it helps to have a political sponsor—county party chairman, legislator or public official—especially if the sponsor is of the governor's party. Opposition partisans can get appointments too: some boards are set up to have bipartisan membership, and some opposition sponsors have clout due to previous favors for the governor.

Senate approval is routine. Nominations usually come in batches of 15 to 40, and are referred to the Senate's Executive Appointments Committee. If there is "trouble" with a nominee, it usually becomes apparent before the committee recommends approval of the nominees to the floor. Should a nominee for a major position have a conflict of interest, or exhibit incompetence or political insensitivity for anticipated responsibilities, senators of the governor's party from the committee may ask informally that the nomination be withdrawn. It is very rare for the committee not to recommend those whom the governor insists on having, and likewise rare for the Senate not to give its consent to those nominees.[3] It is common for a group of nominees to be approved on a single roll call vote, and most of the time there are no negative votes. There is a strong legislative tradition entitling the governor to choose individuals for positions of administrative responsibility. But, the procedural opportunity is there to block appointments, should the opposition choose to do so.

The governor's appointment powers have significant policy impact. Most of what state government does for the people of Illinois is administered through 25 code departments of the state. Because the governor's vast responsibility precludes day-to-day involvement in departmental administration, heavy reliance is placed upon the appointed agency directors. A wise governor will choose people of competence, knowledge and administrative ability to deal with particular policy areas: public health, corrections, agriculture, law enforcement, public aid and so on. The governor also can and does select people who are in basic agreement with administration goals. Agency heads direct their units to implement the law, to fulfill the governor's priorities and to help the governor develop new ways to solve public problems.

The Illinois Constitution (Art. 5, Sec. 11) gives the governor the initiative for changing the structure of the agencies under the governor's authority. This is done by an *executive order* which looks very much like a legislative bill. If the governor's wishes conflict with existing law—as noted before, the structure and organization of state agencies are defined in the state statutes—the executive order has to be submitted to the General Assembly. Either house may disapprove by a constitutional majority (60 votes in the House; 30 votes in the Senate), but if neither house does, the order becomes effective and the law is changed. Several significant executive orders have reorganized government with legislative acquiescence; for example, the combining of the Department of Personnel and the Department of Administrative Services into a unit called the Department of Central Management Services was ordered in 1982. The legislature retains an effective "veto," but the initiative is in the hands of the governor.

Although the General Assembly is a "continuous body," with legal authority to do business at any time, the governor may call it into special session. This power can be used by the governor for policy promotion. The governor's proclamation states the purpose of the special session, and business is limited to that purpose. This power allows the governor to focus attention on a specific goal, perhaps an emergency action. The special session can be held in conjunction with the regular session, or may be called during the part of the calendar year when the legislature does not normally meet. Not only does the governor have this power, but the legislative leaders together—the president of the Senate and the speaker of the House—may also convene special sessions.

OTHER ELECTED EXECUTIVES

The Illinois Constitution provides for a lieutenant governor, who is nominated separately from the gubernatorial candidate, but who runs with the gubernatorial candidate in the general election, and four other state executives, elected separately from the governor. These office holders are the secretary of state, the attorney general, the treasurer and the comptroller.

Lieutenant Governor

This office is similar to that of vice president at the national level; the holder is the governor-in-waiting-in-case-the-governor-is-displaced. Under the 1870 Constitution the lieutenant governor was elected independently of the governor and served as the presiding officer of the Senate. Both those features of the office provided the incumbent more visibility and significance than at present. The last lieutenant governor elected under the 1870 provisions was Paul Simon, a Democrat who served with Republican Governor Richard B. Ogilvie.

Three men have served under the provisions of 1970 constitution. Neil Hartigan held the office under Democratic governor Dan Walker. Elected with Republican Governor James Thompson in 1976, David O'Neal resigned in 1981 after an unsuccessful effort to win the Republican U.S. Senate nomination in 1980. In 1982, former Republican speaker of the House, George Ryan, was elected with Thompson.

Although the candidates for lieutenant governor and governor of each party are teamed together on the general election ballot, just like the president and vice president at the national level, lieutenant governor candidates get on the ballot by solo campaigns in the party primaries. The two members of such a general election team are not necessarily a harmonious pair. In the Democratic primary of 1972 Hartigan's base of electoral support was the Chicago regular Democratic organization. Dan Walker sought the governorship in the primary by opposing the candidate endorsed by the Democratic organization, downstater Paul Simon. Walker chose as his running mate Carbondale mayor, Neil Eckert, who was defeated by Hartigan in the primary. As a result, Walker and Hartigan were elected together despite the fact that they were supported by rival Democratic factions.

The 1976 winners, Thompson and O'Neal, were a combination independently nominated in separate primary contests. Unlike Walker, Thompson did not choose or endorse a running mate. O'Neal, the Madison County sheriff, ran against and defeated Joan Anderson from Western Springs in suburban Cook County. Thompson and O'Neal were renominated and reelected in 1978. Thompson and O'Neal were not close politically, however, and O'Neal felt ignored by the Thompson administration. On certain political issues O'Neal even opposed the governor's positions publicly. In 1981, O'Neal resigned, leaving the lieutenant governorship vacant until January of 1983.

George Ryan was a House member from Kankakee who moved up through the Republican House leadership, becoming speaker in 1981. He asked for Thompson's help to obtain statewide office, and well before the 1982 primary Thompson endorsed Ryan for nomination to the office of lieutenant governor. Ryan defeated two other Republican legislators in the primary, and was elected to office with Thompson in November of 1982. During 1983, as lieutenant governor, Ryan spoke to Republican audiences around the state in support of the governor's proposed tax increase.

Lieutenant governors have few constitutional or statutory powers, and little staff. Informally they may do as much as the governor allows or encourages. They can help the governor's cause before the legislature or with legislators they know. But without the governor's trust and support, the lieutenant governor tends to be shut out of policymaking.

Attorney General

The attorney general has significant law enforcement powers under the constitution and laws of the state. As the state's top legal official, the attorney general directs a staff of about 750 employees, including about 200 lawyers, and deals with three basic tasks. First, the attorney general is the legal advisor to all of state government. While courts, including the Supreme Court, must render final decisions in lawsuits, the attorney general has the authority to render "advisory opinions." Because aspects of governmental authority are sometimes unclear, the attorney general has the authority to interpret the constitution and statutes for other state and local officials—a significant power. The attorney general's official opinions are advisory to agencies of government and are binding unless overruled by a court or superceded by new legislation (Lousin, 1976).

Second, the attorney general is the defense attorney for the state. The state may be challenged in court by a citizen, a corporation, another state, a local government or the federal government, and it is the attorney general who represents the state of Illinois in such cases.

Third, the attorney general is the chief prosecutor for the state. Often the attorney general assumes responsibility for matters that extend beyond a single county, for example, pollution, corporate tax matters or cases against persons who have defrauded the state. Upon the invitation of the county prosecutor or state's attorney, the attorney general assists in local prosecutions, especially in difficult cases which may be appealed to higher courts.

The attorney general has wide jurisdiction and significant legal powers, authority which makes the office important to the making and administration of the law. The attorney general promotes a wide range of public policy through the legislative process. While not as visible as the governor, the person in this position can obtain broad public and political attention, and is in a position to challenge the governor or other statewide officials in the policy process or in an election contest.

Secretary of State

This office has almost no parallel to the position of the same name at the national level. The U.S. secretary of state is thought of as primarily concerned with foreign relations, a matter of no formal interest to states. The Illinois secretary of state is primarily the state's record keeper, keeping records on corporations organized in the state, both for-profit and nonprofit, and records about motor vehicles and driving. The secretary administers the state library and archives, and every other year publishes the *Illinois Blue Book*, a useful source of information on Illinois government. In Illinois the secretary of state is most widely known for licensing vehicles and drivers; almost every adult carries a license signed by the secretary of state.

While the office exercises rather modest discretion, its public service responsibilities are high. Traditionally, the secretary of state employs many people—over 4000—many of whom are required to have few professional skills. The office was long dominated by patronage politics until its employees were put under a merit system in 1973.

The office does have specific policy areas—regulating drivers and the sale of corporate securities—which to some extent involve the secretary of state in policy promotion. So there are significant political opportunities associated with the position.

Treasurer and Comptroller

The state has two elected financial officers, the treasurer and the comptroller. Neither administers very large bureaucracies: the treasurer has about 100 employees, the comptroller about 400. The latter pays the state's bills, screening them and the authorizations to pay them. However, there is relatively little discretion exercised or policymaking innovation.

The treasurer is sometimes referred to as the state's banker. Revenues are put under the treasurer's charge, and investments are made in a variety of state financial institutions. Again, there is relatively little policy discretion, the revenue and spending decisions having been made by the legislature and governor. While the comptroller and treasurer are in positions to be aware when state funds are low, or when the costs of short-term debt are high, and thus can obtain visibility with the press and public, neither administers much legislation. Nor are they very conspicuous in promoting legislation.

BUREAUS AND BUREAUCRATS

Bureaucracy in the American states achieved a new direction when public opinion accepted the following as administrative wisdom: "There are right ways and wrong ways to build a road, but there are no Republican or Democratic ways to build a road." The ideas about nonpartisanship, professionalization of state agencies, management for efficiency and economy, and the separation of partisan politics from the delivery of public services was part of the Progressive Movement around the beginning of the 20th century. A moralistic movement, it appealed to some people and politicians in Illinois more than others. One of the heroes of the movement was Frank Lowden, who became governor of Illinois in 1917. He brought the movement for efficiency and economy to state organizations by getting the legislature to consolidate over 100 more or less independent agencies into nine departments. Over the years there have been hundreds of changes in the code, and there are now 25 code departments. To understand the place of these departments and their administrators in legislative politics, some general attributes must be understood.[4]

Characteristics of Bureaus

1. *Bureaus are the "doing" part of the government.* The legislature enacts the tax laws, but the Revenue Department collects the money. The governor may freeze the hiring of new state employees, but it is the bureaus that get the flack for being slow or unable to provide services. While the politicians get the public attention, it is the bureaus that have day-to-day contact with the citizens: staffing the universities, running the prisons, sending out the public aid checks, issuing fishing licenses, and the like. The impact on the public of the lawmaking process is felt only when statutes are implemented by the bureaucracy. About 125,000 individuals are employed by the state to handle this implementation.

2. *Bureaus are organized and assigned functions by law.* The laws vary in their specificity and clarity. Therefore, the legislature is very important to the bureaus and bureaucrats: new legislation may sharply change the jobs of people at the doing end of government.

3. *Bureaus are funded by law.* Bureaucrats may ask for money, but they function at the mercy of the administrators above them, the Bureau of the Budget, the governor, the appropriations committees and their staffs and the legislature. In the end they can only spend what is granted after the long, and sometimes tortured, appropriations process is over. Moreover, a middle level bureaucrat, who makes a request for "my section" in September may not know for sure until March if his request got into the governor's budget, until July if it made it through the legislature, and if he got all that he asked for until reduction vetoes are signed in October. Even then, it is possible, as in fiscal year 1983, that reductions will be made during the spending year. Authorized funds can actually be called back before the end of the fiscal year.

Consequences of the Characteristics

1. *Bureaus are responsible to policymakers, clients and bureaucrats.* Obviously, the policymakers govern the bureaus—through those laws, appropriations, executive orders and the political appointees at the top. But bureaus and bureaucrats also feel responsible to those they serve. The measure of that responsibility varies from one bureaucrat to another and is affected by the type of client served by the department. Agricultural bureaucrats generally identify very strongly with farmers. University personnel want to serve students. Corrections officers are more ambivalent about their prisoners and parolees, and not all public aid administrators proudly defend the needs of the poor.

But bureaucrats cannot help but try to take care of themselves, and one another. A bureau needs high morale. Bureaucrats need to feel effective and successful. They want a sense of control over their tasks. Sometimes they take their time following orders from above, or they interpret the laws their own way in order to preserve a sense of control, or to meet needs of clients.

2. *While there are exceptions, for the most part bureaus and bureaucrats are committed to serve the public.* Bureaucrats who manage soil conservation, for example, are there because they believe their expertise can help farmers and developers save soil resources for the future. People in the Department on Aging, a small agency of only about 100 people, want to make the lives of older citizens better and more comfortable. Similarly, the administrators in the Department of Mental Health and Developmental Disabilities, the largest of the code departments with about 14,000 employees, believe not only in serving the obvious mental health needs of the people in the state, but wish to do more. They envision new programs far beyond current service levels.

3. *Bureaucrats want their bureaus to survive and flourish.* When bureaucrats believe in their function, they are likely to believe "more is better." It is a rare bureaucrat who will ever come before the legislature to say, "We have solved the problem you created our agency for ten years ago, so now you can eliminate this unit." Bureaus want to grow, increase their authority and add to their budgets.

Implications of the Consequences

1. *Bureau responsiveness to external lawmaking varies in relation to many factors.* Politically appointed agency heads, the governor, the governor's staff and the legislature can make or break bureaus. But not all those centers of power speak with the same voice. Some bureaus thrive better under Republicans while others do better under Democrats. Some ride a wave of popular support—the Environmental Protection Agency in the 70s, for example—while others, such as public aid, wallow in unpopularity. Department directors are usually loyal to the governor, but middle-level bureaucrats may have their own friends in the legislature, the press and particular interest groups. Some agencies have powerful clients, like the Department of Commerce and Community Affairs, which serves businesses and local governments. Others have numerous but weak clients, such as the Department of Human Rights, which serves the victims of discrimination. Prudent bureaucrats know the pressures they themselves can exert as well as the sources and strength of pressures that can be used against them.

2. *Agencies have staff for legislative relations.* A regular feature of large governmental units is that they have a legislative liaison, someone designated to handle inquiries from the legislative branch.[5] The size of the liaison staff depends a good deal on the size of the department. Most departments have one person, but the liaison person can get additional staff support from the agency when needed. For example, in 1983 the Department of Agriculture had three staff people designated to keep in regular contact with legislators concerning legislation affecting the department. On many issues—bills, amendments, information for staff or constituent problems—the liaison is the first agency person that a legislator or legislative staff person contacts. The liaison provides an answer on the spot, or works through the agency to get what is needed. It is the liaison's job to keep abreast of legislative affairs: broad trends in revenue and appropriations as well as any details or concerns legislators may have about aspects of the agency or its programs. The liaison helps the department director and lower department personnel prepare for hearings on budgets, specific bills or any other matters legislators want to know about.

3. *Career administrators are continuing participants in lawmaking and administration.* James D. Nowlan illustrates this fact as follows:

David Kenney, director of the Illinois Department of Conservation, recounts overhearing a conversation . . . among state employees in which he heard himself referred to as "the new director over at Conservation." At the time Kenney had held the job for four years and was a senior director in the Thompson administration. The body of Illinois government bureaucracy is permanent. Agency heads are transient; most stay only three or four years (1982, p. 143).

Even though directors come and go, middle-level program heads, section chiefs, divisional deputy directors, field station managers, and the like, may spend an entire career within a department. These are people who know and are known by many other middle managers in the department, and other departments. They have contacts with career staff in the Bureau of the Budget. They know people in the interest groups—lobbyists and group officers. In fact, they may very well be group members themselves. They have professional peers in county and city governments as well as in parallel departments in other states and the federal government. Often they know veteran legislators and legislative staff. Some have friends in the press. These careerists may not have obvious partisan involvements, but they know the ropes and are deeply interested in the politics—the development and resolution of public issues—of their profession.

Career bureaucrats help create consensus on policy proposals and the evaluation of policies already in effect. They help top executives prepare to defend the department before the legislature. On the other hand, disaffected bureaucrats can funnel tough questions to the legislative staffers for use in hearings where political executives appear. Such bureaucrats, even at middle levels, are not neutral paper pushers. They are knowledgeable insiders who supply information and take part in policy development and application. They have access to, and are called on by, other bureaucrats, administrators, executive staff, legislators, lobbyists and legislative liaisons. Bureaucrats cannot be neutral about the policies they administer. Their careers, their ideas and their day-to-day responsibilities are too strongly affected by the policies they administer.

Keeping the Bureaucracy Straight: Oversight

The primary control over policy administration in the departments is by the governor, through the agency heads and the governor's staff. For the reasons given above, the governor needs to keep a watchful eye on those bureaucrats who put policy into effect because their priorities do not always match those of the governor. With power over appointments for top departmental executives, and loyalty by the Bureau of the Budget and a top-notch staff, the governor has strong control over the bureaucracy.

Legislators also exercise their authority as both legislators and representatives to engage in oversight. "One of the most time-honored and important duties of a legislature is to 'oversee' the operations of the bureaucracy—to make sure they are spending the public's money honestly and efficiently, and running the public's programs properly." That is the judgment of the Citizens Conference on State Legislatures (1971, pp. 126-127).

The legislature has growing resources to keep bureaucrats accountable. The very detailed budget prepared by the governor's Bureau of the Budget is gone over line by line by the legislature in its appropriations process. The governor works from a fairly understandable set of statewide priorities, but the legislature's priorities are varied, complex and shifting. Not only are there two teams—Democrats and Republicans—challenging the bureaucrats, the rivalry goes forward in two environments, the House and Senate.

The work of legislative oversight is accomplished by the partisan staffs. Because those staff members are required to cover agencies both on substantive policy and their spending, they are often well aware of administrative practices at operational levels. So legislators can be thoroughly briefed by hearing time.

The growing careerism that is occurring among legislators contributes to successful oversight. More and more legislators consider themselves full-time politicians. They are well-informed on how government works, and those with specialized policy interests know what the objectives of their bills are. Veteran legislators may have been working on a particular chapter or section of the state statutes over the years, adding paragraphs, deleting others, altering criteria in the law and plugging up loopholes. After a few years such legislators know the law, the spending, the case loads and the local administering facilities of a bureau better than the latest executive appointee.

The legislature also has specialized nonpartisan staffs: the Legislative Research Unit, the Joint Committee on Administrative Rules, the Office of the Auditor General and others. Each can focus attention on administrative operations. Reports from these staff units which suggest that some executive branch agency is operating badly, inefficiently or contrary to legislative purpose often stimulate legislators to sponsor legislation to bring about change. Bills or amendments can close an office of a department, repeal the authority to carry out some function, reduce the automotive equipment line in a budget or transfer an activity to a different department. When bills to do such things go to the committee, executive branch administrators and their legislative liaisons are there to answer, explain, justify and apologize for their real or imagined offenses.

The legislature is not alone in its scrutiny of agencies and their practices. Disaffected citizens, agency clients, interest groups, social critics and the press are also watching. Legislative action often follows investigative reports in the press. All the other information sources mentioned come to the legislature, or to "their" representative, with complaints and concerns. The mere registering of complaints in the legislature brings someone from the agency—usually the director or legislative liaison—to say how the matter complained of has been rectified.

CONCLUDING OBSERVATIONS

Alexander Hamilton, in No. 67 of *The Federalist Papers*, argued that the unity of the executive made it possible for popular control while still giving "energy" to the government. In many respects the governor energizes the system of state government. Even in the realm of lawmaking, the governor plays the primary role in determining priorities for policies of statewide importance, proposing solutions to problems by formulating a legislative agenda. Visibility, staff, expertise and the very expectations people have that the governor "ought to do the job," provide opportunities for policy promotion. In a sense rivals, in another sense allies, the legislature and the governor have differing roles to play in the making of laws.

But the executive branch is not just the governor. There are many other executives, major and minor. The lieutenant governor is limited by and subject to the tasks and opportunities allowed by the governor. The attorney general and the secretary of state have substantial discretion under the constitution and laws of the state. Because they do, they too can engage in policy formulation and promotion. It is not unusual for them to appear before the legislature in support of particular legislation relevant to the tasks of their offices. The treasurer and comptroller have much more limited positions, and are less conspicuous in the legislative process.

The doing end of government—the bureaucracies—despite the low degree of visibility of their directors, have significant and continuing relationships with lawmaking and lawmakers. The bureaus are tremendous repositories of problem-solving expertise. The governor exercises primary control over that expertise, but the legislature can draw upon it also.

Moreover, because bureaucrats may stray from the legislature's intentions in policy application, the lawmakers, who take their own policymaking powers seriously, need to be apprised of how policies work out in practice. So legislators practice oversight. Some do so aggressively; they enjoy "making those bureaucrats sweat" when they appear at legislative hearings. Others do so incidentally, calling the agency's legislative liaison about a problem that a constituent is having with the department. The most systematic oversight is a result of the cyclical patterns such as annual budgets, appropriations and audits.

The separations between the executive branch and the legislature are specific and important. Nonetheless their interdependencies are substantial, as are their interrelations. The legislature expects to hear regularly from executive branch officials; indeed, it sometimes insists upon their appearance. Legislators have the resources to take initiative with or without the help of executives or the bureaucrats. Because that is true, the executives and bureaucrats willingly enter the legislative process so that their interests will not be overlooked. Checks and balances stimulate a lively legislative process in Illinois.

NOTES

[1]See *Opportunities in State Government*, Pub. 164, published in 1982 by the Illinois Legislative Council, Springfield, IL. Known as "the goodie book," it lists over 2400 appointive positions, most of which are appointed by the governor and have no salary.

[2]Cases cited in support of this quotation include the following: *People ex rel. Klinger v. Howlett.* 1972. 50 Ill. 2d 242, 278 N.E. 2d 84; *People ex rel. City of Canton v. Crouch.* 1980. 79 Ill. 2d 356, 403 N.E. 2d 242; *Continental Illinois Natl. Bank and Trust Co. v. Zagel.* 1979. 78 Ill. 2d 387, 401 N.E. 2d 491.

[3]As of early 1986, only one nominee of Governor James R. Thompson had been turned down by the Senate: Helen D. Schmid. She was renominated for a four- year term of service on the Commerce Commission, a five-member body which controls rates for public utilities. During the previous decade, the commission had to deal with tremendous increases in energy costs. Pressed in committee about the numerous instances in which she had previously voted to increase various rates, she was asked if she regretted any of those decisions. She said she did not. This evoked the view that she was insensitive to consumers' interests and on a roll call vote her nomination was defeated—26 in favor, 24 against, 9 not voting. A constitutional majority of 30 is necessary for confirmation. If the Senate takes no action on a nomination within 60 session days, confirmation is automatic. The Senate has used this provision to permit appointments without formal public approval. Former Governor Dan Walker, however, had several nominees defeated. See, for example, "3 more Walker Appointees Turned Down," reprinted from the *Peoria Journal Star*, May 15, 1973, in William K. Hall, ed. 1975. *Illinois Government and Politics*. Dubuque, Iowa: Kendall/Hunt Publishing Company.

[4]I am using the term *bureau* in a nontechnical sense to refer to any governmental administrative unit, and *bureaucrats* as upper- and middle-level decision-makers within bureaus. In the technical language of the Illinois code, *departments* are broken down into *divisions, bureaus,* and *sections.* But other terms complicate structural description: *office, branch,*

group, center, agency, and the like.

[5]For a list, see *Directory of Executive Agencies and Legislative Liaisons*, Pub. 170, published in 1982 by the Illinois Legislative Council, Springfield, IL, or subsequent updated issues.

Chapter Nine

Pressure on Lawmaking: The People, Their Interest Groups and Advocates

The government of Illinois is a representative democracy. All the people of the state directly elect the top executives and, from districts of equal population, choose their lawmakers. All the governing officials are explicitly responsible to the people. The government, therefore, does what people want and what government does has popular support. Right? Not necessarily. A national survey, designed to measure the amount of confidence people have in government, gives a discouraging report (A. Miller, 1983, p. 17). People were asked to respond to the following:

"I don't think public officials care much what people like me think."

Agree 46%
Disagree 49%
Don't know 5%
100%

Clearly, ordinary people feel a great deal of cynicism about the responsiveness of government.

But politicians are also frustrated about the difficulty of maintaining contact with the people. Many work hard to stay in touch with their constituents. They hold town meetings and public forums in their districts, but few citizens show up. So lawmakers go to county fairs, ethnic festivals, fish fries, parades and every other kind of public event. They seize opportunities to speak to the media. They use their office expense allowance ($37,000 per year for senators; $27,000 for representatives) to publish newsletters for constituents, often including questionnaires that they want people to answer.

Legislators who work at contacting people do have successes. So, too, do citizens who take time to contact their legislators. But effective two-way communication between legislators and constituents is difficult to achieve and expensive. The complications of this relationship deserve a bit of elaboration, which will be followed by discussion of the role of some important intermediaries between the people and the lawmakers.

SOCIAL STRATIFICATION AND PLURALISM

While democratic theory emphasizes the equal rights of people, equality is most difficult to demonstrate. That is probably why Jefferson, when he spoke of the created equality of humankind in the Declaration of Independence, referred to that equality as a "self-evident" truth. In most areas of human activity the inequality of people is more obvious than their equality. Some of these disparities are trivial—shoe size and hair color—others are not. The people with more tend to get richer, obtain higher status and win control over still more resources through the institutionalization of these advantages. People good at accounting have established credentials for certified public accountants (CPAs). Similar actions have been taken by physicians, lawyers, academics, nurses, realtors, plumbers, insurance agents, pharmacists, electricians, architects, tree surgeons and a great many others. Certain advantages can be passed on from one generation to another—money, property and a "good" family name—and these can aid some people in obtaining greater advantages in education, employment and social status. Conversely, inherited disadvantages can stunt development. Bright children born into a ghetto culture may sense little incentive or support for intellectual growth.

One of the enduring dicta of political science is that people differ in the degree of their involvement in politics. Robert Dahl pictures society as shown in Figure 9:1. In his discussion of this stratification, he says:

> Because many of us take it for granted that man is naturally a political animal, the existence of active and involved citizens, who make up the political stratum, hardly seems to need an explanation. What is more puzzling is the presence of an apolitical stratum.
>
> It appears to be true, nonetheless, that in most political systems those who show great interest in political matters, are concerned and informed about politics, and are active in public affairs, do not make up a large proportion of adults; usually, it appears, they are a minority. Even in countries with popular governments where opportunities for political involvement are extensive, the political stratum by no means includes all the citizens. On the contrary, . . . a sizeable number of citizens are apathetic about politics and relatively inactive: in short, they are apolitical (1976, pp. 101-102).

Dahl cites a study of American society by Verba and Nie (1972) that put the label "Inactives" on 22 percent of the people who simply avoid any involvement in political affairs. They found five distinguishable categories of participants ranging from 21 percent who merely voted, to the other extreme of 11 percent who were "Complete Activists" and engage regularly and deeply in all aspects of political activity. The other 46 percent were between these extremes or unclassified. It is important to note that the study showed a strong correlation between vigorous political participation and high socioeconomic status. The greater the wealth, income and education, the greater the likelihood of political participation. Still, it must be noted that 14 percent of the Complete Activists were from the lowest third of the population in socioeconomic status (SES), while 10 percent

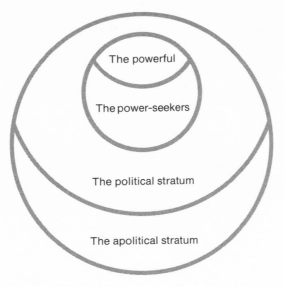

Figure 9:1

Source: Robert A. Dahl, MODERN POLITICAL ANALYSIS, Fourth Edition, ©1984, p. 95. Reprinted by
permission of Prentice-Hall, Inc, Englewood Cliffs, New Jersey.

of the Inactives were from the highest third of the population on SES.
So while there is a high socioeconomic bias among participants, there are
low SES people that are deeply involved in politics at all levels.

People differ not only in their degree of interest in politics, but in
the breadth of their conception of what government should do and how
it should do it. This difference was noted in Chapter Two where the three
cultural streams—moralistic, individualistic and traditionalistic—were
discussed in some detail. Moralists view citizen participation as a matter
of civic duty. For individualists, participation is a take-it-or-leave-it matter; if one is doing business with politicians, helping them out is good practice. For traditionalists political activity is undertaken in defense of stability, even if that activity consists of passive submission to the powers that
be. Traditionalists who are low in the societal pecking order make political
demands cautiously and deferentially, passing them up the line informally from lower to higher planes of influence. Moralists typically demand
that an activist government make improvements in the quality of life in
society through regulation of a great range of social relations. Individualists are much less dogmatic about definitions of "the good life,"
but definitely want it to be negotiable. Traditionalists tend to equate the
quality of life with lack of government regulation. The point here is to

be reminded of the countless societal differences that generate contradictory demands on governments and political parties.

The diversity of socioeconomic and political interests in Illinois is
very great and makes the state's politics highly complex. Northeastern
Illinois has a disparate and interdependent industrial-commercial-service
economy. The state has every kind of farmer, with fruit and timber interests in the south, truck farmers and dairymen in the northeast, soy-
bean and corn farmers in between and red meat and poultry farmers pep-
pered across the landscape. The people of Illinois are unequally distributed
and there are many ethnic enclaves, some of which take pride in their
ethnic identity, while others do not. Illinois is not a melting pot, but as
a microcosm of the nation, it contains a plethora of specialized interests.
Some are regularly involved in the political process, others rarely raise
their voices. Given this mix, if lawmakers take seriously both the *representative* and *legislative* sides of the job, they will face a dilemma. The
lawmaker is willing to represent an array of constituent interests, but
what do the various interests want? How does one determine a course
of action in the face of competing claims forwarded by rival interests?
Are trades and compromises possible? What legislative bills can satisfy
individual needs and desires while simultaneously fulfilling statewide requirements for good policy?

SPECIALIZED SPOKESPERSONS

The same social forces that encourage specialization in other social
enterprises have encouraged a similar pattern in politics. It pays to
specialize. So it is not surprising that there are specialists who articulate
political demands.

Journalists and Editors

Professionals in the news media are a regular source of political
demands. The most familiar position is that of the editorial writer. They
are experts, paid to observe with a keen eye what their communities' needs
are, and to recommend/urge/oppose/deplore what government is doing
and how local legislators are acting in a variety of situations. The press
corps has a big role in determining what problems get high priority in
the legislature. If any of the daily papers or television stations in the state
does a substantial investigative report on treatment of mental health patients, coal mine safety, quack treatment of cancer patients, car theft rings
and chop shops or abuses at abortion clinics, chances are that several
legislators—perhaps a committee—or even the party leaders will jump on
the issue. The greater the visibility of an issue, the likelier the legislative
response. And if media interest continues, legislation in some form will
be enacted.

A moralistic view of politics is especially common among the press. Columnists and TV editorialists regularly call upon government to intervene in whatever situation they view with alarm. They expect government to be rational, programmatic, principled and, above all, open to constant press scrutiny. Nothing raises the righteous wrath of the press more quickly than for politicians to have secret meetings or delay the release of governmental information. In Illinois this leads to routine conflict between the press and the politicians because a majority of the latter take an individualistic, pragmatic approach to politics. The politicians see their job as a business, and believe they can solve some problems better through negotiation and compromise behind closed doors rather than in the public forums. The press is often cynical about such politicians' motives and are, therefore, quick to criticize their modes of action. Similarly, media are frequently enthusiastic about governmental reforms and see nonpartisanship as a cleaner, more public-spirited mode of governing. Listeners and readers often feel that the media moralists look down upon the politicians.

Ambitious Candidates and Officeholders

People who want public office, or want a higher office than they already have, often specialize in demanding new policy changes. They look at the constituency they want to represent and try to imagine policies or changes that would please those constituents. Proposing policies or changes is the way they position themselves to become serious contenders for office at the next election.

This kind of behavior is as common among people already in an office as among first-time candidates. Members in the House often think of running for the Senate. Both representatives and senators keep a close watch on the congressional opportunities. They keep in mind the chances for statewide office, and, if they are of the governor's party, the vacancies in agencies, commissions or the governor's staff. Depending on the size and significance of their hometown or county, they are aware of office opportunities back home too.

Bureaucrats watch for opportunities too, such as higher appointments or perhaps the chance to move to elective position. Because the legislature is such an open, permeable institution for policy proposals, many people in and outside the legislature are drawn to the task of proposing policy ideas and getting them considered in the legislative arena.

Academics and Social Critics

Academics sometimes focus their research, creative thinking and writing on aspects of public policy or the political process. Occasionally they assume temporary or continuing positions on commissions, staffs or in other public offices. While not as conspicuous as such figures at the national level, like Henry Kissinger or Zbigniew Brzezinski, some academics are well known to Illinois political insiders. Similarly, there are occasional gadflies who play the role of social critic like Ralph Nader at the national level. Patrick Quinn, who spearheaded the effort to change the Illinois constitution and cut back the General Assembly to a 118-member House from single member districts, is a conspicuous example. So is Michael Shakman, a persistent opponent of the Chicago Democrats, whose suits concerning public employment have resulted in federal court orders enjoining city and state public officials from firing public employees for political and patronage reasons (McClory, 1983).

Lobbyists

Lobbyists are agents of organized groups who, usually on a continuing basis, attempt to affect the policymakers and the policies of the state. Lobbyists are political information brokers, go-betweens, who link policymakers, especially legislators, with the organized groups that are interested in and feel affected by public policies and regulations.

Organized groups, or interest groups, as they are often called, are commonplace in Illinois. According to David Truman the term *interest group* refers to a set of people who, "on the basis of one or more shared attitudes, makes certain claims upon other groups in the society for the establishment, maintenance, or enhancement of forms of behavior that are implied by the shared attitudes" (1951, p. 33). With that broad definition in mind we can think of companies, softball teams, ethnic groups, professional associations, labor unions, universities, churches, sororities and bird-watching clubs as interest groups. Society encompasses a vast array of groups whose members share certain goals that as a group they seek to advance.

In most instances, such members spend the bulk of their energy pursuing their interests in apolitical processes. Many—corporations, labor unions and farmers groups—focus their attention on making money. Some seek pleasure (bird watchers), skill (softball teams) or intellectual and spiritual enrichment (universities and churches). Sometimes the interests of such groups are affected by public policy and this leads them to the political process. They become *political* interest groups. Bird watchers want protection for endangered species of wild fowl. Ethnic groups want government to open or enhance economic and social opportunities for their people, labor unions want job protection for their members, churches want tax exemptions and universities want scholarship money. Even when the groups get drawn into politics, most of their members concentrate their efforts and concerns on nonpolitical matters.

How do such groups engage in politics? If they have financial resources, they hire a lobbyist. If not, they seek a volunteer to do the job.

The lobbyist is just one more example of the specialized professional in a complex society. As a broker between the interest group and its members on one side and the policymakers, including legislators, on the other, the lobbyist passes information—mostly demands from the group, mostly constraints from the policymakers—back and forth (Cook, 1982, pp. 113ff). The lobbyist uses detailed inside knowledge about the legislature, its members and its process. But he/she also must thoroughly know the interest being represented and how governmental policies can advance or limit the group's interests.

Because of the two-sided, specialized knowledge necessary for the job, it is rare for a person to begin a professional career as a lobbyist. Lobbyists are usually in their thirties or older and have specialized knowledge in a particular interest, or have experiential knowledge of the legislature. Consider Lobbyist A, a successful university lobbyist who was a speech communication professor. Having taught, done research and been involved in faculty affairs at the university for many years, this professor understands the university and its interests. Moreover, politics was a favorite hobby and the professor having helped out in numerous campaigns, knows a great many state politicians. Lobbyist A knows the interest group side of the job (the university) extremely well and is politically knowledgeable, but had to learn about the people and processes at the Statehouse.

Lobbyist B is also a university lobbyist, but B's background is quite a contrast to A's. B began as a staff member for the Illinois House Democratic leadership. There B analyzed bills, mastered the appropriations process and also came to know many of the members and the special characteristics of their various constituencies. When it became clear that career advancement as a legislative staff member was limited, B became a lobbyist, eventually landing a job parallel to that of A.

A and B find contrasting aspects of their jobs difficult. A had to learn a lot about the legislature to do a good job, but did not need much coaching on the university's interests. B enjoys mastery of legislative politics, but the conflicting interests within the university do not always make sense.

Another way to understand lobbyists is to see them in different categories. A leading Illinois lobbyist, Robert Cook (1982, pp. 116-117) whose lobbying experience at the capitol spans 35 years, recently delineated six types:

— The executive director of a trade association. Cook himself was one of these. The executive director is the manager, or chief administrator, of the association. Generally responsible for all the services and affairs of the group, the executive director also deals with government, including the legislature.

— The government relations representative of an association, firm
or union. Such organizations are often large and may have one or
several individuals whose main or full-time job is lobbying. Cater-
pillar Tractor, Central Illinois Light Company (CILCO) and the Illinois Education Association usually have three or four lobbyists.
— A contract lobbyist, like a lawyer or accountant, organizes a firm
to serve several clients that want part-time or occasional representation and lobbying services. Gerald Shea, a former Democratic
House leader, is the senior partner of such a firm.
— A similar, but special type of contract lobbyist is the law firm lobbyist. Some law firms contract with clients who want legal services
and lobbying representation. An example of a lawyer with his own
firm is James L. Fletcher, formerly Governor Thompson's chief
deputy, whose clients include a number of Illinois associations and
businesses.
— Another special type is the governmental lobbyist who may work
for a department, agency, board or university, but usually has the
title "liaison." The Legislative Research Unit, a staff arm of the
Illinois General Assembly, published a *Directory of Executive Agencies and Legislative Liaisons*, which describes a legislative liaison
as a person assigned "to handle inquiries from the legislative
branch." They do more than handle inquiries; they lobby.
— There are a variety of volunteer lobbyists. Some are activists in
groups with little or no formal organization or resources, such as
student groups, retirees, churches, clubs, hobby groups and the like.
Some are from highly organized and informed citizen groups such
as the League of Women Voters. They may be stimulated to action by a particular issue, or they may have the time or interest
to pursue lobbying as an avocational concern. Some are student
interns.

Implicit in the differentiation of these types is the notion that people lobby with varying degrees of skill, experience, involvement and commitment. Illinois statutes have registration requirements for "persons who
undertake to promote or oppose the passage of legislation by the General
Assembly, or its approval or veto by the Governor . . ." (*Illinois Revised
Statutes*, 1984b). We will say more about this law later, but pursuant to
it, most lobbyists register. In 1984, the list included 595 individuals, more
than three registered lobbyists to every elected lawmaker. That does not
include volunteers or liaisons, who are not required to register. On the
other hand, it does include many who lobby irregularly.

WHY LOBBY?

Laws confer advantages and disadvantages, privileges and obligations, benefits and burdens. Laws determine who shall pay taxes, at what
rate, on what income or wealth, who shall get what benefits, services,

or welfare. Obviously, funding for programs is accomplished through legislative appropriations. People, as individuals, and in their positions or roles in groups, have stakes in these legislated matters.

At the same time, lawmakers sense the burden of their task. Typically they are generalists, not elected because of narrowly defined professional expertise like nuclear physicists, agronomists, quality control engineers or cost accountants. Often they come from small businesses, law offices in general practice, teaching careers or the like. In varying degrees they want to reflect their constituents' views while making sensible policy. They are open to expertise on the one hand and political advice on the other.

Lobbyists provide an informational connection between lawmakers and organized groups. Effective lobbyists know the interests of their groups and understand the policy issues. They study the options under consideration, and perceive the consequences for their group (and their rivals) of loopholes, variations and exceptions. Lobbyists pursue advantages for their clients by communicating information, demands and support to the policymakers.

METHODS OF LOBBYING

The image of fat cat lobbyists handing out envelopes stuffed with cash to legislators who voted right will probably never be erased from the minds of Americans. Indeed, less than a generation ago, Paul Simon (1964), then himself an Illinois state legislator, wrote an article for *Harper's* in which he said that a third of the legislators who served with him in the Illinois legislature accepted payoffs. From time to time since then, charges have been made that lobbyists buy legislative support. It is difficult to prove that such activity—which would obviously be done in secret—no longer takes place. What does seem certain is that the social significance of state policymaking has grown substantially. Therefore the processes of government have become more open and visible. Its participants—members, staff, lobbyists and press—are professionals, often with long careers in state politics, who seek upward mobility in government positions. All these factors place a premium on reputations for integrity and honesty. Corruption and payoffs probably explain a very small proportion of the decisions made today in Illinois' state processes.

The traditional lobbying method is direct communication. Lobbyists seek out legislators to present the best, most appealing case for their client's point of view in a particular matter. Both lobbyists and lawmakers like to do that face-to-face, one-on-one. Often, however, legislators cannot or will not take the time. So the communication may be by telephone, often a brief conversation, which the lobbyist follows up with a memo, a report or a briefing paper. On the other hand, the initiative does not always lie with the lobbyist. Lawmakers in need of information go to lobbyists with those needs, especially lobbyists with reputations for knowledge and integrity.

When a lobbyist cannot get to a lawmaker in person, he/she will contact staff or secretaries. Party leaders and committee chairpersons usually work closely with particular staff members. Sometimes lobbyists do well to make their case to such staff. But most lawmakers do not have personal staff. They do have secretarial support, and secretaries become a means of access, channels for passing along information.

Lobbyists engage in many activities that support direct lobbying. They monitor new bill introductions, study relevant bills, attend committee hearings, sometimes testifying, keep track of separate actions in both the House and the Senate and observe floor sessions. Many are visible around the brass rail which circles the rotunda that separates the House and Senate. Lobbyists, legislators, staff, press, bureaucrats and curious observers stand around the rail engaged in every kind of small talk, high jinks and serious negotiation.

There is no such thing as a typical lobbyist or a typical process, but the following description comes from a practicing lobbyist in another state. In all but a couple of trivial details it could have come from an Illinoisan:

> I will get down to the capitol regularly at seven fifteen or seven thirty in the morning and will have breakfast in the capitol coffeeshop. There will usually be some legislators there and I will sit with them and we will talk. Quite often they will be members of one of my committees that will meet at eight o'clock. I will go to the committee meetings whether or not I testify. I cover all the committee hearings as far as I can to be able to answer questions. That period will be over about nine thirty and we'll go back to the coffeeshop with a different group of people and sit down with them. They will go upstairs at ten o'clock to sit through the session. I will go upstairs and call the office, talk to some other lobbyists and go down and have another cup of coffee with some other lobbyists. We will compare notes. The session adjourns at a quarter to twelve. I will pick up a couple of legislators and take them out to lunch in the coffeeshop or somewhere else.
>
> Quite often I will have a one o'clock hearing. If not, by this time the doors to the floor are open. Let us assume that it is still early in the session and they aren't meeting afternoons. I will talk to many legislators on the floor, stand around and wait for them, quite often because they are being called to the phone or someone else is talking to them, and you line up back there and it looks like a bull ring or something. I also will check with committee clerks somewhere in this interim. We will read the bills that were introduced or printed the day before. You will pick up those that apply to you. If you have time, then you will start doing some research or I will go down to the three

o'clock hearing if there is one. If not, then I will spend my time on the floor of the Senate or the House.

Five o'clock or five thirty you will leave. I will go up to the apartment, sit down and have a drink, and, if I am taking someone out to dinner I get dressed for dinner and we go out. If not, we run what we call the track-line, which is running the bars to see who is out with whom. Quite often there is a legislator out by himself. You see who is with whom. Notice how the alliances are building up. About midnight or one o'clock I call it a day and go home (Zeigler and Baer, 1969, pp. 77-78).

Social lobbying is an element of the larger process. Lobbyists who are in the capitol on a daily basis when the legislature is in session are a highly sociable set of people. As the example above suggests, the hours are long, and periods of specific, scheduled activity are irregular. Lobbyists may get chances to chat, have a drink or eat dinner with lawmakers with whom they have no immediate business. But by so doing they learn about lawmakers' interests, abilities and political strengths. Lobbyists in turn let the lawmakers know about their groups and their resources. Social lobbying goes on constantly as a form of keeping in touch.

When lobbyists or their groups reach the lawmaker through the lawmaker's own constituents, it is called grass roots lobbying. For example, the Illinois Education Association may need a particular lawmaker's vote on an upcoming matter, and the member may be undecided about support or opposition. If the lobbyist has no more persuasive arguments (a rare occurrence), he/she might contact local parent-teacher associations in the lawmaker's district. "Get the teachers and parents to write letters to your representative. Say we need a vote for HB 1000." By getting people at the grass roots level involved, lobbyists exert pressure on legislators and also show their clients that they are on the job.

GROUPS AND THE LEGISLATIVE PROCESS

In contrast to many operations in the governor's office, the courts and the bureaucracies, the legislature conducts most of its business and arrives at its final decisions openly. Moreover, its chambers are collegial bodies. Some members may be more influential than others, but on roll calls each lawmaker's vote counts the same. Finally, legislative enactments must go through specific stages. A bill must pass every stage, so lobbyists can deal with the problem of building or opposing supportive coalitions at various decision-making points. Following are some illustrations.

Getting on the Agenda

Groups and lobbyists anticipate the next legislative session. Formulating their ideas well ahead of a session, they can prepare bills suited to their interests. Groups like the League of Women Voters, Illinois Hospital Association and the Illinois State Chamber of Commerce may have extended discussions among constituent members about their priorities. Others may have one very specific legislative goal. Some, like the Illinois Railroad Association or the Illinois Concrete Pipe Association may not have any specific new legislation in mind but are on the lookout for bills that might change their currently satisfactory circumstances.

Of course, some matters appear on the agenda automatically. Appropriations bills for all the agencies of government will be on the agenda every year. Some groups routinely ready themselves for the annual battle of the budget: school boards, public employees, the Illinois Taxpayers Federation, the Illinois Road Builders Association and many others.

Getting Bills Introduced

It is not difficult for groups to get bills introduced. As noted before, it requires little effort for a lawmaker to introduce a bill. A well-formulated idea is transformed into a bill by the Legislative Reference Bureau on the request of any legislator. Groups are very willing to supply such ideas; they may even draft them into legal language, requiring only that the Reference Bureau sign off on proper bill form.

But, once a lawmaker takes up the sponsorship of the bill, it is really his/hers. The lawmaker may sometimes change the definitions and provisions of the proposal. From the point of introduction the group and lobbyist must take their chances with the sponsor and the legislative process, relying on influence and persuasion.

Prior to Committee Consideration

The period between introduction and committee consideration is a quiet one as far as the public processes of the legislature are concerned, but it is during this time that lobbyists are often busiest. Occasionally, determining which committee will consider the bill is quite important, even vital. Groups and lobbyists may care—groups have more influence in some committees than others—but the assignment is usually a matter settled by the sponsor and the leaders without much attention given to the preferences of groups.

Lobbyists spend a great deal of time studying bills that have been introduced. They look both for bills favorable and contrary to their interests. They look closely at specific provisions: where could their interests be advanced by more restrictive language, a loophole or a milder provision? Finding these, lobbyists try to influence the sponsor accordingly.

Often the sponsor is open to suggestions about these fine points. At this early stage the sponsor may have little sense of how easily the bill will move in committee or on the floor. The fine points may not mean as much to the sponsor as they do to the lobbyist. Moreover, the sponsor has risked little or nothing at this point. No "face" is lost by sponsors for making subsequent amendments to their own bills. In fact, it is common practice. So lobbyists often ask sponsors to revise bills with suggested amendments, promising future endorsement of the amended bill. Getting commitments for such amendments is least complicated for the lobbyist at this early stage. Only the sponsor has to be convinced. So the early period of a session can be a crucially important time for productive lobbying.

Committee Consideration

Lobbyists take committee hearings seriously. They attend to let legislators know about their concerns. Some will want to testify, others simply sign a witness slip indicating to committee members that they are for or against a bill. Lobbyists can be effective during committee hearings in other ways. For example, a lobbyist opposing a bill can sometimes do a better job of stopping the bill at the hearing by giving a committee member some penetrating questions about the content and effects of the bill. If questioning reveals that the sponsor does not really know the bill's effects, committee members will be reluctant to vote a "do pass" recommendation. In such a situation the committee usually decides to defer action on the bill, and move to other business. The sponsor is left to decide how to get the bill into a form that can pass. If, at that point of vulnerability, the committee member with the questions and the lobbyist opposing the bill come to the sponsor with some suggested amendments, the sponsor may accept these proposals in order to get support for a revised version of the bill. When the bill is called again, the sponsor starts by moving the requested amendments to the bill. (As a courtesy, committees routinely adopt amendments by sponsors to their own bills.) Then the bill, as amended, is heard on its merits. If no further opposition is heard, such a bill is routinely recommended "do pass as amended." Thus the informal relationships of lobbyists with bill sponsors and committee members in the early part of the legislative process can be very important.

Subgovernments

Recurring phenomena noted by scholars of Congress have been named "subgovernments." According to Ripley and Franklin:

"A typical subgovernment is composed of members of the House and/or Senate, members of congressional staffs, a few bureaucrats,

and representatives of private groups and organizations interested
in the policy area" (1980, p. 8).

An enduring and successful subgovernment in Illinois consists of the
veterans' groups and their lobbyists along with the Department of
Veterans Affairs and the legislative committees that deal with veterans.
Their strategy has been—session after session—to add small benefits and
advantages to the laws affecting veterans. The legislative hero of this
subgovernment was Representative Lawrence DiPrima, now retired from
the House, but for a long time the chairman of the House Veterans Affairs Committee. A loyal regular Democrat, DiPrima got supporting information, ideas and legwork from both the Department of Veterans Affairs and from the lobbyists of various veterans' groups such as the
Veterans of Foreign Wars, the American Legion, Disabled American
Veterans and Amvets. He managed to represent veterans' benefits as
favors to constituents throughout the state and not as a matter of partisan advantage. Legislators from both sides of the aisle (many themselves
veterans) regularly supported DiPrima's bills. Similar subgovernments
appear to have formed around the regulation of horse racing (and the ex-
clusion of dog racing) and support for arts and the Illinois Arts Council.
Subgovernments thrive by distributing tangible benefits to rather inconspicuous, harmless or even honorable beneficiaries. Part of the success of such enterprises depends upon the perceptions that "there appear
to be only winners and no losers" (Ripley and Franklin, 1980, p. 21). Of
course, the public always pays.

Floor Consideration

The bigger the bill and the more groups and lobbyists lined up to
contest it, the less control any lobbyist has at the floor stage. On minor
and middling bills, groups and lobbyists supporting them hope the sponsor knows the bill and can handle floor debate. Lobbyists help get supporters on the floor in time for action and keep track of opposing lobbyists,
who may be trying to arrange for negating amendments on second reading
or defeat on third reading. Sometimes lobbyists resemble coaches at a
football game; they may be able to call the play, but only the lawmaker
can run with the ball. Sometimes lobbyists look more like cheerleaders,
urging on their side, but having little substantive effect on the outcome.

On big bills, legislative leaders working with/against the governor
and major group lobbyists are the primary actors. Specific lobbyists then
spend most of their time trying to keep track of the action so that they
can keep their clients back home informed. The action often is beyond
their control. Strategy is determined in the offices of the legislative leaders
or the governor. Sometimes lobbyists are invited to take part; more often,
once the leaders have basic plans settled, they call on lobbyists to help

line up certain lawmakers. For example, the school aid formula is a perennial concern. It establishes how much money local school districts will receive from the state. Slight changes in the formula can make large dollar differences both to the state and the various local districts. To increase funding for education, legislative leaders and the governor often make trades that affect spending for other state agencies. By the time the larger agreement has been settled among the leaders, the resulting school aid coming to ABC county, part of Representative Y's district, might not seem good enough to Representative Y. But if, to the Illinois Education Association, the deal is the best available, the IEA lobbyist will encourage Representative Y to vote for the school aid formula bill. "It's the best we can get statewide and for your district. If you will vote for it, I'll let the teachers' association in your district know that you voted for the best formula possible at the time." Representative Y may be reluctant to support the new formula, solely out of personal or party loyalty, but with the lobbyist's promise to pass the word to a significant local group, the teachers' association, the compromise is easier to accept.

It is very difficult to assess just how much influence lobbyists have at the floor stage. Some are very close to the action, keeping in constant contact with the bill sponsor. If the sponsor wishes, the lobbyist may, in fact, call the shots, telling the sponsor what amendments to accept, which to fight and even preparing amendments for the sponsor. Typically, however, more seasoned lawmakers are not dependent on the lobbyists' expertise.

Getting to the Leaders

The importance of the leaders in directing the legislative process has been noted repeatedly in this and previous chapters. Knowledgeable and effective lobbyists do not ignore the leaders. Majority and minority leaders develop packages of bills intended to address related problems. Lobbyists try to get provisions advantageous to their interests into the leaders' bills. Sometimes lobbyists keep bringing back a basic idea for legislation year after year, despite recurring defeats. A lobbyist may eventually get the leadership behind the bill and finally get it passed.

An example of the latter, during 1983, was the "Freedom of Information" bill. The bill provided comprehensive procedures for opening up public records of all public bodies in Illinois to the people and the press, including records of the state, municipalities, villages, county governments, school districts and special districts, such as airport authorities, mosquito abatement districts, park districts and other relatively small units. Subject to some constraints, "Each public body shall make available to any person for inspection or copying all public records. . .," and do so within seven days (Illinois Revised Statutes, 1986d).

In previous sessions, the bill had the support of a variety of "good government" interest groups including the American Civil Liberties Union, Common Cause, news media persons organized as the Freedom of Information Council, and others. Opposing the bill was the Illinois Municipal League, which speaks for the public officials of the hundreds of medium and small-sized cities across the state. They consider freedom of information a burdensome and intrusive problem for already overloaded local bureaucracies. In 1983 the bill was sponsored by reform Democrat, Barbara Flynn Currie, from the Hyde Park area of Chicago. She negotiated some amendments with potential opponents of the bill. Speaker Michael Madigan, who authored some changes to the bill, then signed on as a cosponsor. With help from its friends and the speaker, it passed 88 to 18 in the House. The Senate sponsor, the assistant majority leader, Terry Bruce, guided the bill to passage on a 57 to 2 vote. The active support of the speaker and Senator Bruce was instrumental in the bill's passage.

Getting to the Governor

Obviously, the governor is important; so is the governor's staff. The governor may be persuaded to take an interest in the group's bill even before it is introduced. Perhaps it becomes one of the elements mentioned in the State of the State address, or gets incorporated into the governor's budget. Of course, there are risks. Getting a bill into the governor's program may mean the lobbyist "loses control." Moreover, the bill may then pick up enemies, rivals of the governor. Lobbyists are usually willing to take those risks.

Lobbyists do not forget the governor after the session is over. The Illinois governor's broad veto powers can significantly affect the final form of a bill. For example, the Freedom of Information bill passed the legislature in a form very satisfactory to its supporting interest groups. But the governor amendatorily vetoed the bill by making more than a dozen substantive changes, adding language in some places and deleting it in others. Supporters of the bill as passed by the legislature felt that the governor's amendments watered down public rights, and preserved too much discretion for public officials. He had, in their opinion, responded to the views of the Illinois Municipal League lobbyists who opposed the bill.

At this point, the bill's sponsor, Representative Currie, had three choices. She could seek to override the governor's veto, thereby enacting the bill as passed by the legislature. That would take a three-fifths majority in both houses. The Freedom of Information Council urged that approach. The risk in this choice was that if she sought exclusively to override the amendatory veto and got too few votes, the bill would die. The second choice was to ask the House and Senate to concur in the governor's changes. That only would require a constitutional majority in each chamber. Then the governor would certify the concurrences and the bill would become law as he had amended it. The third choice was to do nothing, letting the bill, as amended, die. Wanting something to pass, and fearful that if she only tried an override, Republicans would side with the governor and the attempt to get three-fifths would fail in one chamber or the other, Currie took the only other choice. She asked for concurrences to the governor's amendments, and the bill sailed through both houses easily in its amended form.

Because of the breadth of the veto power (see Sevener, 1985), and the willingness of Illinois governors to use the full range of those powers, the job of interest groups and lobbyists is not over when the session ends in June. To the contrary, they make strenuous efforts to follow up on bills they support, and oppose, by communicating their wishes to the governor after the legislative session is over.

Lobbyists, Interest Groups and Regulation

Policymaking does not stop when the legislative process is over. The bureaus and bureaucrats have significant roles to play as well. This was discussed in Chapter Eight and in the earlier discussion of subgovernments. Much of what state government does by law is regulation. Bureaus put these laws into effect. One very specific job is to make rules for administering laws.

Illinois has a thoroughly specified set of procedures for rulemaking. They are contained in the Illinois Administrative Procedure Act (*Illinois Revised Statutes*, 1986c). Agencies initiate and draft proposed rules which are published in draft form in the *Illinois Register*, a weekly publication of the Secretary of State's Office. Then there is a period of time in which comments and criticisms of the proposed rules can be submitted by any person, lobbyists included. Often the agency makes revisions in response to concerns from the public.

The Illinois Administrative Procedure Act also provides for a legislative committee, the Joint Committee on Administrative Rules (JCAR), with its own professional staff, to review all rules. Its job is to review all administrative rules, making sure that agencies do not write rules that exceed the authority granted to them under the law or any related court decisions. JCAR's authority to review is accompanied by the power to issue a "statement of objection" to any rule of any agency. The agency then has 90 days to change the rule, withdraw it or take no action. "No action" results in the automatic withdrawal of the rule. Changes are reconsidered by JCAR. In order to prohibit a rule, it must introduce a joint resolution to the legislature, which must be passed by both houses. If the resolution fails in either house, the agency can put the rule into effect.

These formal sanctions are the "gun behind the door." Because all agencies must develop and publicize draft rules, and because there are procedures to challenge them, the rulemaking process is thereby opened to the public and to interest group action. Lobbyists, as part of their job, keep tabs on this rule-making. Hard work by an interest group at the rule-making stage can definitely help the interest group's cause.

REGULATING THE LOBBYISTS

Consistent with the individualistic stream of political culture, lobbying is not heavily regulated in Illinois. Political activists in this state expect government to preserve a fair marketplace of business and political rivalry, and then let the competitors seek their own advantages. So the emphasis in the Illinois Constitution and laws is on the rights to participate and seek advantages through the policy process. The constitution sets the stage in Article I, Section 5, "The people have the right to assemble in a peaceable manner, to consult for the common good, to make known their opinions to their representatives and to apply for redress of grievances."

Statutory control is expressed in the Lobbyist Registration Act (*Illinois Revised Statutes*, 1986a). As the title of the act states, the basic feature of this legislation is simply to register people "who undertake to promote or oppose the passage of legislation by the General Assembly, or its approval or veto by the Governor, and to provide a penalty for the violation thereof. . . ." The act is short (less than two full pages in the *Illinois Revised Statutes*) and its requirements are relatively simple: paid lobbyists must make public who they are, whom they work for and what they spend in lobbying efforts, "showing in detail the person or legislator to whom or for whose benefit such expenditures were made." Lobbyists are required to make several reports a year, and these reports are considered public information, available for public inspection and retained for three years from the date of filing.

While the Secretary of State's Office is scrupulous in maintaining these records, the enforcement of the act is, at best, occasional. Lobbyists willingly register and most file timely, sworn reports of expenditures. But documenting them is not required. Penalties for violators are severe. An individual can be found guilty of a class 3 felony, meaning a fine and/or imprisonment for one to 10 years. A corporation can be fined up to $10,000, and a convicted person is prohibited from working as a lobbyist for three years. Cases may be prosecuted by states attorneys or the Office of the Attorney General. However, as of early 1986, no one had been prosecuted under the statute.[1]

LOBBYISTS AND CAMPAIGN FINANCE

The lobbyists who represent well-financed interests groups, such as the Illinois State Medical Society, the Illinois Association of Realtors, the Illinois Education Association, are important participants in decisions about campaign financing. Many interest groups form political action committees, commonly known as PACs. The interest group collects money for political activity from the group members. The PAC funds are distributed to campaign organizations of candidates. Typically, the interest group's lobbyist helps decide which legislative candidates should get PAC money for their campaigns.

Small, or regionally concentrated groups usually contribute directly to particular candidates. Large groups with statewide concerns may likewise contribute to selected candidates. But it is increasingly common for these groups to give funds to the campaign committees of either the House or Senate Republican or Democratic campaign committees.

It is a growing practice for legislators, especially legislative leaders, to hold fund-raising dinners during May and June while the legislative session is at its peak. A brisk business is done with lobbyists, who buy tickets and thereby support the campaign needs of party organizations or individual candidates.

Some interest groups provide other help to legislative candidates. State labor unions and teacher organizations are particularly effective in getting local units of their group to help legislative candidates with campaign work. Usually lobbyists are the key decision-makers about which incumbent lawmakers ought to be helped or opposed by an interest group in particular contests.

PACs are of growing importance to election financing. Gove (1985) notes that spending in campaigns by PACs at the state level alone grew from $5.2 million in 1982 to $8 million in 1984. A *Chicago Tribune* study (9 February 1986, p. A14) reported as follows:

> In all, political action committees, known as PACs, and other special interests, including unions and corporations, contributed $2,234,613 to the campaign funds of Illinois legislators, or 39.6 percent of the $5,644,455 raised last year, state records show.

The PACs are legitimate means for affecting politics, but they can become a corrupting link between lobbyists and lawmakers. To this time very little research has been conducted on this aspect of Illinois legislative politics.

EFFECTIVENESS OF LOBBYING

There are no agreed-upon criteria for evaluating or measuring the effectiveness of lobbying or even the relative power of interest groups on the policymaking process. There are too many variables operating simultaneously to measure such power with any precision. For instance, a specific group may control a small policy matter while another gets a minor concession on a major piece of legislation—which has more power?

One rough, comparative effort to examine the strength of interest groups in the United States separates the states into three categories. States are grouped as having strong, moderate or weak "pressure-group systems" (Morehouse, 1981, pp. 107ff). Illinois is included among the 18 states with a moderate pressure group system. From her perspective, Morehouse included the following as "significant pressure groups" in Illinois:

> Illinois Manufacturers Association
> Illinois State Chamber of Commerce
> Coal operators
> Insurance companies (State Farm and Allstate)
> Illinois Education Association
> Illinois Medical Society
> AFL-CIO unions (Steelworkers)
> Retail merchants
> Race tracks
> Farm Bureau
> *Chicago Tribune*

People actively involved with the legislature will no doubt agree with several of those, and add others. The significance of some groups rises and falls as issues come and go. Other groups possess enduring significance. For example, it is highly likely that by the year 2000 the Farm Bureau and the insurance lobbyists will still be of major significance in Illinois. Coal operators could be weakened or strengthened depending upon what technological and economic changes take place during the coming years in energy use; their significance as lobbying interests could be greatly changed.

It is evident from the regular appearance of hundreds of lobbyists each legislative session that the groups they represent consider their efforts worthwhile. Their real or imagined effectiveness, however, is not ascertainable on the basis of what legislation becomes law. It must be deduced by imagining the negative consequences if a lobby group were not actively lobbying at the same time as its rivals. Unions assume that business groups are powerful. Utilities interests fear the unrivaled pressure from consumer groups. Railroad interests are afraid that the trucking companies will put them out of business.

CONCLUDING OBSERVATIONS

Lobbyists are an easy target for criticism, especially from a moralistic perspective. But lawmakers and bureaucrats consider lobbyists necessary and valuable participants in policymaking. They provide expertise, they enrich the adversarial process and they are an accessible link to specialized publics who have legitimate interests in public policy. Some observers fear that lobbyists, as advocates for particular views, will be too influential. They are concerned about the links between lobbyists, political action committees, the financing of particular lawmakers' campaigns and those lawmakers' votes on the lobbyists' legislative proposals. Lawmakers, on the other hand, expect legislative advocacy, and consider it a useful gauge of pressure. As politicians they feel confident of their ability to evaluate the relative importance of both neutral technical information and political influence.

Zeigler points out that "there is a clear relationship between the extent of professionalism in the legislature and the strength of the groups. The more professional the legislature, the less powerful are interest groups" (1982, p. 121). In Illinois, legislators are not dependent on lobbyists in the absence of professionals on the legislative staff and in executive bureaucracies. As we have made clear throughout this book, the Illinois legislature is among the most professionalized legislatures in the country. Its members are not beholden to a compelling band of lobbyists. Moreover, the Illinois General Assembly is comprised of strongly organized and competently led political parties. The parties and party leaders do not deny lobbyists a role, but they do have the leadership resources to override the influence of lobbyists. Yet the very diversity of Illinois lobbyists adds greatly to the mix of information for policymaking, and the competition of ideas lets the policymakers control their selection. The Illinois policy process is dynamic and flexible.

Finally, most lobbyists protect their own reputations for professionalism and integrity in all their actions. Many lobbyists will be lobbying for years, or engaged in other aspects of politics. Integrity is as valuable as competence. Lobbyists must be candid with lawmakers about what bills do and how they affect people. Lobbyists who want to be effective support the norms of professionalism and integrity. These two informal norms constrain lobbyists just as much as they do members and staff.

NOTE

[1]The source of this information is the Opinion Division for the Attorney General. There is an Attorney General's opinion on the applicability of the statute. See *Illinois Attorney General's Opinions For the Year 1977*, No. S-1319, published in 1977 by the State of Illinois, pp. 210-213. It was issued in response to questions by Senator Don Wooten, from Rock Island, Illinois.

Chapter Ten
Lawmaking in Illinois: Outputs and Outcomes

The Illinois General Assembly does not act alone in policymaking, but as the first branch of state government, and the institution closest to the people, it must both receive praise and accept responsibility for the shape of government and the nature of public policy in the state. This chapter will look at the four kinds of legislative outputs. First, we will briefly reexamine lawmakers' two alternative roles: legislator and representative. Second, we will report on lawmakers' voting patterns on controversial legislation. Third, we will consider levels of state service in several essential policy domains including education, welfare and economic regulation. To gain a sense of how well Illinois delivers services, we will make some comparisons to other states. Finally, we will examine the "self-regarding" actions of the legislature: how it has provided for its own operations and how it might operate differently.

MEMBER OUTPUTS—REPRESENTATION AND LEGISLATION

In Chapter One we sketched out the dilemma in which lawmakers find themselves. On the one hand, they must represent their constituents' interests while, on the other, they have to legislate for the whole state. One way to see how lawmakers deal with this dilemma is to examine their newsletters for a recent year.[1]

One of the services lawmakers have provided themselves is administered through the Legislative Printing Unit (LPU), a service agency of the legislature. The LPU will publish a newsletter, prepared by the lawmaker, in an attractive format. The content is up to the member, who typically obtains help from the leadership's partisan staff. Newsletters must follow the LPU's rules about the content and timing of the letter. Here is an excerpt from those rules:

> A newsletter must be limited to reporting legislative activities to constituents and may not be used for partisan political purposes. A newsletter shall not contain appeals, direct or indirect, for campaign contributions or other funds, and shall not be used to announce or advertise campaign activities. The voting records of other members of the legislature may be included only with the prior written consent of the other member(s) placed on file in the [Legislative Printing Unit] either incorporated into the newsletter or printed as an insert.[2]

According to Legislative Printing Unit records, 42 members published newsletters in 1983; these are the basis for the analysis that follows.[3]

First, notice the breakdown by chamber and party of those sending newsletters:

Senate		House	
Democrats	Republicans	Democrats	Republicans
4 of 33 = 12%	8 of 26 = 31%	23 of 70 = 33%	7 of 48 = 15%

A greater proportion of the newsletters were sent out by House members. About 25 percent used them, while about 20 percent of the senators did so. Only a few of the Senate Democratic majority produced newsletters, but majority Democrats in the House were more frequent users of this medium to communicate with constituents. Within that group we find that 18 of the 23 Democrats were from Cook County. Only a handful of the downstate Democrats sent out newsletters in 1983. Republicans were more evenly divided on this score: three of eight newsletters from Senate Republicans were from Cook County suburbanites and five were from downstaters. In the House, three of seven newsletters were from members representing districts all or partly in Cook County, one was from a collar-county district and three were from downstate.

Predictably, lawmakers emphasize their commitment to the district and its people in these newsletters. A common technique is to include a questionnaire for constituents to fill out and return, which lawmakers can then use to guide their legislative actions. Sometimes members use newsletters to report on the opinions expressed by constituents through previous questionnaires. All told, 18 members used questionnaires or provided reports on earlier questionnaire results. The questions vary from the easy "yes" question, to some very difficult and complex choices about taxes and spending. A popular question in 1983 that easily got "yes" answers was this one:

> Do you favor a proposal currently before the General Assembly which would create a Citizens Utility Board that would argue the consumer's views before the Illinois Commerce Commission?

In a time of rising rates for natural gas, electricity and telephones, the suggestion that consumers will get better utility rates from the Commerce Commission if a board of citizens were established was highly popular.

Some legislators tried to get tax information. For example:

> Do you favor an increase in the state income tax?

A more complicated inquiry came from a member who put two questions together:

> (a) The tax multiplier is used to equalize property tax assessments throughout the state to eliminate disparities in the county assessment

county assessment procedures. Do you favor elimination of the tax multiplier—even if it means less monies from property taxes to all units of local governments, including schools?

Yes   No

(b) Would you favor elimination of the tax multiplier if it was coupled with a requirement for county assessors to assess property at the required 33-1/3 percent value with provisions for penalties if they failed to do so?

Yes   No

We do not know what answers these questions produced, but probably the majority of citizens who read through the last pair would favor the elimination of any mechanism that would multiply taxes, even though the idea of "tax multiplier" is to make taxes fairer rather than higher. This example illustrates one of the problems in member/constituent communications. Members sometimes have difficulty describing their policy choices on complicated issues. Moreover, constituents may offer responses about questions they do not understand. Members proceed at their own risk as they interpret constituents' opinions.

One of the favorite ways members choose to show their association with the district is to have a picture, or more than one, of themselves with constituents. There are such pictures in 24 of the 42 newsletters. Often the member is pictured with school children. Sometimes the picture shows a class of students standing with their lawmaker on the Capitol steps. Or it may picture the lawmaker in a school room, or talking to an attentive citizens' group. Several members are shown with senior citizens. Another graphic means of identifying with the district is to feature a map of the district boundaries. Six members included such maps in their newsletters.

Members use their newsletters to claim credit for bringing home the bacon to the home folks. Six provided very explicit lists of roads in the district to be developed, improved or enlarged at the state's expense. Others referred to specific state projects, or included a picture of state-funded construction going on in the district. One added the following:

> The total number of State employees is the lowest in 15 years. Yet our District has approximately 1500 residents who are employed by the state . . . [in various] government departments.

This representative makes it abundantly clear that the district is getting more than its share of state jobs.

A couple of members have a mail-back portion of the newsletter on which the constituent can fill out an "I advise you of the following . . ."

form. Two more include a form that invites the constituents to "Write your own bill." The invitation states, "Most of you don't have the chance to introduce bills and push ideas that you think would make good laws. Well, I want to give you that chance. Below I have left room for you to write down some ideas that you would like to see made into laws. Just fill out the form and mail it back to me." Another member explained that a bill he had sponsored and had gotten passed actually resulted from a citizen proposal. The idea came through a constituent's letter and later it was further amplified at one of the member's community coffees. "This new law is the result." A couple of lawmakers reported to their constituents that they have, or wish to have, an advisory committee of citizens to meet with them and help them decide how to vote on issues. One invited constituents to volunteer for the committee. Another indicated a list of constituents with whom he consults. In short, lawmakers make numerous efforts to present themselves as representatives.

Nearly all the members use newsletters to present themselves in the legislator role, making significant policy decisions for the whole state. A great many of the newsletters report to citizens on legislative actions taken relating to hazardous wastes, utility reform and senior citizens. Downstate members consistently refer to farmers' concerns and agricultural issues. Cook county members note mass transportation issues. The following is a fairly typical illustration that appeared in the newsletter of Representative James Marzuki, a House Democrat from Park Forest in the 80th district, which includes parts of Cook and Will Counties, directly south of Chicago.

UTILITY COMPANIES FACE TOUGH REFORMS

Consumers will be receiving more protection from unnecessary actions by public utilities under a plan I was proud to support. One bill I introduced required Illinois Commerce Commission rate increase hearings to be open to the public. I was also one of the initial supporters of the bill creating a Citizens Utility Board to represent consumer interests before the ICC. Other important reforms include phasing-out of Construction Work in Progress costs (CWIP) in the rate base; implementing a program whereby consumers will eventually be paid back for CWIP pass-throughs in their utility bills; prohibiting other automatic pass-throughs such as pollution control, advertising, out-of-state-coal transportation costs; and prohibiting winter utility shut offs.

Utilities are essential services, not luxuries, and utility companies have a monopoly on the essential service market. I think utility companies are only too aware of their advantages and they have capitalized on [them] outrageously (Representative James Marzuki, October 1983).

Explaining Hard Choices

Although members do picture themselves in the legislator role, they find it very difficult to explain the truly "hard choices." In 1983, for example, there were thousands of bills and hundreds of important decisions but, everyone agreed, the preeminent issue was what to do about tax increases so the state would not have to live with the governor's "doomsday budget" (Parker, 1984). The final compromise was approved in the House by a 63-55 vote, and in the Senate by a vote of 30-29. Party leaders in both houses voted for it. The compromise increased income taxes temporarily (18 months), permanently added a penny to the sales tax, eliminated sales taxes on food and medicines, provided a deduction on the income tax for residential property taxes and made a few less significant revenue law changes.

Table 10:1 illustrates how difficult it is for legislators to explain their votes in favor of taxes. Of the 42 legislators reporting to constituents, seven did not report on the tax increase because their newsletters were produced before the compromise was settled. The remaining 35 fall into three groups: those who commented directly and explicitly on the tax issue (54 percent), those who treated the issue indirectly or partially (20 percent) and those who did not comment on the tax issue at all (26 percent).

Table 10:1   An Analysis of Lawmakers' Comments on the Income/Sales Tax Increase (1983)*

Vote on Tax Increase	Direct Comment	Indirect Comment	No Comment	Total
Yes	4	5	7	16
No	15	2	2	19
	19 (54%)	7 (20%)	9 (26%)	35

*Of 42 members whose newsletters were analyzed, seven produced the newsletters before the tax issue came up for a vote. Three of those voted "yes" and four voted "no." None made advance statements about their position on the issue.

Of those opposed to the tax, the great majority (15 of 19) were very direct in their reports to constituents. Senator Laura Kent Donahue (R-48) explained the issue and her position in detail. This excerpt is illustrative:

> As for the actions of the 1983 Illinois General Assembly, I am disturbed that once again government has overreacted during a crisis. Short term solutions were offered to problems deserving a long term plan. To bail the state out of a fiscal crunch, the legislature passed and the Governor signed a permanent sales tax increase and temporary income tax increase.
>
> I voted against these measures because I strongly feel that before we considered raising taxes, we must assure the citizens

of Illinois that there is no unnecessary or wasteful government spending (Senator Laura Kent Donahue, Fall 1983).

Representative Larry Stuffle (D-105) put his report into a newspaper style describing his reaction as follows:

> Citing a lack of funding for downstate Rep. Stuffle voted against an income tax increase.
>
> "The people of my area are going through some difficult times. They cannot afford a tax increase that does not directly benefit them or their community," said Stuffle. "As usual, too much money goes to Chicago. For every $3 in tax hikes in our district, we only get $1 back" (Representative Larry R. Stuffle, September 1983).

An atypical description by an opponent of the tax increase was the indirect comment by Representative Ted Leverenz (D-51).

> The cry of Governor Thompson was "Raise Taxes!" and property taxes, the income tax, the gas tax and the sales tax were raised.
>
> I don't believe raising taxes is the answer to the mismanagement, loss of productivity, and the national economic woes which have caused Illinois' fiscal problems (Representative Ted E. Leverenz, November, 1983).

Leverenz did vote no, but nowhere in the newsletter is he explicit about it.

Being direct about yes votes was much more difficult. After sketching Governor Thompson's "unpopular" proposal, Senator Howard Carroll (D-1) bit the bullet this way:

> The issue of increasing state taxes dominated the Spring session of the 83rd General Assembly. After months of negotiations, an accord on a compromise tax package was finally reached by the legislative leaders and the Governor.
>
> Settled only hours before the new fiscal year, the compromise tax package passed as the only responsible solution to the state's fiscal crisis.
>
> Rather reluctantly, I voted for the compromise state income tax package to continue essential services to my constituents, only after I was able to achieve unanimous agreement on how these added funds would be spent (Senator Howard W. Carroll, October, 1983).

Suburban Republican William Mahar was also direct:

> A 20 percent temporary increase in the state income tax and a 1 cent permanent hike in the sales tax were passed during the closing hours of the session. I supported the scaled-down temporary income tax to avoid further budget cuts, particularly in education, mental health and corrections. We could not afford to let the quality of these services deteriorate further (Senator William F. Mahar, August 1983).

The majority of supporters of the tax increase (12 of 16) either commented indirectly or not at all. Senator Arthur Berman put it as follows:

> The problem of declining state and federal revenues combined with an increasing demand for government services dominated the days between wintry January 12 and sultry July 2. The governor had barely been sworn in for a new term before he was asking the Legislature to approve higher income and gasoline taxes. He proposed a budget based on existing revenues and showed as that drastic cuts in state services would result. The state's cash crunch was so bad in early 1983 that I joined many of my colleagues in voluntarily returning a week's pay.
>
> We wrestled with the overall financial problem for months before hammering out a compromise. It calls for additional revenues to help us bridge the gap of recession and cuts in federal funds. I believe that agreement will fund needed services to the poor, the elderly, the unemployed, the schoolchildren and others (Senator Arthur L. Berman, August 1983).

Berman voted for the tax but never quite said so in the newsletter. Rep. Dwight Friedrich (R-109), generally considered to be a pretty conservative downstater, voted for the tax increase as a loyal member of the House Republican leadership team that negotiated the final resolution. His newsletter described the process, but not his vote:

> When we went back into session in January of this year, Illinois was faced with approximately $500 million in borrowed money and delayed payments brought about by reduced sales and income tax revenues. Lawmakers either had to increase taxes or trim almost $1 billion from an already lean budget for fiscal year 1984 (which started July 1st). These cuts would have affected payments to local schools, general assistance, mental health and other vital programs.
>
> The General Assembly passed, and the Governor signed into law, a tax package that will provide enough money to pay off the indebtedness and delayed bills, and provide the same amount of funds available for the year ending July 1st. It also contained a new tax relief deduction for residential property owners. These tax changes are shown in the chart below (Representative Dwight P. Friedrich, November 1983).

Nine legislators did not mention the matter of income tax and sales increases in their newsletters. All but two of those nine voted in favor of the tax increases. The posture of a legislator—a policymaker acting on behalf of the good of the whole state but perhaps at the expense of the district—is politically difficult and potentially painful. The careful language in these excerpts illustrates why the governor, or any other leader, has so much difficulty getting tax increases adopted by the lawmakers, who can only hope their constituents will not punish them for supporting it. Even in the examples noted above, Stuffle and Carroll justify the state policy choices they made in relation to the "good" of their own constituents.

Variations on the Representative-Legislator Dilemma

In a study of U.S. representatives, Roger Davidson observed a "nongeographic focus" among certain lawmakers (1969, pp. 123-124). For example, one black congressman noted that he speaks for black people "everywhere." That perspective seems to be prominent among minority lawmakers in the Illinois General Assembly. For example, black legislators were the only ones to point out in their newsletters legislative action on a bill to provide public assistance through the Department of Public Aid for sickle cell anemia diagnosis and treatment under medicaid. One spoke of his efforts to pass a resolution calling on Congress to amend the U.S. Constitution to grant congressional representation to people who live in Washington, D.C., a mostly black population. These issues got no attention in newsletters from white lawmakers.

Women members, not men, noted issues of gender. One noted her election as the chairwoman of the General Assembly's Commission on the Status of Women, which has promoted legislation on matters such as domestic violence, displaced homemakers and many forms of sex discrimination, such as sexual harassment in the workplace. Women lawmakers tend to take more note than their male colleagues of family issues such as no-fault divorce, birth defects, child pornography and public education policies.

Commentary on the Representative-Legislator Dilemma

In Chapter Five we pointed out the gradual increase in the proportion of professional lawmakers—those who describe their primary occupation as member of the General Assembly. They are highly aware that, although they pass legislation that affects "all the people," the people to whom they owe their jobs are their own constituents. In newsletters members emphasize their stewardship to their constituents.

Not surprisingly, lawmakers claim credit and avoid blame. For example, numerous legislators claimed credit for supporting the Citizen's Utility Board (CUB) bill. Some described their participation in rallies to stir public support and hearings at various places in the state, and implied that a furious battle occurred to bring "powerful utilities" with "high-paid lobbyists" to heel. In fact, at each stage of legislative action there were almost no lawmakers who spoke against CUB. A few industry opponents spoke at committee meetings, but at no time did anyone seriously think they could stop the bill, which passed easily.

Avoiding blame and claiming credit sometimes requires nimble footwork. One suburban legislator, Representative James Marzuki who devoted about 15 percent of the newsletter to explaining his no vote on the tax increase, then turned around and claimed credit for how the tax revenues were appropriated:

> I was greatly disturbed that funding for . . . the Arts Council was eliminated under the Governor's "doomsday budget. . . ." The Illinois Arts Council is the only state-funded program which encourages the cultural development of our citizens. If the Governor's doomsayers had their way, Illinois would be the only state in the union without a state art agency. . . . I am greatly relieved that the General Assembly approved legislation I cosponsored to restore funding for these programs (Representative James Marzuki, October 1983).

The funding only came about as part of the allocations made after the tax increase compromise was approved, an increase Marzuki was content to blame on others.

The dilemma of legislating wise policy while representing one's constituents is real, and the members struggle to explain their decisions to the folks back home. As the newsletters make so evident, lawmakers want to look good in their districts. The compelling need to appear so means that constituents can have significant leverage with their representatives at all stages of the legislative process.

LEGISLATIVE VOTING BEHAVIOR

Voting is one of the chief things that the legislature does. Committees vote on amendments and bills. Each house votes separately on every enactment. There are votes on countless amendments, resolutions and conference committee reports. The very frequency of voting makes it difficult to explain or systematically analyze. Voting records of legislators are difficult to completely assemble because voting is so commonplace. Records of votes taken on the floor are preserved in the House and Senate journals, but because bills are voted on individually, thousands of bits of data must be brought together before any systematic inquiry can be undertaken. The information we will present here is based on a small sample of roll-call votes which is described in more detail in previously published research (Van Der Slik and Brown, 1980).

The investigation focused on roll calls on final passage (third reading) in each chamber between January 1977 and December 1, 1978. Votes on all regular legislation in which not more than 80 percent of the members voted on the winning side were included, thereby ignoring votes that were unanimous or nearly unanimous. By these criteria 412 Senate roll calls and 556 House roll calls were identified. Using random selection, 25 percent of these contested roll calls were coded for statistical analysis—103 in the Senate and 139 in the House.

Participation

Members can respond to the roll call by voting yea, nay, present or by not voting at all. Because a constitutional majority of 30 yea votes is necessary in the Senate, and 89 in the House (the House was comprised of 177 members in 1977-78) for a bill to pass; present is in effect a nay vote. Two findings were immediately apparent. Voting participation on contested votes was high, and members rarely voted present. Present is a way of letting constituents know that the member was there, while not obviously voting against a bill. Voting present is not commonplace on contested votes. The average usage by senators was 3.3 percent, and 5.8 percent for representatives.

Absenteeism varied too. Every member missed a few votes. On average, senators and representatives missed 17 percent of the roll calls. Nonetheless, 26 representatives and 11 senators voted on 90 percent or more of these roll calls, a very high percentage. At the other extreme, five senators and eight representatives missed 40 percent or more of the roll calls.

Party Voting

Partisanship is strong in Illinois and is evident in roll-call voting on contested issues. A "party vote" is one on which a majority of Democrats voted the opposite of a majority of Republicans.[4] In the Senate 58 roll calls, or 56 percent of the contested votes in the sample, were party votes. There were 83 party votes in the House, or 60 percent of the sample. Partisanship is stronger in the Illinois General Assembly than in the U.S. Congress.

Member loyalty to the party can be calculated by determining the percentage of times the member supported the party position on party votes. Party loyalty was much more consistent among Democrats than among Republicans. In the Senate, Democrats averaged 88 percent to only 73 percent for Republicans. Similarly, in the House Democrats scored 86 percent while House Republicans scored 71 percent. This is a substantial difference.

A review of individual scores revealed that the core of the party loyalty among Democrats was concentrated among the Chicagoans. Downstate and suburban Democrats tend to have below-average party loyalty scores.

While Republicans showed lower scores, there was no clear suburban or downstate pattern. Some suburban Republicans showed high party loyalty while others did not. The same is true of downstate Republicans.

An alternative way to analyze conflict in the legislature is to contrast Cook County legislators with those from downstate. Members were scored for their Cook County or downstate loyalty. Only about 25 percent of the roll calls pitted a majority of Cook County against downstate. As might be expected, factional loyalty scores were lower than party loyalty scores. The few exceptions were usually downstate Republicans, members not strong on party loyalty who regularly oppose the Cook faction in Cook-versus-downstate votes.

Changing Patterns

No single factor explains legislative voting patterns more strongly than political party, but party loyalty is not lockstep. There is a substantial amount of tolerance within the parties for deviation by members. Leaders often urge but cannot command loyalty. On contested roll calls, Democrats usually stick together better than Republicans.

In the House, two short-term factors affected partisan loyalty. The reduction to 118 members (each from a single district) has probably increased the average party loyalty scores. A veteran House member put it this way:

> . . . I think that diversity has been lost. There are few people now serving in the General Assembly who are not devoted advocates of their party's philosophy. As a result, many viewpoints are not adequately presented . . . (Josephine Oblinger, December 1983).

That means even higher party cohesion is likely in the 118 member House. On the other hand, the Chicago Democrats, traditionally the core of the Democratic unity, have suffered some divisions because of factional fights in city politics between Mayor Harold Washington and Cook County Democratic party chairman, Edward Vrdolyak. Those divisions carry over into the legislature.

Sometimes party loyalty may be hidden in party loyalty scores. For example, party leaders will allow less than maximum support from legislators of their party on a roll call. In the 1983 tax increase action a compromise was achieved by the four leadership teams and the governor. All the leaders of both parties voted for the tax increase, and both sides in both houses had to supply enough votes for adoption. There were 63—three to spare—in the House, and 30—just enough—in the Senate. But the leaders willingly let some members of their party, those who believed their constituents would insist on a no vote, vote against the bill (see Parker, 1984, especially pp. 83-89). One of the reasons leaders keep close to the members is to know when to "let them off" from matters that may be controversial in their constituencies.

Friends and Neighbors

A great many votes are not for party. They are for friends, for seat-mates, for office neighbors or for the representative of the district neighboring one's own. Logrolling camaraderie supports the individualistic style of legislative politics on bills of minor or middling importance. There is a sense among members that everyone is entitled to push his/her own pet ideas. But it is up to the individual members to herd pet bills through the process. If one of those pets gets into trouble, it is up to the member to decide whether to spend time and effort fixing it, or to let it die while moving others along. When a bill does survive the trip to final passage, colleagues may vote for the bill with little concern about its substantive merits, but with real commitment to a good sponsor who produces "good bills."

The notion of being a "good sponsor" is very important. Because the legislature processes so many bills, and because the bills cover so broad a range of content and specialized information, members take their voting cues from other trusted legislators. Members are constantly sizing each other up; a lawmaker's reputation is crucial to passage of his/her bills. When a good, hard-working member—Representative Dogooder—sponsors a bill that "Amends various Acts regarding vandalism of traffic control signs, devices, structures and related subjects," it goes through with very little discussion. On the other hand, someone—Senator Whizbang—who doesn't do his homework and doesn't know his own bill, may get merciless questioning on the floor revealing his ignorance about a bill that "Amends the Unemployment Insurance Act relating to job retraining programs." On the roll call the votes are not there, more as a reaction to Whizbang than to the bill.

STATE OUTPUTS—AN OVERVIEW OF PUBLIC POLICY

How do the policies enacted in Illinois compare to policies in other states? In previous chapters we have described the legislative process and the people in it. But these facts can be better understood and more fairly evaluated by drawing some parallels with other states. The politics and policies of states are obviously affected by circumstances beyond their control. The desert environment of Nevada dictates starkly different policy problems from those faced by state officials in small, but densely populated Rhode Island. To have any sense of Illinois accomplishments in public policy, comparisons with other states are needed. We will examine some key indicators of economic and social change in Illinois and elsewhere.

Then we will consider tax revenues and the relative effort states must make to get them. We will see the variations in state services and try to connect them to aspects of state political cultures and their legislatures.

For purpose of comparison, Table 10:2 provides data on Illinois, the nation as a whole and five other states. California is in many ways a leading state. In Elazar's terms (see Chapter Two), it is predominantly moralistic, especially southern California, but more individualistic in the San Francisco Bay area. Georgia is a leading deep south state with a traditionalistic culture. Massachusetts, one of the original Yankee moralistic states, is now dominated by the individualism of Irish Catholics and later immigrants. Oklahoma is marked by sunbelt growth and a mix of traditionalism and individualism. Wisconsin is a Great Lakes, neighbor state with a distinctively moralistic culture.

As the population data show, Illinois is one of the largest American states with a relatively high population density and heavy concentration of people in metropolitan areas. What may be surprising is the slow rate of population growth in Illinois compared to the other states. Illinois is not only below average, it even lags behind its snowbelt neighbor, Wisconsin. Personal income is high in Illinois, well above the national average and higher than in the comparison states except California and Massachusetts. A look at state ranks in 1970 and 1983 reveals, that Illinois is standing still while all the others, except Wisconsin, moved up. These two sets of measures for population and personal income provide a sense that Illinois is big, rich and metropolitan, but a mature state whose growth has already occurred and whose decline might be coming.

Revenue Resources

The key to state problem-solving is revenues. The primary means of obtaining the needed dollars is taxation, which is both complex and controversial. Making comparisons from state to state is difficult because taxation takes many forms and occurs at varying levels. Illinois, for example, has a relatively low tax rate on personal and corporate income taxes, but it has high rates for licenses, such as motor vehicle registrations and drivers' licenses. Looking at other states reveals that California taxes corporate income heavily, whereas Oklahoma taxes it very modestly. Georgia's rates are low on estates and gifts, but Massachusetts' rates are high in that category, and even higher on property. Wisconsin is low on licenses, but high on personal income.

The data in Table 10:2 summarize two important aspects of taxation with good analytical tools. The first is tax capacity. The Advisory Commission on Intergovernmental Relations (ACIR) has long been interested in making comparative studies. Its tax capacity index answers this question: "How would each of the 50 states rank on a tax productiv-

Table 10:2   Indices of State Resources and Services: Illinois Compared to Selected States and the Nation

	CA	GA	MA	OK	WI	IL	USA
Population							
A-1 in 000s 1980	23,688	5,463	5,737	3,025	4,706	11,427	226,546
A-2 State Rank	1	13	11	26	16	5	X
A-3 Per Sq. Mile	151.4	94.1	733.3	44.1	86.5	205.3	64.0
A-4 Percent Change 1980-83	6.4	4.9	0.5	9.0	1.0	0.5	3.3
A-5 Percent Metropolitan '83	95.2	63.0	91.0	57.6	66.7	82.0	76.0
Personal Income							
B-1 Per Capita 1983	13,239	10,283	13,089	11,187	11,132	12,626	11,675
B-2 State Rank 1983	4	35	6	26	27	8	X
B-3 State Rank 1970	9	36	11	35	24	8	X
Tax Capacity							
C-1 1967	124	80	98	102	94	114	X
C-2 1977	114	84	95	101	99	112	X
C-3 1982	116	84	101	126	87	99	X
Tax Effort							
C-4 1967	108	92	121	80	124	84	X
C-5 1977	117	89	133	72	113	96	X
C-6 1982	99	96	119	78	128	107	X
Prisoners							
D-1 State and Federal 1982 (per 10,000 adult residents)	19	36	11	28	14	17	25
State Spending Effort							
E-1 Public Schools 1980-81	3.8	3.9	4.9	4.4	4.7	4.0	4.3
E-2 Higher Education 1980-81	1.38	.95	.53	.98	1.37	.86	1.02
State Spending							
F-1 Highways 1982	65	154	73	141	116	102	111
F-2 Public Welfare 1982	427	167	375	230	330	275	244
F-3 Public Aid AFDC 1982	447	170	369	257	422	294	303

SOURCES OF DATA
A-1-3, Table No. 12, U.S. Bureau of the Census, *Statistical Abstract of the United States, 1985.* (105th edition) Washington, D.C., 1984.
A-4, Table No. 13, Ibid.
A-5, Table No. 21, Ibid. Refers to percent of state population in standard metropolitan statistical areas.
B-1 & B-2, Table No. 731, Ibid.
B-3, Table No. 705, U.S. Bureau of the Census, *Statistical Abstract of the United States, 1982-83,* (103d edition) Washington, D.C., 1982.
C-1-6, Advisory Commission on Intergovernmental Relations (May 1985). *1982 Tax Capacity of the*

Table 10:2 (continued)

Fifty States. (M-142) Washington, D.C.: U.S. Government Printing Office.
D-1, Table No. 309, *Statistical Abstract of the United States, 1985*, cited above.
E-1, Table 67, National Center for Education Statistics (December 1983). *Digest of Education Statistics, 1983-84.* Washington, D.C.: U.S. Government Printing Office. Refers to Column 7, current expenditures for public elementary and secondary day schools as a percent of personal income, 1980, by state.
E-2, Table No. 130, Ibid. Refers to Column 4, higher education current-fund revenues from state and local government 1980-81, as a percent of personal income, 1980, by state.
F-1, 2, Table No. 454, *Statistical Abstract of the United States*, 1985, cited above. Refers to general expenditures for functions: highways and public welfare. Dollar per capita calculation by the authors, using population in A-1.
F-3, Table No. 641, *Statistical Abstract of the United States, 1985,* cited above. Refers to average monthly payment per family under Aid to Families with Dependent Children.

ity scale if every state applied identical tax rates to *each* of the 26 commonly used tax bases?'' They examine and compare not only what each state taxes, but what it does not. As a result, "tax capacity" is "the amount of revenue that each state would raise if it applied a nationally uniform set of tax rates." These uniform rates are derived from the average of all states on the 26 commonly used tax bases. Then the tax capacity index reports the per capita capacity divided by the average for all states, and the average state score is 100 (Advisory Commission on Intergovernmental Relations, 1983, pp. 3, 6). The tax capacity index reveals the wealth of a state which is available for taxation on a per capita basis.

The 1982 scores indicate that of all the states we have selected for comparison, the one with the greatest potential for tax revenue is Oklahoma. California is high. Massachusetts and Illinois are almost average, and all the others are below the average, with Georgia at the bottom. Another point that deserves notice is the change in tax capacity over time. Georgia's low tax base is substantially unchanged as is Massachusetts' nearly average one. But the greatest decline over the period has been in Illinois. Illinoisans have been used to thinking of their state as a rich state, but its relative tax capacity has dropped substantially. The economic resources of the state that are potentially taxable have declined over the period, especially in the time between 1977 and 1981.

The tax effort data are also very revealing. The ACIR defines tax effort as follows:

> Mathematically, *tax effort* is the ratio of a state's actual collections to its tax capacity. The relative index of tax effort is created by dividing each state's tax effort by the average for all states. The result may be interpreted as a measure of how much each state chooses to exploit all its potential tax bases relative to the national average. If a state has a tax effort beneath the national norm, it will have an effort index under 100. Conversely, if a state has an average tax effort in excess of the national average, it will have a tax effort index over 100.

An index of 115, for example, indicates that tax effort is 15% above the national average (1983, p. 14; emphasis added).

By 1982 Illinois' tax effort had risen above the national average joining the frostbelt states of Wisconsin and Massachusetts, where people are used to heavy tax burdens. Meanwhile in the fast-growing sunbelt state of Oklahoma, the tax burden is substantially below average. Looking at the trends within states, no state has undergone as substantial a change as Illinois. In 1967, before Illinois had an income tax of any kind, it was a low tax-effort state, nearly as low as Oklahoma. But over the 15-year period, Illinois' index of tax effort rose 23 points. It is true that Massachusetts and Wisconsin make an even greater tax effort, but both have for a long time been "high tax" states, and their rates have been more stable. We should add that while these are the latest comparable data, in 1983 Illinois temporarily hiked its income tax rates, raised the state sales tax from four to five cents and made some selective reductions (most important, exempting food and drugs from the sales tax). The net effect was a permanent tax increase and an even greater tax effort.

By examining the two measures, tax capacity and tax effort, over time, it is evident that Illinois has suffered a painful change. In 1967 its high capacity, 114, and low rate, 84, produced substantial revenues with relatively mild taxpayer pain. None of the other comparison states enjoyed such a comfortable 30-point disparity. But between 1967 and 1981 that disparity disappeared in Illinois, becoming a relationship of 99 to 107. None of the other states endured such a sharp and painful change, although, as noted Oklahoma has experienced the other extreme. Always a low tax-effort state, its burdens have eased while its potential base has grown markedly. Its 1982 disparity was 48 points, the only state in our comparison group that exceeds Illinois' 1967 situation.

Public Service Levels

Recently, Illinoisans have heard a good deal about crowded prisons and the need for public expenditures to solve this problem. One might infer from such discussions that Illinois has a large or disproportionate prison population. Such is not the case. Standardized by population, Illinois imprisons fewer people than the national average for states. The more traditional states, exemplified here especially by Oklahoma and Georgia, have high rates of incarceration. The more moralistic states, such as Wisconsin and Massachusetts, and even California, are low on imprisonment. Illinois is on the low side, more like the moralistic than the traditionalistic states.[5]

The data on state spending for education confirm the complaints that have long been heard from Illinois educators: compared to the national average for states, per capita spending is low in Illinois for public schools and higher education. The data are several years old, but all indications are that the Illinois picture continued to worsen until elementary and secondary education reforms were enacted in 1985.

The variation from the average for public schools is not too great. It is proportionately greater in higher education. California spends more than 2.5 times as much, as a share of personal income, on higher education as does Massachusetts, and over 1.6 times as much as Illinois. The low figure for Massachusetts reflects a common pattern in northeastern states: a much larger proportion of the students are educated in private colleges. But Illinois spends far less than its neighbor, Wisconsin, and a lower share than Georgia and Oklahoma.

The indices of state spending for highways and welfare can be examined together because they are calculated the same way. National averages differ, with state spending for welfare more than twice that for highways. Illinois is close to the average on highways and above average on welfare. By way of comparison, California spends more than six times as much on welfare as highways, but in Georgia the relationship of welfare to highway spending is nearly one-to-one. Another way of looking at welfare assistance is from the perspective of the recipient. In Illinois the average family payment is just below the national average. In the more moralistic states—Wisconsin, California and Massachusetts—payments are substantially higher, but in the more traditionalistic states payments are less, especially in Georgia.

As this brief overview of specific public service levels suggests, Illinois is moderately, not highly, generous in providing state services. Traditionally wealthy, the state population and economy are not growing. Public demands for more and better state services may rise, but any real increases in the amount of services, or the quality of service levels will necessitate increases in tax rates, not a prospect that Illinois legislators and governors will welcome. Until the economic and demographic prospects brighten in the state, these pressures will probably mean that the combination of partisan conflict and interest group rivalry, already so familiar to Illinoisans, will intensify. Interest group pluralism will probably continue to grow. Lobbyists and regional interests will try to retain the benefits they currently have and prevent new groups from butting in, or old groups from getting more. Professionals who provide state services—professors, penologists, welfare administrators, public health officers and the like—will continue to complain that other, even less wealthy states provide higher levels of service than are provided in Illinois. But in recent years public service professionals, many of whom take a moralistic perspective about improving community well-being, have rarely been very successful in convincing governors, much less legislators, that better, higher cost and higher quality service levels should be put in place. Office holders take the individualist perspective that expenditures for social services for "community well-being" provide dubious returns in the long run.

One growing force which may increase pressures for state spending are the public employee unions. Collective bargaining legislation approved in 1983 will encourage unionization in state and local governments, schools and universities. Besides the wage pressures exerted at the job level and in bargaining, growing public employee unions will become increasingly forceful with legislators. That will be true in the traditional lobbying around the statehouse, but also as unions activate grass roots members and union locals to take part in legislative elections. Union bargaining for services and advantages fits the individualistic perspectives of legislators about how policy decisions ought to be made.

THE GENERAL ASSEMBLY AS A SELF-REGARDING INSTITUTION

The Illinois legislature possesses the major characteristics that Nelson Polsby says typify an "institutionalized organization" (Polsby, 1968, p. 145). (1) It is well bounded: the notion of who is in and who is not is very clear, and there is a strict and selective procedure for getting in. (2) The legislature has a complex organization with distinctive functions and specialized division of labor. (3) Operations are conducted by objective rules and criteria, not by mere favoritism or discrimination and the constitution provides legal standing and authoritative status to the legislature. However, the job of making the legislature a significant institution has been left to the political participants themselves.

Two major events outside the legislature's own control stimulated its recent development. One was the reapportionment revolution which mandated districts of equal population and regular decennial redistricting, which made both chambers responsive to popular majorities. The other event was the new constitution, adopted in 1970, which removed many limits on state government and made new fiscal and organizational tools available to policymakers.

Differentiating the Participants

Responding to these developments the Illinois General Assembly has matured into a capable lawmaking body that can maintain and differentiate its information resources and attract able support personnel. Chapters Five and Six provided a wide range of data about the qualitative developments in the membership and staff. Table 10:3 provides information about the changing support system. The data about staff people are differentiated according to professional competencies and tasks. Some staffers are expected, indeed required, to be politically partisan. Others are just as specifically mandated to be nonpartisan.

Executive personnel have their legitimate but specialized support roles as well. Practically every code department and constitutional office has a designated legislative liaison. As noted in the preceding chapter, liaisons behave much like lobbyists. The reason for noting that role here is to emphasize that relations between legislators and their staff are focused upon an executive branch person whose primary job is to maintain contact with and communicate the department's point of view to the lawmaking institution. Moreover, it is routine for the executive departments to respond rapidly to legislative requests. The legislature apprises itself— all its members and staff— of who these liaisons are through the Legislative Research Unit's *Directory of Executive Agencies and Legislative Liaisons*. Requests to executive agencies through these liaisons are common.

Lobbyists, too, have their defined place in the system, and the definition is a matter of law. They are registered with the Secretary of State's Office; the Legislative Research Unit makes available to all legislative per-

Table 10:3   Number of Professional Staff People Serving the Illinois General Assembly in Recent Years*

	FY 65	FY 75	FY 80
Office of Auditor General	0	20	53
Legislative Support Agencies**	14	58	109
Leadership and Committee Staff	2	91	103
Legislative Staff Internship Program	6	16	18
Legislative Study Groups and Commission Staff	2	41	37
	24	226	320

*Estimates compiled from "Personnel Detail, Illinois State Budget," Illinois Legislative Directory, and Illinois Legislative Council File 80-84, February 7, 1980.
**Includes the Legislative Reference Bureau, Illinois Legislative Council, Intergovernmental Co-operation Commission, Illinois Economic and Fiscal Commission, Legislative Audit Commission, Space Needs Commission, Legislative Information Systems and the Budgetary Commission.

sonnel lobbyists' names, the organizations they are paid to represent, their office addresses and telephone numbers in a *Directory of Registered Lobbyists*. Similarly, the Research Unit periodically disseminates its *Directory of State Officials* which, while duplicating some of the information already mentioned, lists all the lawmakers, their committee assignments, office locations and telephone numbers. Likewise, all current staff people are listed by unit and title.

It is significant that the legislature has formalized its boundaries and put into place a specialized information system about its people and the tasks that they perform in the service of the legislative process. Like information systems generally, this adds rationality and order to the General Assembly and its politics.

Pay and Perquisites

Relative to the financial rewards of office in other states, Illinois lawmakers are well-paid at $32,500 per year. Until 1969, salary was paid per biennium. This made sense in those days when special sessions were rare and members only served from January to the end of June in the odd numbered years.[6] According to the 1970 Constitution, the General Assembly is a continuing body, and does business at the call of its leaders or the governor during both years of the biennium. Table 10:4 indicates that the number of regular session days has been fairly stable over the last six biennia, although the time spent in special sessions has varied greatly. Of course the number of days in session is not the full measure of time spent by members at their jobs. Most spend additional days at committee hearings in Springfield, Chicago or occasionally at other locations across the state. Because committees manage their own agendas, the amount of time spent this way varies. Additionally, most members maintain a district office, and a few have two or three. The number of days spent on legislative work in the district is at the member's discretion, which explains why more and more legislators describe themselves as full-time legislators.

In addition to salary, members receive fairly generous travel reimbursement for one round trip on official business per week between home and the Statehouse. For session days members receive money for living expenses at the rate of $65 per day. They receive health insurance benefits comparable to other state employees and take part in a very generous retirement system. Besides secretarial and staff support at the Statehouse office, representatives may spend up to $27,000 per year to operate one or more district offices; senators are allowed $37,000. The money may be spent for rent, equipment, staff and general office expenses. According to recent Illinois state budgets, total appropriations for the General Assembly and its agencies have been approximately $44 million in FY81,

Table 10:4   General Assembly Session Days: House and Senate*

	Senate	House
77th G.A. (elected in 1970)		
Regular Session	165	169
Special Sessions	12	13
78th G.A. (elected in 1972)		
Regular Session	162	171
Special Sessions	121	121
79th G.A. (elected in 1974)		
Regular Session	169	188
Special Sessions	64	57
80th G.A. (elected in 1976)		
Regular Session	157	170
Special Sessions	28	28
81st G.A. (elected in 1978)		
Regular Session	162	168
Special Sessions	13	14
82nd G.A. (elected in 1980)		
Regular Session	146	147
Special Sessions	---	---
83rd G.A. (elected in 1982)		
Regular Session	132	145
Special Sessions	---	---

*Special sessions can be concurrent with regular sessions or other special sessions. Therefore a particular calendar date may be counted more than once.

Source: Legislative Research Unit, 1984b, pp. 71-73.

$46 million in FY82, $47 million in FY83, $44 million in FY84 and $44 million in FY85. The first complete fiscal year following the cutback of the House from 177 to 118 members was FY84; this explains the slight reduction in the cost of operating the legislature. The point is that Illinois has a generously funded, professionally staffed and representatively apportioned legislature. It has the needed authority and resources to legislate effectively.

Changing the Legislature for the Better

To some observers the Illinois General Assembly is chaotic, unintelligible and unpredictable. Therefore, such observers believe it should be reformed to be more orderly and more simply organized. Its decisions should be made openly, deliberately and in an obviously rational manner.

From our perspective, two immediate reactions must be recorded before we can discuss reforms. First, as we made clear at the end of Chapter One, the difference between what is a reform and what is not is often in the eye of the beholder. Rules are sometimes disadvantageous to certain interests, so, in order to win, they want to reform the rules. Second, on the surface, the Illinois General Assembly does appear to be chaotic. But then so do a great many large and complex institutions—the stock market, the commodity exchange, the National Football League and fall registration at a large university. In any complex institutional process, some people engage in aimless activity, there are unmerited successes and failures and there are situations "you had to be there" to understand. But all this does not prove that the institution is ineffective or unproductive.

The major purpose of this book is to sketch out the main lines of order and organization that underlie the lawmaking process in Illinois. It is complicated because it is built upon conflicting presuppositions. One is "Everyone ought to have a chance to affect every law." In fact, literally every citizen has multiple access points to the Illinois legislative process. Each one has "my representative" and "my senator," as well as "my governor" and "my interest group(s)." Members like to respond to citizens by introducing bills that people want, or getting them to appear as witnesses. And they take very seriously their opportunities to engage in these actions themselves in the name of the constituents. The eagerness of lawmakers to serve people by passing legislation is why thousands of bills and amendments are introduced and why the legislative workload is so heavy. That eagerness is the reason why bill-sponsoring legislators say to colleagues at committee meetings, "Please report out my bill so I can see if I can pass it on the floor." The implication is that a mere committee does not have the right to kill bills. Only a majority of the entire house does. As we have stressed, the rights and prerogatives of legislative sponsors over their own bills are very strong in the Illinois General Assembly.

A different presupposition that often conflicts with the first is: "The majority does rule." There are strong majority prerogatives in the General Assembly. A cohesive majority can, and sometimes does, sweep all opposition aside in the enactment of public policy. The notion of an effective party leader means one who can keep a working majority together to pass not only noncontroversial and innocuous bills, but other bills, even unpopular ones, in order to meet many of the needs of most of the legislators in that majority. Sometimes the working majority is a combination of Democrats and Republicans backing a set of bills for which there was a negotiated agreement worked out by the majority and minority party leaders. As time passes and the legislative session moves toward deadlines, party leaders manage the bill process within and across party lines, and they manage relations between the two chambers so that compromises are made on conference committee bills. There is a tremendous amount of interaction, much of it on a face-to-face basis. After agreements have been hammered out, commitments are exchanged: "We will support A and B if you will go along on H and J." Subsequent formalities in floor action and voting may not appear to be deliberate and rational, but in fact they are. Not all aspects of negotiation on "Build Illinois" and educational reform were openly conducted in 1985 for all the world to see. Not all the lawmakers voting on the bills knew why the leaders had agreed to the compromises, but commitments were kept and reflected in publicly recorded roll-call votes.

Having said all this, we have criticisms of how the General Assembly operates. We believe, for example, that committees should kill more bills, and more thoroughly amend bills before sending them to the floor. Standing committees need to have more status, their memberships should be more stable, and committee chairpersons should gain greater legislative influence according to the thoroughness with which their committee discharges its tasks (see Everson, 1984).

The General Assembly could conduct more thorough analyses of the governor's budget. The budget is delivered late—by law on the first Wednesday in March—in relation to the legislature's own deadlines for moving bills through the House and Senate. The four legislative party staffs, House and Senate, Republican and Democrat, cannot really analyze the governor's requests until the budget is delivered. Under current arrangements they work intensely over a very short period of time, not only to examine requests for appropriations but also to assess the adequacy of revenue projections and the possibility of revisions in revenue-raising legislation. The typical result of legislative review is to change some details in the governor's request, and add expenditures popular to legislators. Many of these are reduced or vetoed by the governor. The legislature usually increases the governor's budget, as Table 10:5 shows. By a simple change in the law the legislature could require the budget from the governor earlier (perhaps a month or six weeks), thus giving members and staff more time and opportunity for legislative analysis.

By custom and its own rules the General Assembly considers the odd (first) year of the biennium to be a general legislative session, when all varieties of legislation are introduced, heard and acted upon. But the second year, which is marked by a March primary and a November election, has been characterized as a "limited session" because: "Generally the rules allow appropriations bills, bills of importance to the operation of state government, and emergency bills to be heard. The rules of each house make the determination concerning the eligibility of a bill to be advanced" (Legislative Research Unit, 1984b, p. 3). This pattern could easily be reversed to allow a more generous time for legislators to develop and introduce legislation. For example, the legislature could limit consideration of legislation to just emergency measures and appropriation bills during the first six months of the first year. But every other sort of bill could be introduced throughout that period. In the fall of the first year, emphasis could be placed on committee hearings for general legislation and nonemergency bills introduced during the preceding spring. Then there could be an early deadline in the second year for floor consideration of general legislation in the house of origin. After the March primary, general legislation could be handled in the second house along with the conventional attention given to bills important to the operation of state government and emergency bills.

Table 10:5   Gubernatorial Budget Requests (March) and Final Appropriations after Veto actions: General Revenue and Common School Funds in Illinois ($ in millions)

	Governor's Budget Request	Final Appropriations
FY 74	4,163.6	4,298.0
FY 75	4,478.2	4,995.6
FY 76	5,402.6	5,364.1
FY 77	5,649.7	5,813.0
FY 78	5,992.5	6,032.0
FY 79	6,437.5	6,528.8
FY 80	6,930.2	7,119.6
FY 81	7,629.3	7,795.5
FY 82	8,342.6	8,074.3
FY 83	8,180.7	8,132.4
FY 84	7,717.0	8,861.5
FY 85	9,038.1	9,561.1
FY 86	9,971.5	Not Available
FY 87	10,659.9	Not Available

Source: Bureau of the Budget, April 16, 1986.

Author's note: Governor Thompson's FY 84 request was the so-called "Doomsday Budget," based on projections assuming no additional tax revenues. Final appropriations expended revenues from the temporary income tax increase and the permanent sales tax increase which were adopted after the budget was presented.

This suggestion simply reflects the fact that current deadlines impose heavily on freshman legislators, and sometimes discourage good committee work during the first year of the biennium. The work load of the General Assembly could easily be spread more evenly over the last half of the first year and the early part of the second year.

There are recurring concerns expressed by participants and close legislative observers about whether or not the work and products of conference committees are handled openly, deliberately and rationally. Without reviewing the process (see Chapter Seven, pp. 148-150), it can be noted that the current deadlines and the end-of-session crunch sustain current practices. Recent research (Everson, 1984, p. 19) suggests that the use of conference committees has more than doubled since 1973. But that fact does not necessarily imply an evil. To the contrary, it can also indicate growing discrimination in legislative consideration by the second house.

Current practices make it difficult for all legislative participants to know what is in conference committee reports before they are voted on. The loose rules that permit conference committees to put novel or previously defeated provisions into bills late in the process, but only moments before final adoption, need to be changed. The willingness of members to vote these reports through, too often sight unseen, hurts the credibility of the legislative process. The General Assembly should review the openness of its conference committee procedures and stretch out the time between reports and the adoption of those reports. That would give lawmakers, lobbyists, the press and the public more time to evaluate how the conflicts between the House and Senate have been worked out before the votes on final approval.

We forward these four suggestions undogmatically. They have implications for the legislative workload and unquestionably would affect the distribution of power in the legislature. They encourage the increase of time and effort by legislators at their jobs, and thereby encourage the trend toward full-time legislator-politicians. Such changes would affect recruitment of members and staff, and other aspects of the governing process too numerous to review here. They are, however, all within the capability and authority of the legislature to accomplish on its own, by means of specific changes in its own rules and in the laws of the state. No constitutional or structural changes are needed to accomplish these changes.

We cannot close without some comment on a recent major structural change which was accomplished by constitutional amendment. In 1980 the Illinois electorate approved a change in the House from 177 members elected by cumulative voting from 59 three-member districts, to 118 members elected from 118 single-member districts. The definitive account is in *The Cutback Amendment: A Special Report*, published by *Illinois Issues* in 1982.

In our view, the amendment combined one good and one bad idea. Single member districts with one-person, one-vote elections make lawmakers more accountable to the people than the previous arrangement with cumulative voting. But the cutback to 118 members—which has saved relatively few dollars—costs Illinoisans a great deal in terms of access to the legislature and representation. It has also substantially increased the workload on the remaining members, and reduced the capacity of the House to have an elaborate division of labor in its committees. It discourages House members from specialization. It is likely to encourage members to delegate more of their work to staff.

Given the size of Illinois' population (11.4 million), House district populations average very close to 96,800. Seventeen states have lower houses with more members than Illinois, but only three require House members to represent more constituents (California, New York and Ohio). With 177 members, district populations could be about 64,500, closer to a typical legislative district population in other states, and more like the average for House districts in neighboring states (Indiana, 54,900; Wisconsin, 47,500; Iowa, 29,100; Missouri, 30,200; and Kentucky, 36,600). But the Illinois House size was changed by constitutional amendment. Reversing such a constitutional change in the near future is not very likely, but it deserves consideration.

CONCLUDING OBSERVATIONS

In 1971 the Citizens Conference for State Legislatures published an evaluation of the nation's state legislatures, and reported that the Illinois General Assembly ranked third according to a detailed list of criteria (1971). Since then Illinois has continued to improve its legislative tools and resources. The General Assembly is well-equipped and well-organized to do its work. While both distant and close observers will continue to have criticisms and call for reforms, the General Assembly is as suitably prepared to do its legislative task as Congress is to act for the nation.

The evidence of the legislature's effectiveness is difficult to marshal, however. If liberal state social services were the proof of a good legislature, the Illinois General Assembly would be deemed a failure. Illinois is very moderate in its social services, but that simply shows that the political process, particularly the legislature, faithfully represents the dominant individualistic culture in the state. The heterogeneity of interests across the state has produced a legislature that encourages member individualism (sponsors control their own bills) and strong party leaders with rank-and-file support on matters of statewide significance. Major issues do not pile up, unresolved by the political process. To the contrary, they are combined with issues that can be subdivided into distributable benefits: roads, highways and bridges, school aid formulas, temporary World's Fair financing for Chicago and convention center support for downstate cities. Leaders make deals to resolve many issues in a single package. Talk about issues is often framed in "crisis" terms—bailing out the Chicago Transit Authority (CTA) before a strike or passing appropriations before the fiscal year ends (June 30th)—but Illinois has not suffered deadlocks in its political processes like moralistic California and Michigan (see Peirce and Hagstrom, 1983, pp. 255-258, 749-772). There policymakers have been paralyzed or reversed by direct democracy: "right to work," Proposition 13, the Headlee Amendment and recall campaigns against legislators. The turnover of elected leaders has sharply shifted policies from left to right and back again in California and Michigan. By contrast, partisan turnovers in Illinois have not sharply shifted the pragmatic politics of settling issues by piecemeal compromise.

That is not to argue against future changes or improvements in Illinois political procedures. We have suggested changes, some of which would cost more money. Certain aspects of the legislature can be made more efficient while others should be more open to public view. Perhaps more resources are needed for legislators to stay in touch with their constituents. But from our vantage point the often-derided Illinois General Assembly is professional and effective as a representative and legislative body for the people of Illinois.

NOTES

[1]The individuality of lawmakers shows up in varying newsletter names and formats. All were published during 1983 by the Illinois Legislative Council. We will simply list members by name and provide the date of the newsletter's publication.

Senator Arthur L. Berman, August 1983.
Senator Howard W. Carroll, October 1983.
Senator Laura Kent Donahue, Fall 1983.
Representative Dwight P. Friedrich, November 1983.
Representative Ted Leverenz, November 1983.
Senator William F. Mahar, August 1983.
Representative James Marzuki, October 1983.
Representative Josephine Oblinger, December 1983.
Representative Larry R. Stuffle, September 1983.

[2]"Rules on Printing by Legislative Service Units of the Illinois Legislative Council" (effective July 1, 1982), p.2. The rules were originated

by the Illinois Legislative Council. Since then it has been divided into two agencies (see Chapter Six). The Legislative Printing Unit continues to operate with the rules as quoted.

[3]A few of the 42 members sent two newsletters. In some cases the first mailing, sent early in the session, was primarily a questionnaire. For purposes of our count, we refer to all the newsletters of the 42 members who produced newsletters through the LPU.

[4]To calculate party votes, "present" votes were counted as "nay" votes. However, absentees were ignored in our calculation.

[5]For further consideration of this line of discussion, see Frederick M. Wirt, "Institutionalization: Prison and School Policies," in Virginia Gray, Herbert Jacob and Kenneth N. Vines, eds., *Politics of American States: A Comparative Analysis*, 4th ed., Boston: Little, Brown, especially pp. 294-295.

[6]"Salaries for legislators in Illinois have risen from the 1895 level of $3,000 per biennium to $3,500 in 1915, $5,000 in 1937, $6,000 in 1947, $10,000 in 1953, $12,000 in 1959, $12,000 annually in 1969, $17,500 and $20,000 in 1975" (Gove, Carlson and Carlson, 1978, p. 107n). In a highly controversial action at the very end of the 80th General Assembly, salaries were raised to $25,000 effective in 1979 and $28,000 in 1980. See "The pay raise and the petitions: Catalyst for the cutback," in *Illinois Issues Special Report: The Cutback Amendment* (1982, pp. 14-22). In 1985 legislative pay went to $32,500 on July 1, 1985. According to *The Book of the States 1984-85*, only Alaska ($48,000), Michigan ($33,200), New York ($32,960), and Pennsylvania ($35,000) paid legislators salaries that were higher than those in Illinois (Council of State Governments, 1985).

AFTERWORD

The politics and government of Illinois remain pretty much as we described them in *Lawmaking in Illinois* in 1986. The machinery of government works effectively even while accompanied by loud sounds of partisan politics.

Despite the partisan din, there have been almost no changes in the top political office holders. Republicans still serve as governor, lieutenant governor and secretary of state while Democrats continue as attorney general, comptroller and treasurer.

There has been gradual turnover among members in the General Assembly since the 1984 results analyzed in Chapter Four, but stability in the partisan balance has been remarkable. Very few incumbents were upset in the partisan primaries of 1986 and 1988, and there were but a handful of partisan reversals in the general elections. As Charles R. Scolare (1988) of the Illinois General Assembly's own Legislative Research Unit observed after the general election:

> For the first time since at least 1920, the numerical division between parties in both houses will remain the same for the third General Assembly in a row. After the 1984, 1986, and 1988 elections, the Senate has been divided between 31 Democrats and 28 Republicans, and the House between 67 Democrats and 51 Republicans. Also, in the Senate every incumbent at the end of a term [in 1988] ran for re-election and all 39 were re-elected. This may be without precedent in Illinois history.

Similarly, there has been great continuity among the party leaders of the House and Senate: Democrat Michael J. Madigan (D-30) is the speaker of the House, and Lee A. Daniels (R-46) is the minority leader for the Republicans; the Senate president is still Democrat Philip J. Rock (D-8), and his counterpart Republican, James "Pate" Philip (R-23), continues as minority leader. Partisan conflict continues to be sharp in day-to-day legislative life, and the two parties have targeted specific incumbents for electoral challenge. Nevertheless, incumbents have usually been rewarded with reelection. The patterns and processes we described in 1986 continue pretty much unchanged.

The few turnovers that have occurred hint at some possibilities for change. Democrats continue to hold most of rural southern Illinois, extending that control in 1986 to the 109th House district, which includes Centralia. Democrats also captured the adjacent Senate district 51, which includes Decatur. In 1988 they added the 95th district, which is in west central Illinois. Republicans have made inroads into the 85th House district including some of Kankakee. They won Senate district 24 on the western edge of Chicago, also capturing House district 47 and almost winning its other half, House district 48. These districts rim the southwest side of Chicago, extending into Cook County. The white ethnic voters in and close to Chicago have increasingly voted for Republican presidential candidates. This promises to continue as the battle zone for Democrats to keep or Republicans to gain partisan control of the House and Senate.

The electoral dynamics relate to a continuing legislative issue: Should the state raise its income tax rates or not. In something of a reversal of traditional party patterns, the Republican governor strongly urged higher taxes and spending in 1987 and 1988, only to be defeated by Democratic Speaker Madigan's opposition. While legislative support was not publicly tested on roll call votes, Madigan insisted the tax increase was not needed. In neither legislative year could the four legislative leaders and the governor agree to terms, so no bill was passed.

The Democratic legislative majorities are built on the redistricting maps that Madigan put in place in 1981. A calculated risk by Democrats at that time was to draw legislative districts extending out from Chicago's western rim into Cook County and beyond. Populated by ethnic whites with strong traditional ties to the Democratic party, these voters have been increasingly attracted to candidates emphasizing low taxes, strong national defense, patriotism, law and order. They have been splitting their votes—for Republicans at the presidential level and for Democrats for state and local offices. These voters are politically organized, economically middle class, socially conservative and committed to self-help, and educationally served by parochial schools as much as public. They could shift their partisan identity from Democrats to Republicans. Indeed, Edward Vrdolyak, former Cook County Democratic chairman, made a much publicized switch to the Republican party and promptly denounced his former associates as "tax and spend" Democrats, a label that has worked to Republican advantage in recent presidential elections.

Before the 1988 election, Speaker Madigan carefully eschewed the possibility of being cast as a tax-and-spend Democrat. His opposition to a permanent, state income tax increase helped to immunize a dozen of the Democratic incumbent legislators from that charge by Republican challengers in 1988. In the following legislative session he sought to allow a small, temporary tax increase to benefit schools and local governments, but not general state spending. This unexpected move may signal more political surprises in future revenue legislation.

Unless a sharp economic downturn drives Illinois' tax revenues down, tax policy changes are not likely to radically affect state policies and the level of services in the next few years. This means that the pattern of interest group pluralism and moderate public service levels that we described in Chapter Ten can be expected to continue. The likelihood of change in political forces is small until after the 1990 census and the redistricting that must follow. It is too early to predict the outcomes from that extremely partisan process. However, redistricting could put into place a set of districts that would change the current partisan complexion of the legislature.

Since our last report, the pay and perquisites of legislators have risen. In the 85th General Assembly (1987-88) the annual salary of members was $35,661 per year, up from $32,500 (p. 222). Near the end of the session there was speculation about the prospects for an increase, some suggesting that the salary should be increased as much as $6,000 per year. However, the legislature did not act to increase the salaries. Since 1984 salaries have been handled under the Compensation Review Act, a twelve-member board that recommends salaries for legislators, judges and top executive officials by May 1 of each even-numbered year. These become effective automatically unless rejected or reduced by both chambers. In 1988 the recommended increase in legislative salaries was rejected. Currently the living expense money to legislators for lodging, meals and expenses is $72 per day. Their district office allowance has been raised to $45,000 per year for each senator and $35,000 for each representative. Most legislators have one or more district offices in which to meet with constituents and conduct legislative business when they are not in the capital.

The Illinois General Assembly is a strong and stable organization. The fact that Governor Thompson actively campaigned for a significant tax increase in 1987 and 1988 without success, and that 1989 brought only incremental increases, makes clear that the General Assembly is capable of acting independently of the governor. On the other hand, the governor remains the legislature's chief agenda setter. The legislature considers his proposals and generally enacts the governor's budgetary priorities with only marginal revisions. In short, the legislative process remains one of give and take. It is a proving ground for newcomers that offers enough rewards to engender long service from many members. It is an arena for representation in which most major issues continue to be resolved through bipartisan consensus.

Jack R. Van Der Slik
May 1989

NOTE

Scolare, Charles R. 1988. "Precedents on Partisan Division Shattered," *First Reading*, Vol. 3, No. 10. Springfield: Legislative Research Unit, Illinois General Assembly, pp. 1, 7.

APPENDIX A
The Illinois Legislative Staff Intern Program

The Illinois Legislative Staff Internship Program (ILSIP) provides an opportunity for outstanding individuals to be actively involved with the policymaking and politics of the Illinois General Assembly. Interns gain direct experience through assignments as legislative analysts with one of the partisan leadership staffs or as research analysts with the Legislative Research Unit (LRU).

The internship is a work experience program that benefits individuals with a wide range of interests. For those pursuing a public-service career or a private-sector career related to government, it provides skills, experience and insights that will allow them to function effectively in governmental settings. For the person seeking an advanced degree, the internship provides direct experience in the political process combined with the support of an academic seminar.

The program began in 1961 when the General Assembly appropriated funds to the Legislative Council to match a Ford Foundation grant to the University of Illinois. Dual financing continued until 1967. The program then became a permanent program of the Illinois General Assembly through the Legislative Council, the University of Illinois and other cooperating universities. In 1972, Sangamon State University assumed responsibility for the direction of the program from the University of Illinois. The program is coordinated by the Illinois Legislative Studies Center at SSU for the Legislative Research Unit (formerly the Legislative Council). Funds for the ILSIP are appropriated by the General Assembly to the LRU. The number of positions and the amount of the stipend are subject to approval by the General Assembly and the governor of the State of Illinois.

In the past 25 years only 349 men and women have been chosen to participate in the program—a very special group. Among the alumni are an Illinois secretary of state, U.S. congressmen, state legislators and numerous state agency directors, legislative and gubernatorial staff members and representatives of business and trade associations. Applicants must have completed work for a bachelor's degree before the internship. They should have outstanding academic records during their junior and senior years, or graduate or professional study. Students from all disciplines are encouraged to apply. The academic majors of recent interns include political science, journalism, law, economics, history, business, finance, English, engineering, chemistry and psychology. All applications are screened by a committee of academic members from the

Intern Sponsoring Committee. Finalists are interviewed by representatives of the leadership staffs and the Legislative Research Unit. Final selections are made upon their recommendations.

Interns work full-time for the staff with which they are placed. They are supervised by the legislative officer to whom they are assigned and by the coordinator of the internship program, a Sangamon State University faculty member. Twenty interns are appointed each year for 10 1/2 month nonrenewable terms that begin October 1. A generous monthly stipend is paid for the duration of the internship. Four interns are assigned to each of the following: Senate Democratic staff, Senate Republican staff, House Democratic staff, House Republican staff. Four interns are assigned to the Legislative Research Unit: two are with their Science Office and two with their general research staff. The deadline for applications is March 1 with appointments announced in early April.

Applications can be obtained from:

> Illinois Legislative Staff Internship Program
> Legislative Studies Center
> Sangamon State University
> Springfield, Illinois 62708

How to Read a Bill

When a member of the Illinois General Assembly wants to change current law or create a new law, he or she introduces a bill. The subject of that bill may be a substantive, non-appropriation matter such as tax rates or the death penalty, or it may be the appropriation of money for expenditures on a public purpose. Whether that bill is a substantive or an appropriation bill, it will fall into one of two categories: a new act or an amendatory act. Both have a standard set of required features, but each has a distinctive form. Some complex bills will be combinations of amendatory and new acts.

A new act is a bill which creates an entirely new law. Most appropriation bills are new acts, which create new appropriations for the coming fiscal year. Amendatory acts are bills which amend (change) an existing law. While substantive bills may be either amendatory or new acts, most are amendatory acts. Appropriation bills which transfer funds or appropriate supplemental (new) funds for the current fiscal year are amendatory acts because they change previously enacted appropriations. A special case of an amendatory act is a repealer which repeals an entire law or section of an existing law.

The following outline contains an item-by-item delineation of a legislative bill. A sample bill keyed by number to this outline follows; additional types of bills are also included.

Amendatory Acts
   I. Amendatory Act—Substantive
      The following references are shown on a sample amendatory act, HB1606, from the 84th General Assembly.
    A. Cover Page
      Every bill has a cover page, but there is nothing on the page which actually becomes law. It is an information device for the legislature. The cover page of a bill has the following features.
        1. Bill Number
        HB for a House Bill and SB for a Senate Bill.
        2. Sponsor's Name
        There may be one sponsor or a long list of sponsors. The first name is the chief sponsor. Other names are cosponsors if they are separated from the chief sponsor by commas. The names of two or more chief sponsors who are equal in status are separated by hyphens.

3. Statutory Reference

This reference tells what existing paragraphs of the Illinois Revised Statutes are being affected by the bill. In this case it is paragraph 2-1205 of Chapter 110. If an entirely new act is being created, the words "New Act" will appear in place of the statutory reference.

4. Synopsis

This is a short summary of the bill's purposes. It is usually written by the Legislative Reference Bureau (LRB). Summaries are generally accurate, but they are sometimes incomplete or misleading. They are *not* revised when the bill is amended.

5. LRB Number

This is an identification number assigned by the LRB to each bill it drafts. A typical number, "LRB 80-3953-GAN/mf," has three parts. LRB 80 refers to the 80th General Assembly. 3953 identifies the bill as the three thousand, nine hundred and fifty-third bill drafted by the LRB during the 80th General Assembly. GAN/mf are the initials of the person who drafted the bill and the person who typed it.

6. Printing in Second Chamber (Not shown on sample)

A House bill introduced in the Senate will have an "S" written on the cover page. A Senate bill introduced in the House will have an "H" written on the cover page. If the bill was amended in the house of origin, it will have the word "amended" stamped on it prior to printing in the second chamber. This is important because all amendments adopted in the house of origin will be incorporated into the body of the bill prior to its introduction and printing in the second chamber.

B. Body of a Bill

The body of a bill contains the changes which become law if the bill passes both houses and is signed by the governor. Following are the standard features.

7. Title

This sentence states what the bill does. It may be very specific (see example) or it may be very general. "AN ACT in relation to Civil Procedure" would be a proper substitute for the title of the sample bill.

8. Enacting Clause

This official statement, which is required by the state constitution, declares that the General Assembly is acting on behalf of the people of the state.

9. Act and Section Being Amended
While the title may be general, this part of an amendatory act must be specific, listing the act and section to be changed.

10. Statutory Reference
This sets out the paragraph and chapter in the statute books where the act and section are located. Usually the section number of the act will correspond with the paragraph number from the statutes. However, in some cases the section and paragraph numbers will not correspond. This is because the act when it is drafted becomes part of the law when it is passed and signed, while the chapter and paragraph references are assigned to a law by the Legislative Reference Bureau and most chapters of the statutes contain more than one law.

11. Complete Text of Section Being Amended
Although this bill changes only two sentences, the entire section must be printed as part of the bill. This is a constitutional requirement intended to insure that the significance of the change being made can be evaluated from reading the bill. In this case, only one page was needed to print the entire section. Some sections require 20 pages or more to be completely printed out.

12. New Language Being Added
When language is added to an existing act, it must be underlined.

13. Old Language Being Deleted
When language is deleted from an existing act, it must be crossed through.

14. Effective Date Clause
House Bill 1606, as introduced, did not have an effective date clause, but one has been added here. It specifies when the bill will become law. In the absence of an effective date clause, a bill becomes law under a uniform effective date specified by the General Assembly. Currently for bills passed prior to July 1 the uniform effective date is January 1 of the following year.

15. Page Number (not shown on this sample)
The page number appears at the top of each page (except the first page).

16. Line Number
The line number appears along the left margin of each page. Each page of the body of a bill will have a page number at top center and a set of line numbers in the left hand column beginning with line 1. These page and line numbers are used

to identify specific words and sentences of a bill. Thus, an amendment might talk about making a change on "page 2, line 16." (The numbers on the right hand column are used by the Legislative Reference Bureau and have no external significance.)

The following samples, though not marked with numbers, contain the same types of information listed above.

II. Amendatory Act—Supplemental Appropriations
The next sample bill is an appropriation bill which amends current law. HB 2547 is a bill making a supplemental appropriation. Since existing law is being changed old language is stricken through and new language is underlined.

III. Amendatory Act—Transfer Appropriations
The next sample bill, HB 30007, also amends current law. In this type of bill funds are transferred from one line item to another in an appropriation act. Old language is stricken through and new language is underlined.

IV. Amendatory Act—Repealer
The next sample bill, HB 1956, repeals an entire existing act. It differs from a regular amendatory act in that the text of the act or section being repealed does not have to be printed out.

V. New Act—Substantive
The next sample bill, HB 0116, is an example of a new act. It differs in form from amendatory acts on two key points. The text is all new language, but it is not underlined. Underlining is only needed when new language is being added to an existing act. There is also no statutory reference because no current act is being changed and statutory reference is not assigned to a new act until it becomes law.

VI. New Act—Appropriations
The final sample bill is HB 0665. It is a regular appropriation bill. There is no underlining because it is all new language, creating an appropriation for the coming fiscal year. There is no statutory reference because it is a new act, nor is one assigned once an appropriation bill becomes law because it is a temporary law in effect for a one-year period only.

I. Sample Bill: Amendatory Act — Substantive

A. Cover Page

---

(1) **HOUSE BILL 1606**

84th GENERAL ASSEMBLY
State of Illinois
1985 and 1986

Introduced April 11, 1985, by Representatives Wait, Stange and White (2)

SYNOPSIS
(3) (Ch. 110, par. 2-1205)

Amends the Code of Civil Procedure. Provides that in medical malpractice cases the damages awarded shall be increased by the amount of any insurance premiums or other direct costs paid by the plaintiff for such benefits in the (4) two years prior to plaintiff's injury or death or to be paid by the plaintiff in the future for such benefits. Deletes the provision that reduction of a judgment by the amount of benefits to the plaintiff shall not exceed 50% of the verdict.

LRB8403491ESpf (5)

A BILL FOR

B. Body of a Bill

HB1606

LRB8403491ESpf

(16) 1   AN ACT to amend Section 2-1205 of the "Code of Civil (7) 66
2   Procedure", approved August 19, 1981, as amended.   68

3   Be it enacted by the People of the State of Illinois, (8) 72
4   represented in the General Assembly:

5   Section 1. Section 2-1205 of the "Code of Civil (9) 74
6   Procedure", approved August 19, 1981, as amended, is amended   75
7   to read as follows:
        (Ch. 110, par. 2-1205) (10)   77
8   Sec. 2-1205. Reduction in amount of recovery. An amount   79
(13) 9   equal to 50% of the benefits provided for medical charges,   81
10   hospital   charges,   lost wages, private or governmental   82
11   disability income programs, or nursing or caretaking charges,
12   which have been paid, or which have become payable to the   83
13   injured person by any other person, corporation, insurance   84
14   company or fund in relation to a particular injury, shall be   85
15   deducted from any judgment in an action to recover for that   86
16   injury based on an allegation of negligence or other wrongful   87
17   act, not including intentional torts, on the part of a
(11) 18   licensed hospital or physician; provided, however, that: 88
19   (1) Application is made within 30 days to reduce the   90
20   judgment;
21   (2) Such reduction shall not apply to the extent that   92
22   there is a right of recoupment through subrogation, trust   93
23   agreement, lien, or otherwise; and   94
24   (3) The damages awarded shall be increased by the amount   97
25   of any insurance premiums or other direct costs paid by the (12) 98
26   plaintiff for such benefits in the two years prior to   99
27   plaintiff's injury or death or to be paid by the plaintiff in
28   the future for such benefits. The reduction shall not reduce (13) 101
29   the judgment by more than 50% of the total amount of the   102
30   judgment entered on the verdict.   105
31   Section 2.   This act takes effect upon becoming law.   (14)

II. Sample Bill: Amendatory Act — Supplemental Appropriations

HB2547

LRB8406822THjs

1	AN ACT to amend Section 3 of "An Act making certain	64
2	appropriations to the Illinois State Scholarship Commission",	65
3	approved July 19, 1985, Public Act 84–57.	66
4	Be it enacted by the People of the State of Illinois,	70
5	represented in the General Assembly:	
6	Section 1. Section 3 of "An Act making certain	72
7	appropriations to the Illinois State Scholarship Commission",	73
8	approved July 19, 1985, Public Act 84–57, is amended to read	74
9	as follows:	
10	Sec. 3. The following named amounts, or so much thereof	76
11	as may be necessary, respectively, are appropriated from the	77
12	General Revenue Fund to the Illinois State Scholarship	78
13	Commission for the following purposes:	
14	Grants & Scholarships	82
15	For payment of grant awards to	84
16	full-time and part-time	85
17	students eligible to receive	86
18	such awards, as provided by	
19	law........................... $121,902,000 ~~$118,303,000~~	87
20	For payment of merit recognition	89
21	sch̶ undergraduate	90

2	dependents of correctional		
3	officers killed or permanently		
4	disabled in the line of duty,		103
5	as provided by law............	50,000	104
6	For payment of Illinois National		106
7	Guard and Naval Militia		107
8	Scholarships at		
9	State-controlled universities		108
10	and public community colleges		
11	in Illinois to students		109
12	eligible to receive such		
13	awards, as provided by law....	1,200,000	110
14	~~(Total, this Section $123,403,000)~~		112
15	Section 2. This Act takes effect upon becoming law.		114

III. Sample Bill: Amendatory Act — Transfer Appropriations

HB3007

LRB8409789SPcs

1	AN ACT to amend Section 1 of "An Act making	62
2	appropriations to the Supreme Court," Public Act 84–72,	63
3	approved July 19, 1985.	64

4 Be it enacted by the People of the State of Illinois,   68
5 represented in the General Assembly:

6   Section 1. Section 1 of "An Act making appropriations to   70
7 the Supreme Court," Public Act 84–72, approved July 19, 1985,   71
8 is amended to read as follows:
9   Sec. 1. The following named sums, or so much thereof as   73
10 may be necessary, respectively, are appropriated to the   74
11 Supreme Court to pay certain officers of the court system of   75
12 Illinois as follows:

Line	Item	Amount	
13	For Judges of the Supreme Court	$ 595,000	78
14	For Supreme Court Clerk.......	50,000	79
15	For Judges of the Appellate Courts	2,720,000	80
16	For Clerk of the Appellate Court		81
17	of the First District....	45,000	82
18	For Clerks of the Appellate Court		83
	in the 2nd, 3rd, 4th and		

Line	Item	Amount	
26	Recalled................	00	
27	For 21 Administrative Secretaries	525,000	92
28	For 94 Law Clerks for Judges of the		93
29	Appellate Courts.........	2,600,000	94
30	For Court Reporters Serving on		95
31	Assignment..............	315,000	96
32	For Shorthand Reporters, appointed		97
33	by Judges............... 20,172,500	30,313,500	98

Line	Item	Amount	
5	Circuit Judges / Appellate Judgeships.....	91,000	102 / 103
6	For State Contribution to State		104
7	Employees' Retirement System 1,336,912	1,196,912	105
8	For State contribution to Social		106
9	Security................	1,780,207	107
10	(Total, Section 1, 687,206,100)		109
11	Section 2. This Act takes effect upon becoming law.		114

IV. Sample Bill: Amendatory Act — Repealer

HB1956

LRB8402009BDpf

```
1        AN ACT to repeal "An Act to protect stock breeders within      60
2   the State of Illinois", approved June 10, 1887, as  amended.       61


3        Be  it  enacted  by  the People of the State of Illinois,      66
4   represented in the General Assembly:


         (Ch. 25, rep. pars. 25 through 31)                            68
5        Section 1. "An Act to protect stock breeders within  the      70
6   State  of  Illinois",  approved June 10, 1887, as amended, is      71
7   repealed.                                                          73
```

V. Sample Bill: New Act — Substantive

HB0116

LRB8400705JMcb

```
1        AN ACT designating Retired Teachers' Week.                    63


2        Be it enacted by the People of  the  State  of  Illinois,     67
3   represented in the General Assembly:


4        Section  1.  The  progress of this State, this nation and     69
5   in fact  all  civilization  is  due  to  the  passing  on  of     70
6   knowledge from one generation to the next.  The burden of the     71
7   transmittal  and  expansion  of  this  body  of knowledge has     72
8   historically been borne by our  teachers.   The  teachers  of     73
9   this  State have tirelessly and selflessly taken on the noble
10  and sacred trust of educating and training our children.  The     74
11  State of Illinois is proud to be the home  of  many  teachers     75
12  who have retired after spending most of their lives rendering     76
13  this   priceless   service.    The   State  of  Illinois,  in     77
14  appreciation  of  this  service,  bestows  upon  the  retired
15  teachers of the State the recognition and honor they deserve.     78
16       Section  2.  The  fourth  week  of  May  of each year is     80
17  designated  as  Retired  Teachers'  Week.   The  Governor may     81
18  annually  issue a proclamation designating the fourth week of     82
19  May as Retired Teachers' Week and calling upon public schools     83
20  and citizens of the State to observe the occasion  and  honor
21  the retired teachers of the State.                               84
22       Section 3.  This Act takes effect upon becoming law.        88
```

VI. Sample Bill: New Act — Appropriations

HB0665

BOB006—85

1	AN ACT making appropriations for the ordinary and	62
2	contingent expenses of the Military and Naval Department.	64
3	Be it enacted by the People of the State of Illinois,	68
4	represented in the General Assembly:	
5	Section 1. The following named sums, or so much thereof	71
6	as may be necessary, respectively, for the objects and	72
7	purposes hereinafter named, are appropriated to the Adjutant	73
8	General to meet the ordinary and contingent expenses of the	74
9	Military and Naval Department.	
10	FOR OPERATIONS	76
11	OFFICE OF THE ADJUTANT GENERAL	77
12	For Personal Services .... $ 810,700	82
13	For State Contributions to State	83
14	Employees' Retirement System 45,400	84
15	For State Contributions to	85
16	Social Security 57,600	86
17	For ...ices 59	

	Social Secu...	284,700	
2	For Contractual Services	2,387,500	111
3	For Commodities	257,700	112
4	For Equipment	18,900	113
5	Total	$7,183,300	114
6	(Total, Section 1: $8,528,800)		115
7	Section 2. The sum of $34,100, or so much thereof as may		118
8	be necessary, is appropriated from the General Revenue Fund		119
9	to the Military and Naval Department for rehabilitation and		120
10	minor construction at armories and camps.		121
11	No contract shall be entered into or obligation incurred		123
12	for any expenditure from the appropriation made in this		124
13	Section until after the purpose and amount of such		125
14	expenditure has been approved in writing by the Governor.		
15	Section 3. The sum of $108,300, or so much thereof as		127
16	may be necessary, is appropriated from the General Revenue		128
17	Fund to the Military and Naval Department for administrative		129
18	costs related to the maintenance of the Broadway Armory in		130
19	Chicago, Illinois.		
20	Section 4. This Act takes effect July 1, 1985.		134

REFERENCES

Adkins, Gary. 1978, August. "Roll Calls," *Illinois Issues*, pp. 28-29.
_____. 1979, August. "The Suburbs Also Rise," *Illinois Issues*, pp. 2, 29.
Advisory Commission on Intergovernmental Relations. 1983. *1981 Tax Capacity of the Fifty States*. A-93. Washington, DC: Government Printing Office.
Ahlen, John. 1983. *Identifying the Causes of Failure: A Selected Survey of Science Advisory Mechanisms*. Urbana: Institute of Government and Public Affairs, University of Illinois and the Illinois Legislative Council.
Andrews, James H. 1966. "Illinois At-Large Vote," *National Civic Review*, 55:253-257.
Baker v. Carr. 1962. 369 U.S. 186.
Bazzani, Craig S. 1982. "The Executive Budget Process," in James D. Nowlan, ed., *Inside State Government: A Primer for Illinois Managers*. Urbana: Institute of Government and Public Affairs, University of Illinois, pp. 41-51.
Beyle, Thad L. 1983. "Governors," in Virginia Gray, Herbert Jacob, and Kenneth N. Vines, eds., *Politics in the American States: A Comparative Analysis*. 4th ed. Boston: Little, Brown, pp. 180-221.
Bibby, John F., Cornelius P. Cotter, James L. Gibson, and Robert J. Huckshorn. 1983. "Parties in State Politics," in Virginia Gray et al., eds., *Politics in the American States: A Comparative Analysis*. 4th ed. Boston: Little, Brown, pp. 59-96.
Briggs, Michael. 1984. "Springfield's Hidden Persuaders," *Chicago Sun-Times* (May 13).
Campbell, Angus, Phillip E. Converse, Warren E. Miller, and Donald E. Stokes. 1960. *The American Voter*. New York: Wiley.
Carlson, Richard J. 1982. "The Office of the Governor," in James D. Nowlan, ed., *Inside State Government: A Primer for Illinois Managers*. Urbana: Institute of Government and Public Affairs, University of Illinois, pp. 15-39.
The Chicago Tribune, Chicago, IL.
Citizens Conference on State Legislatures. 1971. *The Sometimes Governments: A Critical Study of the 50 American Legislatures*, written by John Burns. New York: Bantam Books.
A Citizen's Guide to the Illinois Administrative Procedure Act. 1983. Springfield, IL: Joint Committee on Administrative Rules.
Colby, Peter W. and Paul M. Green. 1978, August. "Voting Patterns in the 96 Downstate Counties," *Illinois Issues*, pp. 15-21.
_____. 1979, February. "The Consolidation of Clout," *Illinois Issues*, pp. 11-20.
_____. 1979, October. "Patterns of Change in Suburban Voting," *Illinois Issues*, pp. 17-23.
Colegrove v. Green. 1946. 328 U.S. 549.
Commission on the Organization of the General Assembly (COOGA). 1967. *Improving the Legislature*. Urbana: University of Illinois Press.
_____. 1977. *COOGA: 10 Years Later*. Springfield, IL: Commission on the Organization of the General Assembly.
In Re Contest of Election for Governor. 1983. 93 Ill. 2d 423.

Cook, Robert E. 1982. "Lobbyists and Interest Groups," in James D. Nowlan, ed., *Inside State Government: A Primer for Illinois Managers*. Urbana: Institute of Government and Public Affairs, University of Illinois, pp. 113-122.

Council of State Governments. 1985. *The Book of the States 1984-1985*. Vol. 25. Lexington, KY: Council of State Governments.

Crane, Edgar G., Jr. 1980. "The Office of Governor," in his *Illinois: Political Processes and Governmental Performance*. Dubuque, IA: Kendall/Hunt, pp. 60-86.

Dahl, Robert A. 1984. *Modern Political Analysis*. 4th ed. Englewood Cliffs, NJ: Prentice-Hall.

Davidson, Roger H. 1969. *The Role of the Congressman*. New York: Pegasus.

Davidson, Roger H. and Walter J. Oleszek. 1981. *Congress and Its Members*. Washington,DC: Congressional Quarterly Press.

Dawson, Richard E. and Kenneth Prewitt. 1969. *Political Socialization*. Boston: Little, Brown.

Elazar, Daniel J. 1972. *American Federalism: A view from the States*. New York: Crowell.

Elazar, Daniel J. and Joseph Zikmund II. 1975. *The Ecology of American Political Culture: Readings*. New York: Crowell. See especially Elazar, "Competing Political Cultures in Illinois," Chap. 13.

Emerson, Judy. 1985, March. "A Question of Status for Women's Issues," *Illinois Issues*, pp. 33-36.

Everson, David H. 1981. "Illinois," in "State Legislative Developments," Loren M. Carlson, ed., *American Review of Public Administration* 15:339-341.

_____. 1984, May. "Legislative Committees v. Legislative Individualism," *Illinois Issues*, pp. 15-20.

_____.1985, April. "The Case of the Missing Voter!" *Illinois Issues*, pp. 15-17.

Everson, David H. and Joan A. Parker. 1981, February. "Voter Turnout Drops Again," *Illinois Issues*, pp. 9-10.

_____. 1982. "Congressional Elections: The Advantage of Incumbency," in Caroline A. Gherardini, J. Michael Lennon, Richard J. Shereikis, and Larry R. Smith, eds., *Illinois Elections*. 2d ed. Springfield, IL: Sangamon State University, pp. 55-59.

_____. 1983, March. "Legislative Elections: Reviving an Old Partnership," *Illinois Issues*, pp. 14-17.

Everson, David H. and Joan A. Parker, with William A. Day, Rita A. Harmony, and Kent D Redfield. 1982. *The Cutback Amendment: A Special Report*. Springfield: Illinois Issues, Sangamon State University.

Everson, David H. and Kent Redfield. 1980, March. "Regional Interest Further Party Decline," *Illinois Issues*, pp. 12-13.

The Federalist Papers. 1961. New York: New American Library of World Literature, Mentor Books.

Fenno, Richard E. 1978. *Home Style*. Boston: Little, Brown.

Fenton, John H. 1966. "Political 'Clout' in Illinois," in *Midwest Politics*. New York: Holt, Rinehart & Winston, pp. 194-218.

Franklin, Tim. 1986. [Article on political interest group funding for legislative campaigns.] *Chicago Tribune* (February 9):A14, A18.

Galligan, Mary C. 1977, April. "Democrats Compromise in Senate," *Illinois Issues*, p.26.

Gherardini, Caroline A., J. Michael Lennon, Richard J. Shereikis, and Larry R. Smith, eds. 1982. *Illinois Elections*. 2d ed. Springfield, IL: Sangamon State University.

Gonet, Philip M. and James D. Nowlan. 1982. "The Legislature," in James D. Nowlan, ed., *Inside State Government: A Primer for Illinois Managers*. Urbana: The Institute of Government and Public Affairs, University of Illinois, pp. 69-91.

Gove, Samuel K. 1980. "The Illinois General Assembly," in Edgar G. Crane, ed., *Illinois: Political Processes and Governmental Performance*. Dubuque, IA: Kendall/Hunt, pp. 94-108.

_____. 1985, July. "Living down the past in Illinois politics," *Illinois Issues*, pp. 36-37.

Gove, Samuel K., Richard W. Carlson, and Richard J. Carlson. 1976. *The Illinois Legislature: Structure and Process*. Urbana: University of Illinois Press.

Graham, Jory. 1973. *Instant Chicago: How to Cope*. Chicago: Rand, McNally.

Green, Paul. 1983, January. "How Thompson Did It: Downstate Again the Key," *Illinois Issues*, pp. 6-10.

_____. 1983, April. "Washington's Victory: Divide and Conquer," *Illinois Issues*, pp. 15-20.

_____. 1983, August. "Chicago Election: The Numbers and the Implications," *Illinois Issues*, pp.13-18.

_____. 1984, June. "Vrdolyak Wins Opener in Cook County Power Politics," *Illinois Issues*, pp. 15-17.

Handbook of Illinois Legislature. 1985. Compiled by Kenneth Wright and John F. O'Brien. Springfield: State of Illinois.

Harris, Fred R. and Paul L. Hain. 1983. *American Legislative Process: Congress and the States*. Glenview, IL: Scott Foresman.

Heinecke, Burnell. 1976, January. "New Force in Senate—They Call Themselves 'The Crazy 8', *Illinois Issues*, pp. 21-23.

Hill, David B. and Norman R. Luttbeg. 1980. *Trends in American Electoral Behavior*. Itasca, IL: Peacock.

House Republican Staff Report. 1981. *Veto Book 1981*. Springfield, IL: Office of the Speaker of the House.

Howard, Robert P. 1982, October. "Thompson v. Stevenson: A Long View," *Illinois Issues*, pp. 6-11.

Illinois Blue Book 1963-64. 1964. Springfield: State of Illinois.

Illinois Blue Book 1983-84. 1984. Springfield: State of Illinois.

Illinois Issues. 1976, May. "Walker carries 85 counties, but loses: Daley's candidate, Howlett wins primary," p. 24.

Illinois Legislative Council. 1980. *Directory of State Officials*. Pub. 159. Springfield: Illinois Legislative Council.

_____. 1982. *Directory of Executive Agencies and Legislative Liaisons*. Pub. 170. Springfield: Illinois Legislative Council.

_____. 1982. *Manual of the Procedures of the Illinois House of Representatives*. 5th ed. Pub. 171. Springfield: Illinois Legislative Council.

_____. 1982. *Preface to Lawmaking: Legislators'Introduction to the General Assembly*. Pub. 172. Springfield: Illinois Legislative Council.

_____. 1983. *Directory of Registered Lobbyists, 1983 Session*. Pub. 180. Springfield: Illinois Legislative Council.

_____. 1984. *Directory of State Officials*. Pub. 183. Springfield: Illinois Legislative Council.

Illinois Revised Statutes 1967. 1968. "Chap. 63, Par. 131.1, 132." St. Paul, MN: West.

Illinois Revised Statutes 1969. 1970. "Chap. 63, Par. 131.1, 132." St. Paul, MN: West.

Illinois Revised Statutes 1983. 1984a. "Chap. 46, Par. 8.8." St. Paul, MN: West.

_____. 1984b. "Chap. 63, Par. 171ff." St. Paul, MN: West.

Illinois Revised Statutes 1985. 1986a. "Chap. 63, Par. 171-182." St. Paul, MN: West.

_____. 1986b. "Chap. 127, Par. 63b, 101-119." St. Paul, MN: West.

_____. 1986c. "Chap. 127, 1001-1021." St. Paul, MN: West.

_____. 1986d. "Chap. 116, Par. 203, 3a." St. Paul, MN: West.

Jacobson, Gary C. 1983. *The Politics of Congressional Elections*. Boston: Little, Brown.

Jurgens, Nora Newman. 1983, June. "Legislative Action," *Illinois Issues*, pp. 22-23.

Kahn, Melvin A. and Frances J. Majors. 1984. *The Winning Ticket: Daley, the Chicago Machine, and Illinois Politics*. New York: Praeger.

Kenney, David. 1974. *Basic Illinois Government: A Systematic Explanation*. Rev. ed. Carbondale: Southern Illinois University Press.

Knoepfle, Margaret S. 1979, September. "Thompson's Reorganization Efforts," *Illinois Issues*, pp. 2,27.

Legislative Research Unit. 1984a. *Economic and Social Profiles of Illinois Counties*. File 9-476. Springfield: Illinois Legislative Research Unit.

_____. 1984b. *Preface to Lawmaking: Legislators' Introduction to the General Assembly*. Pub. 191. Springfield: Illinois Legislative Research Unit.

_____. 1986. *Directory of State Officials*. Pub. 202. Springfield: Illinois Legislative Research Unit.

List of Individual Lobbyists as of September 2, 1983. 1983. 83rd General Assembly, 1983 Session. Springfield, IL: Secretary of State Index Dept.

Lockport, William B. 1981. *The American Constitution: Cases-Comments-Questions*. 5th ed. St. Paul, MN: West, pp. 970-986.

Lousin, Ann. 1976, April. "Attorney general's opinions: Take 'em or leave 'em—at your peril," *Illinois Issues*, pp. 20-22.

McClory, Robert J. 1983, September. "Shakman: the man and his battle against patronage," *Illinois Issues*, pp. 7-12.

McDowell, James L. 1967. *The Politics of Reapportionment in Illinois*. Carbondale: Public Affairs Research Bureau, Southern Illinois University.

Mackay, Robert. 1982, April. "The New Congressional Districts," *Illinois Issues;* reprinted in Caroline A. Gherardini et al., eds., *Illinois Elections*. 2d ed. Cited above, pp. 64-67.

Malbin, Michael J. 1980. *Unelected Representatives: Congressional Staff and the Future of Representative Government*. New York: Basic Books.

Michaelson, Ronald D. 1975. "An Analysis of the Chief Executive: How a Governor Uses His Time," in William K. Hall, ed., *Illinois Government and Politics: A Reader*. Dubuque, IA: Kendall/Hunt, pp. 111-119.

Miller, Arthur. 1983. "Is Confidence Rebounding?" *Public Opinion* 6:16-20.

Miller, David R. 1983. *The 1970 Illinois Constitution Annotated for Legislators*. Pub. 177. Springfield: Illinois Legislative Council.

Morehouse, Sally McCalley. 1981. *State Politics, Parties and Policy*. New York: Holt, Rinehart and Winston.

National Center for Education Statistics. 1980. *Digest of Education Statistics 1980*. Washington, DC: Government Printing Office.

Netsch, Dawn Clark. 1970. "The Executive," in Samuel K. Gove and Victoria Ramsey, eds., *Con Con: Issues for the Illinois Constitutional Convention*. Urbana: University of Illinois Press, pp. 144-182.

Nowlan, James D. 1982. "Practical Guidance for New Agency Heads," in James D. Nowlan, ed., *Inside State Government: A Primer for Illinois Government*. Urbana: Institute of Government and Public Affairs, University of Illinois, 143-155.

O'Grady, Patrick. 1981, November. "What's it like to work for the General Assembly?" *Illinois Issues*, pp. 27-31.

_____. 1982, September. "Running the Legislature's Law Firm," *Illinois Issues*, pp. 13-16.

Olson, Russell E. 1954. "Illinois Faces Redistricting," *National Municipal Review* 43:343-348,363.

Parker, Joan A. 1984. *The Illinois Tax Increase of 1983: Summit and Resolution*. Springfield: Illinois Issues, Sangamon State University.

Patterson, Samuel C. 1968. "The Political Cultures of the American States," *Journal of Politics* 30:187-209.

_____. 1983. "Legislators and Legislatures in the American States," in Virginia Gray et al., eds., *Politics in the American States: A Comparative Analysis*. 4th ed. Boston: Little, Brown, pp. 135-179.

Peirce, Neal R. and Jerry Hagstrom. 1983. *The Book of America: Inside 50 States Today*. New York: Norton.

Peters, Cynthia. 1984a, August. "The Legislature Decommissions Commissions," *Illinois Issues*, pp. 25-26.

_____. 1984b, August. "World's Fair Gets $8.8 million in $82.8 million Package," *Illinois Issues*, pp. 26-28.

Polsby, Nelson W. 1968. "The Institutionalization of the U.S. House of Representatives," *American Political Science Review* 62:144-168.

Pomper, Gerald M., Ross K. Baker, Kathleen A. Frankovic, Charles E. Jacob, Wilson Carey McWilliams, and Henry Polkin. 1981. *The Election of 1980: Reports and Interpretations*. Chatham, NJ: Chatham House.

Preston, Michael B. 1982. "Black Politics in the Post-Daley Era," in Samuel K. Gove and Louis H. Masotti, eds., *After Daley: Chicago Politics in Transition*. Urbana: University of Illinois Press, pp. 88-117.

Przybylski, James. 1976, August. "As goes Illinois . . . .The state as a political microcosm of the nation," *Illinois Government Research*; reprinted in Gherardini et al., eds., *Illinois Elections*. 2d ed. Cited above, pp. 21-25.

Rakove, Milton L. 1975. *Don't Make No Waves, Don't Back No Losers*. Bloomington: Indiana University Press.

Ranney, Austin. 1965 and 1976. "Parties in State Politics," in Herbert Jacob and Kenneth N. Vines, eds., *Politics in the American States: A Comparative Analysis*. 1st and 3d eds. Boston: Little, Brown.

Ripley, Randall P. 1983. *Congress: Process and Policy*. 3d ed. New York: Norton.

Ripley, Randall P. and Grace A. Franklin. 1980. *Congress, The Bureaucracy, and Public Policy*. Rev. ed. Homewood, IL: Dorsey Press.

Rosenthal, Alan. 1981. *Legislative Life: People, Process, and Performance in the States*. New York: Harper & Row.

Ross, Diane. 1980, January. "Governor Thompson Talks About His Administration," *Illinois Issues*, pp. 13-15.

_____. 1981, March. "The Day the Republicans Stole the Senate," *Illinois Issues*, pp. 4-8.

_____. 1983, May. "The Ascension of Michael Madigan," *Illinois Issues*, pp. 6-11.

Salisbury, Robert H. and Kenneth A. Shepsle. 1981. "U.S. Congressman as Enterprise," *Legislative Studies Quarterly* 6:559-576.

Schattschneider, E. E. 1960. "The Contagiousness of Conflict," in his *The Semisovereign People: A Realist's View of Democracy in America*. New York: Holt, Rinehart and Winston, pp. 1-19.

Schoeplein, Robert N. with Hugh T. Connelly. 1975. *The Illinois Economy: A Microcosm of the United States?* Urbana: Institute of Government and Public Affairs, University of Illinois.

Sevener, Don. 1985, February. "The amendatory veto: to be or not to be so powerful," *Illinois Issues*, pp. 14-17.

Shin, Kwang S. and David H. Everson. 1979, May. "What's the Turnover Rate in the Illinois Legislature?" *Illinois Issues*, pp. 18-19.

Simon, Lucinda S. 1979. *A Legislators Guide to Staffing Patterns*. Denver: National Conference of State Legislatures.

Simon, Paul, as told to Alfred Balk. 1964, September. "The Illinois Legislature: A Study in Corruption," *Harper's Magazine*, pp. 74-78.

Sixth Illinois Constitutional Convention of 1969-1970. 1972. *Record of Proceedings*. 7 vols. Springfield: State of Illinois.

Steiner, Gilbert Y. and Samuel K. Gove. 1960. *Legislative Politics in Illinois*. Urbana: University of Illinois Press.

Temporary Rules of the Senate of the Eighty-Fourth General Assembly. 1985. Prepared by Kenneth Wright, Secretary of the Senate. Springfield: State of Illinois.

Truman, David B. 1951. *The Governmental Process: Political Interests and Public Opinion*. New York: Knopf.

U.S. Bureau of the Census. 1982. *Statistical Abstract of the United States, 1982-1983*. 103d ed. Washington, DC: Government Printing Office.

U.S. Supreme Court. Important cases concerning legislative districting:
Gray v. Sanders. 1963. 372 U.S. 368.
Wesberry v. Sanders. 1964. 376 U.S. 1.

Reynolds v. Sims. 1964. 377 U.S. 533.
Lucas v. Forty-fourth General Assembly. 377 R.S. 713.
Kirkpatrick v. Preisler. 1969. 394 U.S. 526.
Wells v. Rockefeller. 1969. 394 U.S. 542.
Mahan v. Howell. 1973. 410 U.S. 315.
Gaffney v. Cummings. 1973. 412 U.S. 735.
White v. Regester. 1973. 412 U.S. 755.
Van Der Slik, Jack R. 1977. "The Chief Executive Subsystem," and "The Legislative Subsystem and Its Client Systems," in his *American Legislative Processes.* New York: Crowell, pp. 97-151.
_____. 1977. *American Legislative Processes.* New York: Crowell. See especially Chap. 2.
Van Der Slik, Jack R. and Jesse C. Brown. 1980. "Legislators and Roll Call Voting in the 80th General Assembly," in Edgar G. Crane, ed., *Illinois: Political Processes and Governmental Performance.* Dubuque, IA:Kendall/Hunt, pp. 109-118.
Verba, Sidney and Norman H. Nie. 1972. "The Modes of Participation: An Empirical Analysis," in *Participation in America: Political Democracy and Social Equality.* New York: Harper & Row, pp. 56-81.
Wheeler, Charles N., III. 1978, August. "Reapportionment Begins Now!" *Illinois Issues*; reprinted in Gherardini et al., eds. *Illinois Elections.* 2d ed. Cited above, pp. 46-53.
_____. 1982, April. "Redistricting '81: A Democratic Decade?" *Illinois Issues*; reprinted in Gherardini et al., eds. *Illinois Elections.* 2d ed. Cited above, pp. 68-77.
_____. 1984, June. "The Real Path for Legislation," *Illinois Issues*, p. 2.
Willard, Debbie. 1985, October. "Citizens Councils Replace Seven Commissions," *Illinois Issues*, p. 29.
Wirt, Frederick M. 1983. "Institutionalization: Prison and School Policies," in Virginia Gray et al., eds., *Politics of the American States: A Comparative Analysis.* 4th ed. Boston: Little, Brown, pp. 287-328.
Zeigler, L. Harmon. 1982. "Interest Groups in the States," in Virginia Gray et al., eds., *Politics in the American States: A Comparative Analysis.* 4th ed. Boston: Little, Brown, pp. 97-131.
Zeigler, L. Harmon and Michael Baer. 1969. *Lobbying: Interaction and Influence in American State Legislatures.* Belmont, CA: Wadsworth.

INDEX